S0-AXJ-085

CHARLES DARWIN SLEPT HERE

Compliments of . . .

GALÁPAGOS
DIRECT

http://www.galapagosdirect.com

Charles Darwin Slept Here

Copies may be purchased at Barnes & Noble, Borders Books & Music, or may be ordered online at:

http://www.amazon.com   *http://www.bn.com*
http://www.rockvillepress.com

For free shipping within continental United States, please mention
Galápagos Direct and mail check for US $ 22.00 to:
Rockville Press, Inc.
45 Lakeside Drive
Rockville Centre, NY 11570

for more details: *info@rockvillepress.com*

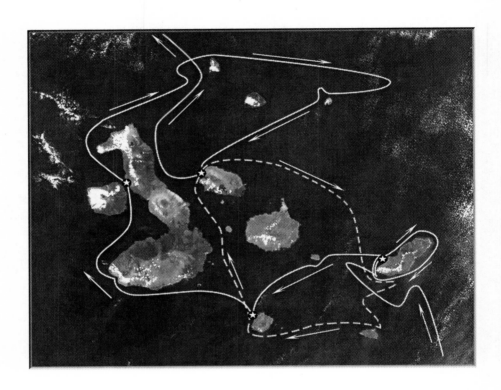

The Galápagos Islands, from a satellite photo taken on
March 12, 2002. © 2002, NASA Visible Earth Program.

Track of H. M. S. *Beagle* added. Dashed line indicates
segment sailed while Darwin remained on James Island.
Four stars indicate places where Darwin went ashore.

Charles Darwin Slept Here

Tales of Human History at World's End

John Woram

Rockville Press, Inc.
Rockville Centre, New York

© 2005 by John Woram, All Rights Reserved

First Edition

Printed in the United States of America

Rockville Press, Inc.
45 Lakeside Drive
Rockville Centre, NY 11570

Rockville Press website: *http://www.rockvillepress.com*
  e-mail: info@rockvillepress.com

author's Galápagos website: *http://www.galapagos.to*
  e-mail: info@galapagos.to

ISBN-13: 978-0-9769336-0-1
ISBN-10: 0-9769336-0-8

Library of Congress Control Number: 2005927683

CONTENTS

to John Jr.,
Susan Mary, and
Christina Marie

*Very few things happen at the right time,
and the rest do not happen at all:
The conscientious historian will correct
these defects.*

PREFACE

This little opus got its start some years ago, after the first of what would become many trips to the Galápagos Islands (#16 at last count). On returning home from #1, I read Herman Melville's *The Encantadas, or Enchanted Islands,* and was immediately confused, for some of his islands were not where one would expect to find them—or at least, not where *I* would expect to find them. So perhaps these isles were enchanted after all and had moved about in the years between his visit and mine.

A bit more reading put that notion to rest, and at the same time sent me off looking for other books—books written by buccaneers turned authors, by sea captains turned authors, by physicians turned authors. The books shared several common traits: they were travel narratives first, they covered lengthy voyages to faraway places, and for most, Galápagos was just one of those places. Many of their authors were engaged in enterprises which might not be considered scientific—looting and pillaging, attacking the British, killing whales, and so on. Some took little notice of the wildlife beyond a passing mention, although one of the early buccaneer authors was an interesting exception, writing extensively of the flora and fauna of Galápagos and elsewhere. And of course there was that one 19th-century gentleman who did go on about natural history at some length, turning a visit of a few weeks into what amounted to a lifetime career.

As my little book collection crept out over more and more shelf space, I had the chance to watch evolution in action — no, not *that* evolution, but a rather different one that was quietly going on between the covers. The literature of Galápagos was changing, in fact, *had* changed; travel and exploration were out, natural history was in. Examine any specimen of *liber Galápagensis* today and you'll find a species that bears little resemblance to its ancestors — those travel narratives of centuries ago. Galápagos today is Animal Planet, and if ever humans were there, they've long since been forgotten. Or when remembered, the recollection is hazy.

And so it seemed I might find room on the shelf for one more book, a book that would tell a little something of the human history of these islands, and nothing at all of their natural history. Or *almost* nothing. After all, each of the literary visitors to be covered in its pages would have made at least that passing mention of bird or of beast, and often the unusual circumstances under which they made their observations are part of their story. But beyond that, the stories should be of the visitors themselves, and of the circumstances that brought them to Galápagos in the first place. Their tales would be told in chronological order, or as near to it as possible, for in some cases one story is intertwined with another. Yet one must read one of them before reading the other. But which one to read first? As this book was evolving, I did notice that the chapters had a habit of rearranging themselves before they settled down into their current arrangement, which seems to work reasonably well.

To begin at the beginning, the first chapter tells of the first visitor, even if there is some doubt that he had legitimate rights to that title. But he's part of the Galápagos legend, and so deserves at least a few pages. Chapter Two is about a man who surely did get there, and about another first—

a 16th-century chart on which the Galápagos Islands are introduced to cartography. The next two chapters introduce a pair of literary buccaneers, and in the case of one of them there's quite a bit about his life beyond Galápagos. But it was such an interesting life that it seemed a shame not to include at least parts of it.

When Herman Melville wrote about Captain David Porter's own book, he warned his readers that "… they will recognize many sentences, for expedition's sake derived verbatim from thence, and incorporated here." The present book follows Melville's example, but with a variation: most sentences derived verbatim from David Porter and others are placed in indented paragraphs, to make it clear at all times just who is telling the story. But the reader should be cautioned (again, for expedition's sake) that these lifted lines have often been edited—sometimes for clarity, other times to trim a fair amount of material that wandered away from the subject at hand. The Bibliography at the end will direct the reader to the source of each such excerpt if a fuller account is wanted (or to find out what each writer *really* said).

The chapters proceed through the centuries until finally arriving in the present, where no doubt some sort of literary law is broken in Chapter 19, in which the author lapses into the first person (pp. 317-318). However, the author assures me that he couldn't figure out a better way of telling a tale in which he played a part without getting clumsy about it.

Perhaps Chapter 22 should be re-titled "Time out for a little fun"—taken at the expense of various conscientious historians, most of whom have gone on to their rewards, or should consider doing so at their earliest opportunity. For reasons unknown to scholarship, there's rarely a book about Galápagos birds and beasts in which the author doesn't feel compelled to toss off a chapter about history.

Perhaps these writers feel that since such coverage is only history, there's no need to go to the bother of getting it right. And so each one simply "borrows" from someone who has gone before, which is ever so much easier than consulting original sources. But for the sake of originality, each such account is "improved" with new tidbits found nowhere else. But more of that in the chapter mentioned.

And on the subject of borrowing from an earlier writer, the reader is reminded that according to the learned philosopher Stephen Wright (who doubles as a standup comedian), stealing from one author is called plagiarism; stealing from many authors is called research. This book is definitely in the latter category, and to reinforce that claim most literary liftings are identified as such within the text, with more details provided in the Notes at the end.

The photographs and other images taken from out of the past are of variable quality. Some come from old books, others from old newspapers, and only a few come from high-quality prints. Some have been "tweaked" a bit to coax a little more detail out of their shadows. But still, they do show their age. As for any less-than-perfect modern photos, there must have been something wrong with my camera.

ACKNOWLEDGEMENTS

At first, I thought I'd claim that "I did it all by myself."
But with so many people still living who know better,
I had second thoughts and decided it might be best to
share the blame with many of those whose assistance has
been so vital to this little project. After a bit of wrestling
with the problem of who to thank first, I came upon the
ideal way to get out of making a decision about who to
thank first. So here they are, in alphabetical order.

Daniel Baldwin and the Customer Service folks at Dover Publications
were most helpful in tracking down some of the illustrations that
introduce, and punctuate, many of these chapters.

Map Librarian (now retired) *Tony Campbell* at the British Library
was of immense help in tracking down the maps and charts of
Herman Moll and William Hacke, and letting me have a look at
the originals.

Ecuadorian film producer *Nicolás Cornejo* wanted to do a film
about the wartime occupation of the Galápagos Islands, and
mutual friends put us in touch. This eventually led to the
documentary "The Rock" which premiered in Ecuador in 2004
and may one day be shown here in el norte. Working with
Nicolás on the film gave me the chance to renew acquaintances
with many WWII veterans, to accompany them on a return visit
to Galápagos, and to gather more background information for
the chapters pertaining to the occupation years.

In England, *Tony Wenman Cowley*—whose middle name has been
in the family for several generations—has long wondered about
a connection between himself and the hero of Chapter Four.
Although he still hasn't found the conclusive link, or proof that
there isn't one, he's done a lot of reseach on his possible ancestor,
and has shared much of his knowledge with me over the years.

A special thanks to *Brian Crain, Don Fuson* and the production crew at Lightning Source for transforming my electronic files from pixels into paper.

Many years ago I had the good fortune to meet Dr. *John Garth,* the only scientist who participated in all ten of Captain G. Allan Hancock's *Velero III* expeditions. Dr. Garth, now deceased, allowed me access to his Galápagos diaries, and provided many of the photos taken on the expeditions.

Thalia Grant Estes and I have kept up a running conversation for years on such matters as the legend of Irish Pat, 19th-century whaling voyages, and American forces in Galápagos.

Mackenzie Gregory was a great help in tracking down details of Count Felix von Luckner, who visited Galápagos between the two world wars.

My thanks to *Don Harrsch* for chatting with me on several occasions about his experiences as leader of the colonization project of 1959-60, and for referring me to contemporary newspaper accounts that chronicled both the colony and the settlers.

For information about the Norwegian settlers, *Stein Hoff* offered me a "Help Yourself" to excerpts from his *Drømmen om Galapagos.* An English translation of his Norwegian text is on my website at *http://www.galapagos.to/texts/hoff-0.htm*, and I hope that before too long it will also be available in print.

The meaning of John Dryden's odd remark about William Dampier was explained to me by Dr. *David Hopkins* at the University of Bristol, and by so doing he no doubt doubled the number of people who can explain what Dryden was talking about.

At Sonoma State Universty, Prof. *Matt James* has shared much of his research on the California Academy of Sciences expedition of 1905-06, and has also been a big help in the search for the various appearances of "Johnson from London" in the Galápagos literature.

At the Seattle Public Library's Jane and Hugh Ferguson Seattle Collection, Librarian *Stephen Kiesow* was of great assistance (in fact, he did all the work) of tracking down the local newspaper accounts of the Island Development Company colonization project.

Major *Fred Laing, Jr.* (USAF., retired) is the son of Captain Fred Lang, one of the participants of a pre-WWII search for the 1813 gravesite of Lieutenant Cowan. From his days at the U. S. Naval Academy, Laing's graduation thesis supplied valuable background information on the subject of the duel.

Martine de Lajudie contributed the illustrations of Charles Island from the 1841 edition of Abel du Petit-Thouars' *Voyage Autour Du Monde.*

Ed Larson, author of *Evolution's Workshop*, tipped me off to the existence of a massive U. S. Naval Intelligence report on pre-war Galápagos, which was a great help in sorting out the details of American activities in Galápagos in the years before Pearl Harbor.

Jacob Lundh grew up in Galápagos, but eventually returned to the Norway of his birth. From there, I've enjoyed an ongoing discussion with him about the early Norwegian and other settlers, much of which has provided valuable background information.

At the United Kingdom Hydrographic Office in Taunton, Research Manager *Adrian Moore* and his staff cheerfully put up with repeated visits and endless requests to see just about everything pertaining to the Galápagos Islands in their vast collection of navigation charts.

Galápagos Direct president *Judie Muggia* was the first—and so far, the only—tour operator to see the potential for organizing tours to you-know-where that would offer a bit of human history to supplement the natural history that is of course the main attraction of a visit to Galápagos. Thanks to her efforts, we've organized a series of such tours, and that in turn has been a great help in putting much of the information found here into a format that would make it (I hope!) interesting to both the armchair and the actual voyager.

At the Virginia Historical Society, *Frances S. Pollard* was of great assistance in making William Ambrosia Cowley's letter to an unknown "Your Grace" available for close inspection.

Photos of Victor Wolfgang von Hagen are not easy to find, but *Keith Richmond* located one at his villa in Tuscany, Italy, where Dr. von Hagen spent his later years.

Veterans of the U. S. *Sixth Air Force* have been generous in sharing their wartime recollections of life on "The Rock" and have invited me to attend several of their annual reunions. In particular, *Alan Beucher, Bob Houston, Bill Knight, Vernon Lange* and *Ernest Reimer*—all members of the 29th Bombardment Squadron—have helped greatly in retelling at least a small part of their story.

Heidi Snell has spent much of her adult life either in a small plane flying over, or in a small boat sailing between, various Galápagos landmarks, always with camera in hand. She knows as much as— and in many cases, more than—anyone else about the vagaries of getting from one island to another and living to tell about it. You'll find several photos from her collection in these pages.

Barbara West, who knows her way around in the archives of the California Academy of Sciences, rendered valuable assistance in sorting out some of the details of the regime of Manuel J. Cobos.

Until her passing a few years ago, a visit with *Margret Wittmer* was always a high point of my visits to Isla Floreana. Although I never asked "Who killed the Baroness?" the questions I did put to her were readily answered, and she was good enough to find— and let me photograph—pages from her wartime guestbook.

At the University of Oregon Library, *Aimee Yogi* was very helpful in tracking down a 1971 issue of the school's alumni magazine with an account of the 1960 colonization project, and then getting the magazine shipped to the opposite coast, to be put to good use as a reference for Chapter 21.

And finally, a special thanks to anyone whose name I have accidentally omitted from these pages. I'll make amends in the next edition (if there is a next edition).

A GALÁPAGOS TIMELINE

A few important dates in the human and cartographic history of the Galápagos Islands are given here. A number in brackets indicates the chapter in which the event is described.

ca. 1480   Voyage of Tupac Inca Yupanqui to the islands of Avachumbi and Ninachumbi. [1]

1535   Bishop Tomás de Berlanga arrives. [2]

ca. 1535   First known appearance of "Galapagos" on a chart. [2]

1569   Islands appear on Gerard Mercator's map. [18]

1570   Islands appear on Abraham Ortelius's map. [18]

1684   William Dampier and William Ambrosia Cowley, aboard the *Batchelors Delight*. [3, 4]

1697   Publication of William Dampier's *A New Voyage Round the World*. [3]

1699   Publication of *Cowley's Voyage Round the Globe*. [4]

1711   William Dampier, aboard the *Duke*, Captain Woodes Rogers. [3]

1795   James Colnett, on H. M. S. *Rattler*. [6]

ca. 1812   Establishment of "Hathaway's Post Office" on Isla Floreana. [6]

1813	Captain David Porter, on American frigate *Essex*. [5-7]
1813	August 10th. Lieutenant John S. Cowan shot in duel and buried on James Island. [7]
1815, 22	Publication of David Porter's *Journal of a Cruise*. [5-7]
1825	George Anson Byron, on H. M. S. *Blonde*. [8]
1832	Islands annexed by Ecuador. [19]
1835	Charles Darwin, aboard H. M. S. *Beagle*, Captain Robert FitzRoy. [8]
1854	Publication of Herman Melville's *The Encantadas, or Enchanted Islands*. [9]
1869	Manuel J. Cobos begins operations on Isla San Cristóbal. [10]
1892	Ecuador renames islands *Archipielego de Colón*, in honor of the Columbus quatrocentenary. [19]
1904	January 15th. Death of Manuel J. Cobos. [10]
1905-06	California Academy of Sciences Expedition, aboard the schooner *Academy*. [11]
1909-41	Pre-war intelligence missions by various American naval vessels. [17]
1925	First Norwegian settlers arrive. [13]
1929	September 19th. Friedrich Ritter and Dore Strauch arrive on Isla Floreana. [15]
1932	August 28th. Heinz and Margret Wittmer arrive. [15]
1932	October. The Baroness and friends arrive. [15]
1932-38	Five Galápagos voyages of the *Velero III*, Captain G. Allan Hancock. [14]

1934   Mid-March. Disappearance and presumed death of the Baroness & Phillipson. [15] Mid-July. Lorenz leaves Isla Floreana with Nuggerud. [15] November 19th. Bodies of Lorenz & Nuggerud found on Isla Marchena. [15] November 21st. Death of Friedrich Ritter. [15]

1935   September 15th. Victor Wolfgang von Hagen dedicates Darwin monument on Isla San Cristóbal. [16]

1938   President Franklin D. Roosevelt, aboard the U. S. S. *Houston*. [15]

1941-46   Occupation by American military forces. [15-17].

1944   August 18th. Congress debates acquisition of Galápagos Islands. [20]

1959   Establishment of the Charles Darwin Foundation. [16]

1959-60   Failed attempt by Island Development Company to establish a colony on Isla San Cristóbal. [20]

1964   Dedication of Charles Darwin Research Station in Puerto Ayora, Isla Santa Cruz. [16]

1971   "Lonesome George" is discovered on Isla Pinta and brought to the Charles Darwin Research Station [4].

2005   Publication of *Charles Darwin Slept Here*.

CHAPTER ONE

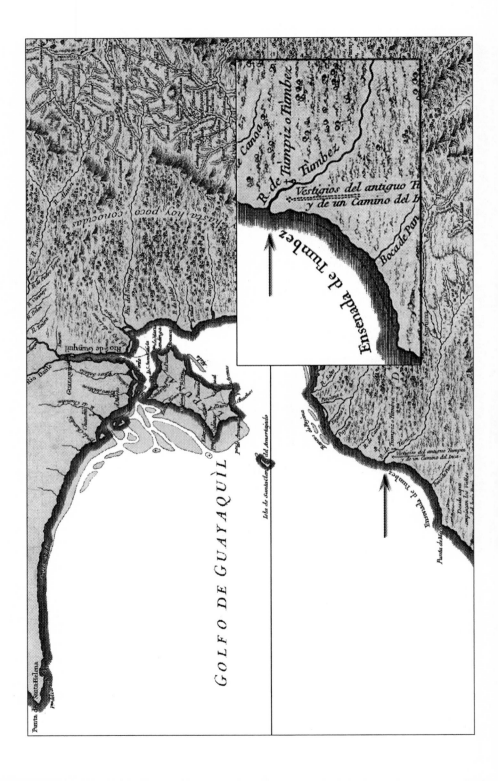

THE INCA VISITS GALÁPAGOS

*Navigating merchants, ... being great
talkers, ought not to be credited too easily.*

Pedro Sarmiento de Gamboa

There arrived at Tumbez some merchants who
had come by sea from the west, navigating
in balsas with sails. They gave information of
the land whence they came, which consisted
of some islands called Avachumbi and
Ninachumbi, where there were many people
and much gold. Tupac Inca did not lightly
believe the navigating merchants, for such men,
being great talkers, ought not to be credited too
easily. In order to obtain fuller information, and
as it was not a business of which news could
easily be got, he called a man named Antarqui,
who was a great necromancer and could even fly
through the air. Tupac Inca asked him whether
what the merchant mariners said was true.

Facing page: The Gulf of Guayaquil and Bay of Tumbez.
The arrows point inland to the village of Tumbez.

And Antarqui answered, after having thought
the matter well out, that what they said was
true, and that he would go there first. They say
he accomplished this by his arts, traversed the
route, saw the islands, their people and riches,
and, returning, gave certain information of all
to Tupac Inca.

The Inca, having this certainty, determined to
go there. He caused an immense number of
balsas to be constructed, in which he embarked
more than 20,000 chosen men. Tupac Inca
navigated and sailed on until he discovered the
islands of Avachumbi and Ninachumbi, and
returned, bringing back with him black people,
gold, a chair of brass, and a skin and jaw bone
of a horse. The duration of this expedition
undertaken by Tupac Inca was nine months,
others say a year.

THE LATE 16TH-CENTURY HISTORIAN Pedro Sarmiento de
Gamboa tells this tale of the tenth Inca and conqueror
of the kingdom of Quito. But Tupac Inca Yupanqui lived
one hundred years before Sarmiento, so the historian is by
no means a first-hand recorder of the event. Nevertheless
he knows—or *thinks* he knows—where the islands visited
by Tupac Inca are located. Writing in his 1572 *History of the
Incas,* Sarmiento claims that he too had visited Avachumbi
and Ninachumbi.

These are the islands which I discovered in
the South Sea on the 30th of November, 1567,
200 and more leagues to the westward, being
the great discovery of which I gave notice to
the Licentiate Governor Castro. But Alvaro de
Mendaña, General of the Fleet, did not wish to
occupy them.

In 1586, Miguel Cabello Valboa wrote of Tupac Inca's voyage, but he had his doubts about whether it was fiction or fact, and if the latter, where these islands might be found:

> I dare not confirm this deed, however, nor determine the islands in question, but the Indians report that the Inca brought back from this expedition a great number of prisoners whose skin was black, much gold and silver, a throne of copper, and skins of animals similar to horses. One is quite ignorant of where in Peru or the ocean washing its coast he could have found such things.

When Sir Clements Markham translated Sarmiento's *History of the Incas* at the beginning of the last century, he explained that the names Avachumbi and Ninachumbi mean "Outer Island" and "Fire Island" and "They were no doubt two of the Galápagos Islands." Markham may have based his conclusion on Sarmiento's account of islands "200 and more leagues to the westward" or about 600 miles off the mainland coast. But he says nothing about the chair of brass, nor is there a word about the other items brought home by the Inca. And surely he would know that a place "where there were many people and much gold" could not possibly be the Galápagos Islands.

Yet despite all indications that Avachumbi and Ninachumbi are someplace else, they are to this day occasionally said to be the modern Islas Isabela and Fernandina. Some would say the legend is nothing more than that: a little fiction invented by some imaginative Inca to encourage the Spaniards to look (or better yet, to go) beyond the mainland for the gold they so anxiously sought.

But even if the tale of a voyage has some foundation in truth—notwithstanding the Inca's crew of 20,000—Tupac Inca certainly discovered neither black people, nor gold,

nor chair of brass or throne of copper in Galápagos. If those
"skins of animals similar to horses" were actually taken
from sea lions, then he may indeed have stopped off at
Galápagos on his way home from another distant island.
But what island?

The legends of Polynesia tell of an ancient visitor named
"Tupa" who spoke of distant lands and of great kings.
Perhaps this visitor was Tupac Inca, although the legends
offer no account of a lost copper throne—nor anything
about a brass chair gone missing.

Even if the Inca did not visit Galápagos on the long way
home to Tumbez, perhaps Sarmiento did, although he can't
claim to be the first Spaniard to do so. That honor goes to a
banana importer from Panama whose real business was to
settle a dispute in Peru.

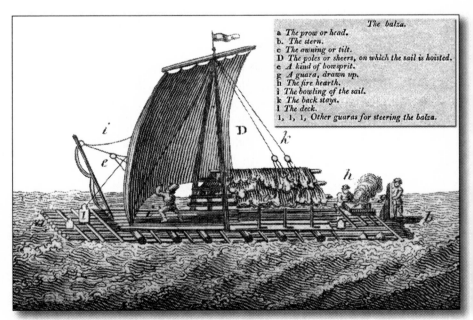

A balsa raft of a type in use more than two centuries after
the voyage of Inca Tupac Yupanqui. Did 20,000 chosen men
accompany him to Galápagos or beyond in such vessels?

CHAPTER TWO

THE BISHOP PAYS A CALL

*It seems as though at some time God
had showered stones; and the earth that
there is, is like slag.*

Tomás de Berlanga, 1535

At ABOUT THE TIME OF COLUMBUS—the day and date are unknown—a child was born in the little town of Berlanga de Duero in Spain. Señor and Señora Gómez christened their son Tomás Martínez, and in 1508 the lad was ordained in the Dominican order. Within a very few years Fray Tomás found himself Prior of a convent in Santo Domingo on the Caribbean island of Hispaniola. It was at this place that the young priest made his first mark on history by presenting the New World with the banana, which he had brought along from the Canary Islands. But banana imports were not the end of his accomplishments, and within the decade he was made Provincial of the province of Santa Cruz—a province created by himself in 1528. And then looking beyond his own boundaries, Tomás sought to bring parts of Mexico under his authority, but that didn't work out. Instead, the Church awarded him a larger prize: the diocese of Panama, which would need another four centuries until a canal-builder from up north engineered its dissection from Colombia to become the small country we know today. In earlier times Panama was the territory surrounding a village of that name, and its diocese embraced all that was known, and unknown, in western South America. In short, the former banana importer was now His Grace Fray Tomás de Berlanga, Bishop of Everything between Panama and Peru.

Fray Tomás's earlier designs on Mexico were not the only territorial claims that came to the attention of the authorities at home. Francisco Pizarro and Diego de Almagro could not resolve their own territorial disputes, and eventually Spain's Charles VI dispatched Fray Tomás to Peru to resolve the issue. In obedience to the royal command, the Bishop departed Panama for Peru on February 23rd of the year 1535, with an unexpected detour into Galápagos history. The first week of the voyage went well enough, with a favorable breeze to assist the Bishop's vessel down the coast of South America. But then the wind died and the ship drifted westward on a strong current against which neither sail nor prayer had influence. Six days passed. And then finally, "… on Wednesday, the tenth of March, we sighted an island." With little water left there was no choice but to make for it and hope for the best. But there would be no relief here: Berlanga reports that "they found nothing but seals, and turtles and such big tortoises that each could carry a man on top of himself, and many iguanas that are like serpents." His Grace sailed on.

> On another day we saw another island,
> larger than the first, and with great sierras;
> and thinking that, on account of its size and
> monstrous shape, there could not fail to be
> rivers and fruits, we went to it. At this juncture
> the water on the ship gave out and we were
> three days in reaching the island on account
> of the calms, during which all of us, as well as
> the horses, suffered great hardship.

The situation was not getting better, a two-day search for water found nothing, and in desperation they turned to squeezing moisture from cactus leaves. The drink was "not very tasty" and much resembled "slops of lye." Nevertheless there are those times when Bishops can't be choosers; Berlanga and his men "drank it as if it were rose water." Next, the crew set up an impromptu alter and on Sunday morning, March 14th, 1535, the Bishop of Panama celebrated the Mass of Passion Sunday in his open-air cathedral in the Pacific. At the concluding *ite missa est*, his flock went off in twos and threes to seek their worldly salvation, and they found it: a ravine among the rocks yielded some eight barrels of water and they were saved—all but one, and then two days later, another. Ten horses also perished.

They might have drawn even more water, but Berlanga thought they were no more than 75 miles or so from Peru. It would be imprudent to push their luck; better to make all haste for the mainland. Eleven days later they were down to one barrel of water and still the ship's master was uncertain of their location. His Grace took the altitude of the sun to discover they were now at three degrees south latitude and sailing slowly into nowhere. He had the ship change course, then set about rationing a blend of water and wine which lasted another week. When that was gone they sighted land but were kept away by a two-day calm. And so they waited, and made do with the few sips of wine that remained. But at last they found their way into the Bay of Caraques on Friday, April 9th, docking in company with a galleon just in from Nicaragua which had been at sea for eight months. Berlanga drew his conclusion: "We considered our trip good in comparison with theirs." The distance from the Bay of Panama to the Bay of Caraques is about 700 miles, the duration of his voyage 45 days and that works out to a speed of some 15 miles per day, or about five times better than that enjoyed by the Nicaraguans. It was indeed a good trip, especially—as His Grace observed—in comparison with others.

In his subsequent report to Charles VI—from which the above quotes are drawn—the Bishop gave no name for the place where he said Mass, although there's little doubt that it could be none but one of the Galápagos Islands. But which of those enchanted places could it be? There are clues:

> The distance around the first one was about four or five leagues and around the other, ten or twelve leagues.

And from that second island,

> ... we saw two others, one much larger than all, which was easily fifteen or twenty leagues around; the other was medium. I took the altitude [of the sun] to know where the islands were and they are between half a degree and a degree and a half of the Equator, in the south latitude.

It's not much to go on, but the likely candidates for the visited islands are the present islas Española and Floreana, which are roughly four or five, and ten or twelve leagues around—or on a modern measure, some 14 and 33 miles in circumference.

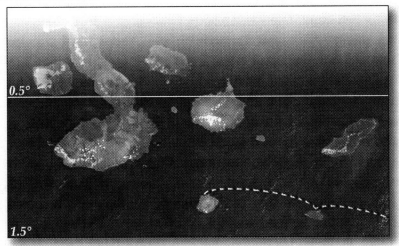

Berlanga's Galápagos: If His Grace celebrated Mass on Isla Floreana (lower center), the "two others" may have been Islas Isabela and Santa Cruz, off to the northwest, and north, respectively.

Floreana fits something else the Bishop wrote:

> On the sands of the shore there were some small
> stones that we stepped on as we landed, and they
> were diamond-like stones, and others amber colored.

Today tourists step on small diamond-like stones at the Green Beach near Floreana's Flamingo lagoon. Berlanga's "much larger island" may have been the southern extremity of the present Isla Isabela, and the "medium" island Santa Cruz. Both are visible from Floreana.

The Bishop was apparently skilled in navigation, as revealed by something he wrote in his letter to Charles:

> The bay of the Caraques is at half a degree south
> latitude and on the maps it is at three degrees; from
> this bay to Puerto Viejo, it is nine leagues along the
> sea coast.

Fray Tomás was correct: the modern Bahia de Caraques is situated near 0.5° south latitude, and from there it's about nine leagues, or 27 miles, to the present Portoviejo. So if that first Galápagos Mass was celebrated on Isla Floreana, then Berlanga's Galápagos were indeed between half a degree and a degree and a half below the equator, just as he said.

But why did he leave them nameless? Since His Grace did take notice of the turtles and tortoises—*tortugas e galápagos* as he put it—we might have expected him to write of the islands as "Galápagos" too, if that name were already known to him in that context. If so, surely he would have mentioned it, as he did every other waypoint along his extended journey. But if the islands were truly *terra incognita* to the Bishop, why did he not say as much? And known or unknown, why did he not at least honor the site of his altar with a name? For so many questions there is just one answer: "Unknown."

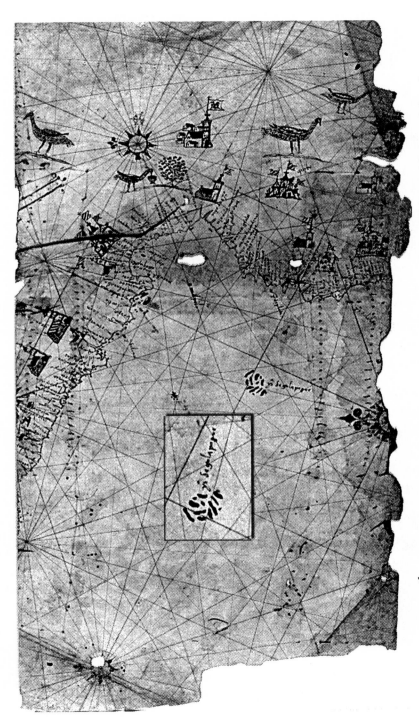

This 16th century vellum chart fragment may be the first to identify the Galápagos Islands by name (rotated 90° in inset). Did Fray Tomás de Berlanga have a hand in its production?

There is an old vellum chart at the Library of Congress that may have been created after Berlanga arrived in Peru. It shows the Galápagos Islands, and there's a tenuous clue that it also shows a Bishop's influence. The chart covers the Pacific coast of Central and northern South America, and the appearance of part of a compass rose at the lower border suggests this surviving fragment is the upper portion of a considerably larger sheet. What became of the rest is unknown, but it's probably safe to write if off as a casualty of the centuries, now permanently lost. The chart was tentatively dated in a *Report of the Librarian of Congress for the Fiscal Year ending June 1929:*

> It appears likely that it was not made until after the year 1561, because it contains the place name *Landecho* for a village in Guatemala. The village seems to have been named for a president of the Audiencia of Guatemala, named Landecho, who assumed office in 1561.

Although this would make it too late to be associated with Fray Tomás, the chart's general style suggests it might be earlier than that date—a possibility not ruled out by the Landecho place name. In the absence of reliable information, we may speculate that the village was not named in honor of el Presidente, but that el Presidente became identified with the village, just as Fray Tomás was known as Berlanga, after his birthplace in Spain. If the same might be said of Señor Landecho, then the village could have existed long before he took office, and there is circumstantial evidence to support this view: The *Audiencia* (High Court) of Guatemala was created in about 1540, and a Juan Nuñez de Landecho served as its president in 1559 or earlier. Also, the *Archivo General de Indias* contains a reference to a "gobernador Juan Martínez de Landecho de 1563-1568." In both cases, the "*de* Landecho" style suggests the men were from a village of that name. And that would allow the name to appear on a chart drawn before either was in office. But is there a connection between the chart and the Bishop? Perhaps there is. After all, he did write that "The bay of the Caraques is at half a degree south latitude and on the maps it is at three degrees." We don't know which maps he means, but the vellum chart is not one of them. We know that because here the bay is not at three degrees. It's at half a degree south latitude—just as the Bishop said.

Why is this chart so different from "the maps" mentioned by the Bishop but otherwise unknown? Is it because he supplied corrected information? If so, perhaps he also passed along information about islands populated by *tortugas e galápagos*. Although at first he underestimated their distance from the mainland, he knew better by the time he reached the Bay of Caraques and may have revised his original estimate accordingly. That would account for the islands—now shown with a name—appearing on the chart about 500 miles off the coast.

Was the chart therefore commissioned by the Bishop to correct errors he found on other charts? It does seem to go beyond a mere navigational aid, for it displays a decorative sprinkling of inland churches and towns, with many flags flying. It's just the sort of thing one might find on a chart prepared for—or under the direction of—a distinguished person. Or if the chart were in existence before the Bishop's arrival, perhaps the islands were added to it according to his description. That's not impossible, because the rhumb lines that crisscross its surface run beneath the islands. The same lines run on top of other locations, which tells us the islands were a later addition to the chart. In any case, *someone* named them "Galápagos" to commemorate those "big tortoises that each could carry a man on top of himself." And then someone wrote that name on a vellum chart. Was that someone a Bishop?

A Bishop's Birthplace. The village of Berlanga (inset) is
seen on a 1570 map of Spain by the famous cartographer
Abraham Ortelius.

The complete text of Fray Tomás de Berlanga's letter to
Charles VI is given here. The original letter is in the Archives
of the Indies in Seville, Spain.

Puerto Viejo:—April 26, 1535

Sacred Imperial Catholic Majesty:

It seemed right to me to let your Majesty know the
progress of my trip from the time I left Panama, which
was on the twenty-third of February of the current year,
until I arrived in this new town of Puerto Viejo.

The ship sailed with very good breezes for seven days,
and the pilot kept near land and we had a six-day calm;

the currents were so strong and engulfed us in such a
way that on Wednesday, the tenth of March, we sighted
an island; and, as on board there was enough water for
only two more days, they agreed to lower the life-boat
and go on land for water and grass for the horses. And
once out, they found nothing but sea lions, and turtles
and such big tortoises that each could carry a man on
top of himself, and many iguanas that are like serpents.
On another day we saw another island, larger than
the first, and with great sierras; and thinking that, on
account of its size and monstrous shape, there could not
fail to be rivers and fruits, we went to it. The distance
around the first one was about four or five leagues and
around the other, ten or twelve leagues. At this juncture
the water on the ship gave out and we were three days
in reaching the island on account of the calms, during
which all of us, as well as the horses, suffered great
hardship.

The boat once anchored, we all went on land and some
were given charge of making a well, and others of
looking for water over the island: from the well there
came out water saltier than that of the sea; on land they
were not able to find even a drop of water for two days,
and with the thirst the people felt, they resorted to a leaf
of some thistles like prickly pears, and because they were
somewhat juicy, although not very tasty, we began to eat
of them, and squeeze them to draw all the water from
them, and drawn, it looked like slops of lye, and they
drank it as if it were rose water.

On Passion Sunday, I had them bring on land the things
necessary for saying Mass, and after it was said, I again
sent the people in twos and threes, over different parts.
The Lord deigned that they should find in a ravine
among the rocks as much as a hogshead of water, and
after they had drawn that, they found more and more. In
all, eight hogsheads were filled, and the barrels and the

jugs that were on the boat, but through the lack of water we lost one man and two days after we left that island we lost another; and ten horses died.

From this island we saw two others, one much larger than all, which was easily fifteen or twenty leagues around; the other was medium. I took the altitude to know where the islands were and they are between half a degree and a degree and a half of the Equator, in the south latitude. On this second one, the same conditions prevailed as on the first; many seals, turtles, iguanas, tortoises, many birds like those of Spain, but so silly that they do not know how to flee, and many were caught in the hand. The other two islands we did not touch; I do not know their character. On this one, on the sands of the shore, there were some small stones that we stepped on as we landed, and they were diamond-like stones, and others amber colored; but on the whole island I do not think that there is a place where one might sow a bushel of corn, because most of it is full of very big stones, so much so that it seems as though at some time God had showered stones; and the earth that there is, is like slag, worthless, because it does not have the virtue to create a little grass, but only some thistles, the leaf of which I said we picked.

Thinking that we were not more than twenty or thirty leagues from the land of Peru, we were satisfied with the water already mentioned, although we might have filled more of our casks; but we set sail, and with medium weather we sailed eleven days without sighting land, and the pilot and the master of the ship came to me to ask me where we were and to tell me there was only one hogshead of water on the ship. I tried to take the altitude of the sun that day and found that we were in three degrees south latitude, and I realized that with the direction we were taking we were becoming more and more engulfed, that we were not even heading for land, because we were sailing south. I had them tack on the other side, and the hogshead of water I had divided as follows: half was given for the animals and with the other half a beverage was made which was put into the wine cask, for I held it as certain that we could not be far from land, and we sailed for eight days, during all of which the hogshead of the beverage lasted, by giving a ration to each one with which he was satisfied. And when the hogshead gave out and there was no relief for us, we sighted land and we had calm for two days, during which we drank only wine, but we took heart on sighting land. We entered the bay and river of the Caraques on Friday, the ninth of April and we met there the people of a galleon from Nicaragua who had left Nicaragua eight months before. So we considered our trip good in comparison with theirs.

The bay of the Caraques is at half a degree south latitude and on the maps it is at three degrees; from this bay to Puerto Viejo, it is nine leagues along the sea coast. The said bay is one of the most beautiful ports that there can be in the world, and the boats can moor there, and they can sail up it three or four leagues and they do not know whether any more. Commander Pedro de Alvarado landed here and destroyed a town of Indians that were there, and frightened others, and it is a pity to see the havoc wherever he went with his men.

> Facing page: The Bay of Caraques, at just the latitude mentioned by the Bishop. Puerto Viejo is at the lower center, and Charapoto is seen about midway between these two locations.

From this bay, I landed with the passengers and we set out on foot because our animals were worn out from coming to this town from Puerto Viejo, and walking we came to a valley which is called Charapoto, which has a very good river, where there are many Indians now peaceful, because Captain Francisco Pizarro had behaved so well that he is at peace with about thirty chiefs. This Captain and Lieutenant-Governor is so well looked upon by them that they bring him food of corn and fish and venison and whatever is necessary, and if by chance when they go to see some land they capture some Indians, they immediately return them to their native soil and they give them a cross so that on account of it no Spaniard will do them any harm, and anyone who wants to come to see it should bring some sign and that way no harm will be done them. If he learns that any gold or silver is taken from them, he immediately has it returned to them, and some of them have brought it to him and he tells them that he has not come for their gold or their silver, but rather so that they may know God and Your Majesty, and that Your Majesty will give them masters, who will have charge of teaching them the things of the Holy Catholic Faith, and that on account of that solicitude, they must undertake to feed them. The keeping of this said Captain seems to me very good for the serving of our Lord and Your Majesty,

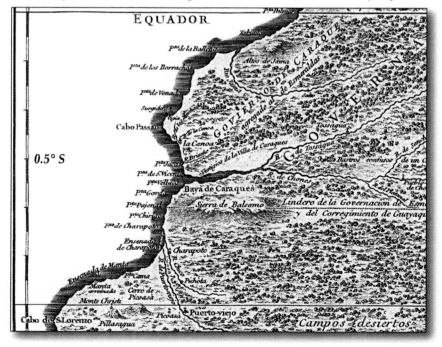

and for relieving your royal conscience; and since he
has a great thing to do, I have told him Your Majesty's
intention in this matter, and he is determined not to
deviate from it very soon. There are grand mines of gold,
and here I gave them information from those who were
with Alvarado that six or seven leagues from this town
there are very good gold mines. There is thought to be a
bed of emeralds, because the Indians have them in their
jewelry. Frequently, the said Indians have touchstones
and copper with [emerald] points of 22 karats, and
also plate with points, some of very good quality. It is
thought that before half a year a good part of this land
will be peaceful, owing to the good treatment given
them by the already mentioned Captain and Lieutenant;
and Your Majesty should support him in it, and it is
necessary considering the importunities of the men that
he has, because they follow with longing eyes every trace
of gold that they see.

God willing, I shall leave for the town of San Miguel
in four days. Of the Governor, Don Francisco Pizarro,
I know nothing at present. He is quite far from here,
although some believe that he is coming to the town of
Truxillo, which is between San Miguel and Xauxa.

The Lord fill Your Sacred Majesty with holy love and
grace for many years and with the conservation of your
realms and an increase of other new ones, as I hope.
From this new town of Puerto Viejo, the twenty-sixth
of April, of one thousand, five hundred and thirty-five
years.—of Your Sacred Imperial Catholic Majesty.—I
am your most true servant and subject and perpetual
Chaplain, who kisses your royal feet and hands.—Fray
Tomás eps locastelli aurii.—(his signature).

CHAPTER THREE

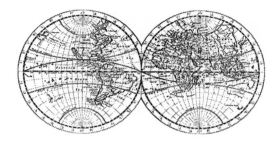

CAPTAIN WILLIAM DAMPIER, PIRATE AND HYDROGRAPHER

*I dined with Pepys, where was Captain
Dampier. He seemed a more modest man
than one would imagine by the relation of
the crew he had assorted with.*

The diary of John Evelyn
entry for 6th August, 1698

A YOUNG BRITISH NATURALIST set out on an extended voyage round the world and after more than a year at sea, tarried awhile at the Galápagos Islands. An inquisitive sort he was, and while his shipmates busied themselves with other activities, he busied himself studying the unique flora and fauna. A few years later he wrote the first book about it all, which was quite well received and established the writer as an authority on such matters. One hardly need be told that his last name begins with "D" and the book's title contains the word *Voyage* to know his identity.

No, that's not it. The famous *Voyage of the Beagle* author was neither the first naturalist to explore the islands, nor the first to write a book about it. Both honors go to William Dampier, who wrote his *A New Voyage Round the World* more than a century before the birth of Charles Darwin. In fact, Darwin's predecessor was a contemporary of his great-grandfather, William Darwin of Elston, although there's no reason to suspect these two Williams ever met.

19

Even if the intervening centuries had not separated Darwin and Dampier, their respective social positions might have done the job, for the one set forth as country gentleman, the other as buccaneer. Yet they did have a few things in common, and one was an uncommon curiosity for natural history. Darwin satisfied his as an invited and unpaid guest aboard H. M. S. *Beagle,* Captain Robert FitzRoy.

WILLIAM DAMPIER.

A ca. 1785 engraving, unknown artist, after a 1781 engraving by Charles Sherwin, which was in turn after a ca. 1697 portrait by Thomas Murray.

Dampier accomplished much the same thing by signing on to the good ship *Revenge,* Captain John Cook, where he too was unpaid. And although he could not fall back on a Darwinian inheritance, he might look ahead to earning a little something along the way. But that would depend on what ships might be captured, what towns might be plundered, what prisoners might be ransomed. Given the right turn of events, he might even return to England with the resources to become a gentleman himself.

Darwin and Dampier also shared a common habit: they kept journals. Dampier's tells us much about his surroundings, but little about himself. Some say he was an officer—a conclusion drawn from little more than an offhand remark committed to paper. Commenting on his shipmates, Dampier wrote:

> For altho' these men were more under
> command, than I had ever seen any privateers,
> yet I could not expect to find them at a
> minute's call.

Just the sort of thing a disgruntled ship's officer might say, but also just the sort of thing any perceptive shipboard scribe might jot down on observing the action—or perhaps the inaction—of his shipmates. One needn't be in charge of anything to recognize a crew that needs work. In fact, Dampier described his own status—or lack of it—when he prepared his journal for publication:

> It may be demanded by some why I call these
> voyages & discoverys myne seeing I was neither
> master nor mate of any of the ships.

The ship's Master indirectly supports Dampier's claim: William Ambrosia Cowley notes in his own journal that he performed his navigational chores "without the assistance of a mate."

And yet Dampier drops contradictory hints. He reports the ship's latitude in his narrative, and of course he'd need an instrument for that. And in fact he had one, as he explains when describing "...the island *Lobos*, which lieth in Lat. 6. d. 24 m. South Lat. (I took the Elevation of it ashore with an

Astrolabe)." To have such a tool would certainly suggest that Dampier had some responsibility beyond that of the ordinary deck hand. And it would be a bit odd if Cowley were not assisted by a man with an astrolabe at hand, unless of course Cowley didn't want assistance, or Dampier didn't want to offer it. Or as another possibility, both men had books to write, and neither wanted to acknowledge the competition. But with no direct comment from either man about his relationship with the other, the link between them remains a mystery.

There is however a link of a different sort, tenuous as it is, between William Dampier and Robert FitzRoy. In 19th century British Society, Captain FitzRoy claimed his gentlemanly pedigree by virtue of his paternal grandfather Augustus, third Duke of Grafton. The first Duke was Henry, son of King Charles the Second, who had not troubled himself to marry Henry's mother, which was understandable since His Majesty already had a wife back at the palace and apparently saw no pressing need to be both King and Gentleman. (Learned comparisons between this and any other Royal Charles are beyond the scope of this little essay.)

Given the delicacy of 17th-century society, the boy could not assume the royal Stuart surname, and so became Henry Son-of-the-King, or as they say in polite society, *Fitz Roy*.

The first Duke did not follow the royal example and actually married his lady, who was thereupon transformed into the first Duchess of Grafton, and shortly thereafter into the first widow Grafton when the 27-year-old Duke was killed on his ship, also named *Grafton*. For the sake of the aristocratic pretensions of the future FitzRoy of the *Beagle*, it should be noted that the second Duke's birth was within a time frame which permitted the lad to claim with a straight face that he really was the legitimate son of the first Duke.

But to return to William Dampier from this digression on the mating habits of British aristocracy, we turn to Chapter 15 of his *New Voyage* where he tells us he took advantage of an old seaman's privilege, while sailing beyond the southern coast of today's Taiwan. There he found an island which "I called the Duke of *Grafton's* Isle, as soon as we landed on it; having married my Wife out of his Dutchess's Family, and left her at Arlington House, at my going Abroad." If Captain Robert FitzRoy had read William Dampier, surely he would have noted that the buccaneer's wife lived in the home of his ancestors. But if he did have any reaction to this little bit of intelligence, it has not been recorded.

Dampier's wife did not necessarily marry beneath her station, since at that time the word "family" simply defined "those who live in the same house" (and Duchess was spelled with a "t"). Arlington House—after Lord Arlington, father of the Duchess—was the Grafton family seat, where the new Mrs. Dampier may have earned her keep as servant to the Duchess. Or her station may have been higher, or lower: Dampier says no more of her, and precious little about himself either, for he thought his world more interesting than himself.

He set about describing it in his *New Voyage,* where he tells of his departure from England early in the year 1679, bound for Jamaica and beyond. On a previous trip he had spent three years in Central America as a log-cutter, and now expected to resume that career. Fortunately for us, he didn't, for

> ... upon some maturer Considerations of my
> intended Voyage to *Campeachy,* I changed my
> Thoughts of that design, and continued at
> *Jamaica,* in Expectation of some other Business.

Business? *What* business? As a non-answer, we have an early example of Dampierian obscurity: "I shall not trouble the reader," he writes, "with the Particulars of my own Affairs

during my Stay there." His "Business" and "Affairs" must
have gone off rather well though, for he purchased a small
estate in Dorchester and was about to return there when a
Mr. Hobby persuaded him to go on a short trading voyage
to the Moskito Coast. Hobby and company got as far as the
west coast of Jamaica, where they met a fleet of buccaneers,
or privateers as Dampier preferred to call them. Sensing
golder pastures elsewhere, Hobby's crew deserted—all
except the faithful Dampier who stayed with him. For about
three or four days. Then he deserted too, and we hear no
more of the unfortunate Mr. Hobby.

Shortly after Christmas, 1679, Dampier and friends
plundered the city of Portobello, then made their first
overland crossing of the Isthmus of Darien the following
April. They spent a pleasant year under the command of
Captain Bartholomew Sharp, looting and pillaging selected
villages and ships along the western coast of South America,
then celebrated their next Christmas at the isle of Juan
Fernandez, or *John Fernando* as Dampier called it. While there,
they deposed Captain Sharp in favor of Captain Watling.
Unfortunately, one of Watling's first official actions was to
get himself killed, after which the fickle crew re-elected
Sharp as Captain, much to the displeasure of Dampier and
some of the others:

> I, who had never been pleased with his
> Management, though I had hitherto kept
> my Mind to my self, now declared my self
> on the side of those that were Out-voted;
> and according to our Agreement, we took
> our Shares of such Necessaries, as were fit
> to carry over Land with us, (for that was our
> Resolution) and so prepared for our Departure.

The departure took Dampier's group back to the Isthmus of
Darien, which they hoped to re-cross with the assistance of

local Indian guides. Negotiations got off to a bad start with a grumpy Indian who offered to escort them west or east into lands known to be held by enemies of the English. With Spaniards to the left, Spaniards to the right, and Indians occupying center ground, the way to safety was clearly north. Yet all agreed it would not be a very good idea for these few dozen Englishmen to get nasty just now. Or as Dampier dead-panned, "It was neither time nor place to be angry with Indians."

After unsuccessfully tempting their host with money, axes and various trinkets, one of the men remembered he had a sky-colored petticoat in his bag. No one asked why he had a sky-colored petticoat in his bag, but there it was. And a good thing too, for on putting it on the Indian's delighted wife, she prevailed on her husband to lighten up, and "soon brought him into a better humour." A guide was arranged and the men were off at last, if not yet home free.

On encountering a river they could not easily ford, they decided to send a man across with a line. Once safely on the other side, the plan was to make it fast and send their goods across, followed by the non-swimmers in the crowd. The man chosen for the job was one George Gayne, or perhaps it was John Gayny. He's George in Dampier's manuscript, but becomes John in the printed book, where the final letter in his last name also changes. But whatever his name, perhaps he was selected because he was a good swimmer, or perhaps because he was a few coins short of a full treasure chest. To support the latter theory, he tied the line around his neck, strapped his share of accumulated loot to his back, then plunged into the stream.

From the safety of the shore, the crew closely watched Gayny but not the line, which got caught on something, flipping him on his back. The men on shore eventually freed their end of the line and tossed it into the torrent. Gayny's end, with Gayny still attached, disappeared downstream. Some days later, stragglers found him with his entire estate of $300 still intact. Unfortunately, he was dead. The stragglers left him and his money in peace, and Dampier had the last word: "This put a Period to that Contrivance."

Their next contrivance was to chop down a tree and crawl across it to the other side. Of no comfort to the late George Gayne or John Gayny, but it worked. But even if it hadn't, Dampier might have had better luck in the water than did his late colleague, since he had brought along a life preserver of sorts.

> Foreseeing a Necessity of wading through
> Rivers frequently in our Land-march, I took
> care before I left the Ship to provide my self
> a large Joint of Bambo, which I stopt at both
> Ends, closing it with Wax, so as to keep out
> any Water. In this I preserved my Journal and
> other Writings from being wet, tho' I was often
> forced to swim.

Dampier was always concerned about his journal and other writings: some ten years later we find him in the Far East. The canoe in which he was riding had just overturned, dumping him and its contents overboard. After swimming ashore, he reports that

> I had nothing of value but my Journal and
> some Drafts of Land of my own taking, which
> I much prized, and which I had hitherto
> carefully preserved. Mr. *Hall* had also such
> another Cargo of Books and Drafts, which were
> now like to perish. But we presently opened
> our Chests and took out our Books, which,
> with much ado, we did afterwards dry; but
> some of our Drafts that lay loose in our Chests
> were spoiled. We lay here afterwards three
> Days, making great Fires to dry our Books.

Later the same year he would be obliged to escape from a fort to a waiting ship.

> I brought with me my Journal, and most of my written Papers; but some Papers and Books of value I left in haste, being glad I was my self at Liberty, and had hopes of seeing *England* again.

But to return to the Darien adventure, it took the men three weeks and two days to make the crossing, for there was no other way to do it without encountering hostile Spaniards. If it were not for that little obstacle, Dampier tells us that "A Man may pass from Sea to Sea in three Days time with ease. The Indians can do it in a day and a half."

Once in the safety of the North Sea, which we know as the Caribbean, he says little about business, preferring to describe the cedars, the Corn Islands and their inhabitants, and to offer an account of manatee and tortoise, and of the manner in which the Moskito Indians hunt them. He even includes a description of the harpoon, the fish hook and the tortoise iron. And then, "So much by way of Digression" says Dampier, and goes back to describing the voyage, frequently punctuated with an account of an interesting bird or a mangrove tree. With some effort, he puts off a further dissertation on turtles for a later chapter:

> I would here give a particular Description of these, and other sorts of Turtle in these Seas; but because I shall have occasion to mention some other sort of Turtle when I come again into the South-Seas, that are very different from all these, I shall there give a general Account of all these several sorts at once, that the Difference between them may be the better discerned.

And then, it's on to nuts: Dampier assures us that "My worthy Consort Mr. *Ringrose* commends most the *Guiaquil* Nut; I presume, because he had little Knowledge of the rest." But of course his worthy consort is mistaken—Dampier assures us that the finest chocolate comes instead from the Caraccos Nut.

After a year of this, Dampier joined a group on a voyage to Virginia, during which he finds time to describe the habits of a sucking-fish which he thinks is "the *Remora*, of which the Antients tell such Stories." And then he loses his voice:

> We met nothing else worth Remark in our Voyage to *Virginia*; where we arrived in *July* 1682. That Country is so well known to our Nation, that I shall say nothing of it, nor shall I detain the Reader with the Story of my own Affairs, and the Trouble that befel me during about Thirteen Months of my Stay there.

Trouble? *What* trouble? Dampier won't detain us with details, so it's anyone's guess.

But to return to the story, as Dampier himself would often remark after an extended look into the mating habits of the sea turtle or some other little digression. To return to the story, the year 1683 saw Captain John Cook lead a pack of rogues outward bound from Virginia, destination the great Southern Sea and eventually the Galápagos Islands. Dampier was one of them.

A month or so before Galápagos, the company captured a few Spanish vessels off the coast of Peru. The event may have recalled a similar seizure off Cartagena in 1681, where at the cost of a few men killed and a few more injured, the ship and its cargo were theirs:

> She was laden with Sugar and Tobacco, and
> had 7 or 8 Tuns of Marmalett on board.

And now, in 1683, . . .

> In this ship were likewise 7 or 8 Tuns of
> Marmalade of Quinces.

Dampier paid more attention to description than to spelling, but of this we were forewarned in his preface:

> I have not been curious as to the spelling of
> the Names of Places, Plants, Fruits, Animals,
> &c. which in any of these remoter parts are
> given at the pleasure of Travellers, and vary
> according to their different Humours.

Although Dampier's own pleasure allowed him to serve up marmalett in 1681 and marmalade in 1684, he might have been put in better humour if the ship had not put in to Guanchaco shortly before it was captured. While taking on flour there, it was learned that buccaneers were nearby, and some 800,000 pieces of eight bound for Panama were instead put ashore at Guanchaco. And there was little chance of going in after it, for even now the residents were building a fort to repulse unwelcome visitors. So the buccaneers had to content themselves with marmalade, flour, and two bonus prizes: "a stately Mule sent to the President, and a very large Image of the Virgin *Mary* in Wood, carved and painted to adorn a new Church at *Panama*."

With no money in their pockets and a hostile reception committee on shore, the English thought it best to revise the itinerary. "We steered away N. W. by N. intending to run into the Latitude of the Isles *Gallapagos*," and that's just what they did, taking three of their captured ships with them as prizes. Dampier uses the occasion for a geography lesson.

> The *Gallapagos* Islands are a great number of
> uninhabited Islands, lying under, and on both
> sides of the Equator. They are laid down in the
> Longitude of 181, reaching to the Westward
> as far as 176, therefore their Longitude from
> *England* Westward is about 68 degrees. But I
> believe our Hydrographers do not place them
> far enough to the Westward.

Perhaps Dampier's typesetter had a problem with this
excerpt. In order for the longitudes to make sense, they must
be re-written as 281 and 276, then converted into modern
notation, which would place the islands between 89°13′ W
and 84°13′ W longitude. Their actual location is between
92° W and 89°14′ W longitude. So Dampier was correct:
17th-century English hydrographers had *not* placed them
far enough to the westward. But now, some questions: Who
were "our Hydrographers" and on what map, or maps,
did they place the islands not far enough to the westward?
Dampier doesn't offer any answers, and in fact confuses the
issue in the sentence immediately following:

> The *Spaniards*, who first discovered them, and
> in whose draughts alone they are laid down,
> report them to be a great number stretching
> North-West from the line, as far as 5 degrees
> North.

If Dampier thought that only the Spaniards had charted
the islands, then what on earth did he mean by "our
hydrographers" in the previous sentence? He doesn't say.
And as to their longitude westward from England, if the
islands were indeed at 68 degrees, we'd find them up in
the Andes somewhere East of Quito. Even Dampier would
have been surprised at that. But if we speculate that he really
meant 86 degrees, this becomes 91°13′ if we reckon from
Greenwich, and it puts him and us almost in the center of
Galápagos.

Although Dampier's own *New Voyage* is not illustrated, an artist on his later voyage with Woodes Rogers sketched the islands and their residents for Edward Cooke's account of the trip. The islands seen here are the modern Isla Santa Cruz (top) and Santa Fe.

Dampier uses the occasion of the Galápagos visit for a digression on turtles on land and turtles at sea. Of the land turtle, ...

> They are extraordinarily large and fat; and so sweet, that no Pullet eats more pleasantly."

Recalling his earlier promise to describe the differences between one turtle and another, "that the Difference between them may be the better discerned," he digresses from the digression to recall that

> There are 3 or 4 sorts of these Creatures in the West-Indies. One is called by the *Spaniards*, *Hecatee*; these live in fresh Water-ponds. Another sort is called *Tenapen*; these are a great deal less than the *Hecatee*."

He describes how Spanish hunters would "brand" the turtles they caught, then bring several hundred of them to Cuba to sell, "for they are very good Meat, and every Man knows his own by their Marks." And then, it's back to Galápagos: "These Tortoise in the Gallapagoes are more like the *Hecatee*, except that, as I said before, they are much bigger. And in the water,

> There are 4 sorts of Sea-turtle. The Trunk-turtle is commonly bigger than the other, their Backs are higher and rounder, and their Flesh rank and not wholsome. The Loggerhead is so call'd, because it hath a great Head, much bigger than the other sorts; their flesh is likewise very rank, and seldom eaten but in case of Necessity. The Hawks-bill Turtle is the least kind, they are so call'd because their Mouths are long and small, somewhat resembling the Bill of a Hawk. These are but ordinary food, but generally sweeter than the Loggerhead: Yet these Hawks-bills, in some places are unwholsome, causing them that eat them to purge and vomit excessively.

And finally,

> The green Turtle are so called, because their shell is greener than any other. Green Turtle are the sweetest of all the kinds: but there are degrees of them, both in respect to their flesh and their bigness. I have heard of a monstrous green Turtle once taken at *Port-Royal,* in the Bay of *Campeachy* that was four foot deep from the back to the belly, and the belly six foot broad. The leaves of Fat afforded eight Gallons of Oil.

And then he remembers variations found on the Mexican coast. Perhaps Charles Darwin should have studied William Dampier before setting out on his own voyage.

Dampier tells us that Captain Cook took sick while the ship was at Juan Fernandez, and he didn't get any better in Galápagos. He hung on for about another month, then died as the vessel approached the Spanish Main. Dampier explains:

> It is usual with sick Men coming from the Sea,
> where they have nothing but the Sea-Air, to
> die off as soon as ever they come within the
> view of the Land.

The Captain was brought ashore for burial shortly after the buccaneers were safely at anchor. As Dampier tells us, the little fleet now consisted of "the ship I was in, Captain *Eaton*, and the great Meal Prize." Those who are keeping score may wonder, therefore, what happened to the other two ships? Characteristically, Dampier does not detain the reader with such boring details as the fate of unneeded prizes. But he does provide a few clues. On September 3rd, 1684, they "… left the *Indians* in possession of the Prize which we had brought in hither." And one year later, to the day,

> We turned ashore all our Prisoners and Pilots,
> they being unacquainted further to the West,
> which was the Coast that we designed to visit.

The unnamed island is the modern Isla San Cristóbal, with Kicker Rock on the left.

Once safely ashore, the former prisoners didn't mind detaining their readers at all. Antonio Rodea and Miguel Antonio Bachi reported to the Spanish authorities that the buccaneers burned one ship and ran another aground while still in Galápagos. From the third, they stored some flour ashore against future need. The ship itself remained in their custody and accompanied the buccaneers to Mexico. This therefore was the great Meal Prize which was given to the Indians. Its unfortunate commander was a Captain Bicuña, whose fate goes unrecorded.

A fortnight before turning the prisoners loose, Dampier said goodbye to Captain Davis and joined the crew of the *Cygnet*, under the command of the well-named Captain Swan. Dampier explains:

> It was not from any dislike to my old Captain,
> but to get some knowledge of the Northern
> Parts of this Continent of Mexico: And I knew
> that Capt. Swan determined to coast it as far
> North, as he thought convenient, and then pass
> over for the East-Indies; which was a way very
> agreeable to my Inclination.

Indeed, Dampier had an apparently cordial reunion with Captain Davis some years later in London, during which Davis told him of another visit to Galápagos.

> Capt. *Davis* came hither a second time. He
> found such plenty of Land-Turtle, that he and
> his Men eat nothing else for three Months that
> he staid there. They were so fat that he saved
> sixty Jars of Oil out of those that he spent;
> This Oil served instead of Butter, to eat with
> Doughboys or Dumplins, in his return out of
> these Seas.

Although Davis returned out of these seas by sailing around Cape Horn, back to the Caribbean and then to Virginia, Dampier and company returned to England via the Pacific Sea, which he felt had been ill-named.

> Tho' it be usual with our Mapmakers to give that Name to this whole Ocean, yet, in my Opinion, the Name of the Pacifick-Sea ought not to be extended from South to North farther then from 30 to about 4 Deg. South Latitude, and from the American Shore Westward indefinitely, with respect to my Observation; who have been in these parts 250 Leagues or more from the Land, and still had the Sea very quiet from Winds.

Dampier felt strongly on this point, for when dining with Samuel Pepys and John Evelyn some fifteen years later, the latter diarist tells us Dampier "assured us that the maps hitherto extant were all false as to the Pacific Sea, which he makes on the south of the line, that on the north end running by the coast of Peru being extremely tempestuous."

Above: Cartographer Herman Moll apparently took Dampier at his word, applying "The Pacifick Sea" to the area south of the line.

Fortunately for our author and his captain, their ship eventually traversed the tempestuous and ill-named Pacific Sea before its provisions were exhausted. Otherwise—or so Dampier was later informed—the crew had planned to have their Captain for dinner, followed by Dampier and the others who had persuaded them to attempt this crossing. When Captain Swan learned how close they had both come to the dinner plate, he offered the following observation: "Ah! Dampier, you would have made them but a poor meal," for as Dampier explains, "I was as lean as the Captain was lusty and fleshy."

The Pacific was not the only ocean he thought ill-named. In his day, the pond separating the Americas from Europe and Africa was commonly called the Aetheopian Sea slightly below the equator, and the North Sea above it. Dampier disapproved.

> Upon mention of the *Atlantick* Sea, there is one
> thing I would observe to the *Reader*, that I use
> that name not only for the *North-Sea*, as 'tis
> called, but for this whole Ocean, on both sides
> of the *Equator*. If I be questioned for taking this
> Liberty, I should think it enough to say, that I
> wanted a general name for this whole Ocean,
> and I could not find one more proper.

Perhaps Dampier was unable to persuade his publisher on the propriety of this point, for the maps in his own books still show the old *Aethiopian* and *North Sea* labels. But eventually his judgement prevailed, and few today have even heard of an Aethiopian Sea. And as for the North Sea, that body of water has long since receded to the East coast of Great Britain.

There is not much record of the married life of Mr. and Mrs. William Dampier. Her first name, Judith, comes from an early will, and given her husband's penchant for extended trips, there may be no record of anything else simply because there was no anything else. In fact, we may speculate that Dampier either outlived his Judith, or that she grew sick of waiting up and left—perhaps even to find companionship in the arms of a landsman. But for whatever reason, a later will stipulates that his goods, "household stuffe" and nine-tenths of his estate should go to "… my loving cousin Grace Mercer of London, spinster." The remaining tenth was for his "loving brother, George Dampier." In characteristic silence, Dampier says almost nothing about brother George in his printed works, and even less—that is, nothing at all— about cousin Grace.

Is it worth mentioning that Samuel Pepys retained a servant named Mercer? Although identified as his wife's "woman," now and then Miss Mercer would help Samuel get dressed, at which time he enjoyed fondling her breasts. He'd record such indiscretions in his diary, yet it never occurred to him to jot down Mercer's first name. He does however describe coming home one day to his wife and a few others, and that "they and we and Mrs. Mercer, the mother, and her daughter Anne, and our Mercer, [went] to supper to a good vension-pasty and other good things." In another entry, he notes that "This day, Mercer not being at home, but against her mistress's orders gone to her mother's." And still elsewhere he reports visiting Mrs. Mercer and her two daughters, or, of being accompanied by "the two Mercers" which may have meant mother and daughter, or servant and sister. About all we can do here is state that Pepys' Mercer was the sister of Anne, the daughter of Mrs. Mercer, and for all we know, a relative of Grace Mercer, spinster. If so, perhaps it was she who introduced cousin William to master Samuel. Or perhaps not; we shall never know.

We do know, however, that Dampier had another cousin, like himself a voyager of some repute. The celebrated travel writer Lemuel Gulliver prefaces his description of a voyage to Lilliput with a mention of hiring some university gentlemen to correct his own style "... as my cousin Dampier did by my advice, in his book called, *A Voyage round the World.*" Mr. Gulliver's buccaneer cousin admits as much about his later book, *A Voyage to New Holland:*

> I think it so far from being a Diminution to
> one of my Education and Employment, to
> have what I write, Revised and Corrected by
> Friends; that on the contrary, the best and most
> eminent Authors are not ashamed to own the
> same Thing, and look on it as an Advantage.

But did Dampier's unidentified "friends" have a hand in the earlier work, as cousin Lemuel states? Maybe. Or maybe not, for Dampier is a bit defensive about his own writing in his first opus:

> As to my Stile, it cannot be expected, that
> a Seaman should affect Politeness. ... I am
> perswaded, that if what I say be intelligible,
> it matters not greatly in what words it is
> express'd.

He might not have felt the need for such an up-front apology if his *New Voyage Round the World* had been polished by some university gentlemen or other friends. But if not the recipient of friendly polish, Dampier's first work does reveal a few facts that he did not gather at first hand. His critics may have noticed this too, for he feels the need to defend himself in his *New Holland* book: "I assure the Reader, I have taken nothing from any Man without mentioning his name." He does allow an exception though, in the case of "credible Persons who desired not to be named; and these

I have always expressly distinguished in my Books from what I relate as of my own observing."

Well, *almost* always. But Dampier had an apparent lapse in Galápagos, where he arrived on the last day of May, 1684, and after landing on two islands, was gone within a fortnight. Yet he tells us of large islands with "some pretty big rivers; and in many of the other lesser Islands, there are Brooks of good Water." And as for that water,

> The time of the Year for the Rains is in
> *November, December* and *January.* Then there is
> oftentimes excessive hard tempestuous weather,
> mixt with much Thunder and Lightning. ...
> but in *May, June, July* and *August,* the Weather is
> always very fair.

Now how did he know that? One might suspect that Captain Davis filled him in, for Dampier's manuscript journal reports that

> What I have not of my own knowledge I had
> from Captain Davies who was there afterwards
> and carreened his ship at neither of these
> [islands] that wee were at but at others to the
> westward of them.

In print, the captain's misspelled name is corrected, but the direct acknowledgement of him as a source does not appear here. But much later in the book, Dampier offers credit to his resource person: "I shall add what Captain Davis told me lately, ..." Well then, what might Captain Davis have told the author about the rains of Galápagos?

Nothing. We know this indirectly from the work of yet another shipboard scribe, Lionel Wafer, with whom we shall spend more time later on. Davis himself was illiterate (and we'll get to that too in another chapter), but Wafer, who was with Davis, made a passing remark about their return visit: "We were got again to the *Gallapago's*, under the Line; and were then resolv'd to make the best of our Way out of these Seas." Wafer offers no dates, but from another comment we can tell when this second visit took place. Shortly after leaving the enchanted isles,

> ... our Ship and Bark felt a terrible Shock;
> which put our Men into such a Consternation,
> that they could hardly tell where they were.

The ship's company subsequently learned of an earthquake that badly shook Peru – and themselves – at about 4:00 am on a day not recorded by Wafer. But from other sources we know that the unhappy event occurred on October 20th, 1687, and therefore Davis and Company had left Galápagos for the last time earlier in the same month. Since they were gone before the rains came, we know that Dampier got his weather information from someone else, whom he does not identify.

At another point we read a stream of disconnected thoughts.

> I took the height of the sun with an *Astrolabe*.
> These Isles of the *Gallapago's* have plenty of
> Salt. We stay'd here but 12 Days.

Right: An astrolabe of the type William Dampier may have used when he took the height of the Galápagos sun.

He has nothing further to say about Galápagos salt, perhaps because he had not found it on his own. Perhaps he was repeating local knowledge. For example,

> The *Spaniards*, with whom I have discoursed,
> have told me, that there is a very high Land all
> the way between *Coquimbo* and *Baldivia*.

Dampier did not see this area for himself, and so he tells us what others told him. Did those others also speak of rains, and of salt? He doesn't say.

William Dampier may have seen more of Galápagos in less than a fortnight than Charles Darwin saw in more than a month. Still, when we think of Galápagos today we think Darwin, not Dampier. The naturalist even has an island named in his honor. The buccaneer has nothing. But perhaps that's understandable; Darwin's *On the Origin of Species* surely made more of an impact on this world than anything written by his predecessor. And Galápagos played such an important role in his theory that it's fitting he be remembered there.

Darwin studied variations in pigeons back home in England some years after his Galápagos visit. Dampier also studied avian differences after his own Galápagos visit. But his observations referred to variations in the "clocking-hens" he saw in Brazil and the Caribbean. Darwin's conclusions are of course known to all, and we would not be surprised if he wrote of birds that were "…near akin to each other, as so many sub-species of the same kind." But although the observation introduces the concept of "sub-species" to the literature, it is not Darwin's. It was written a century before his birth. The author was William Dampier.

> Overleaf: Herman Moll's map of the world from
> William Dampier's *New Voyage Round the World*.

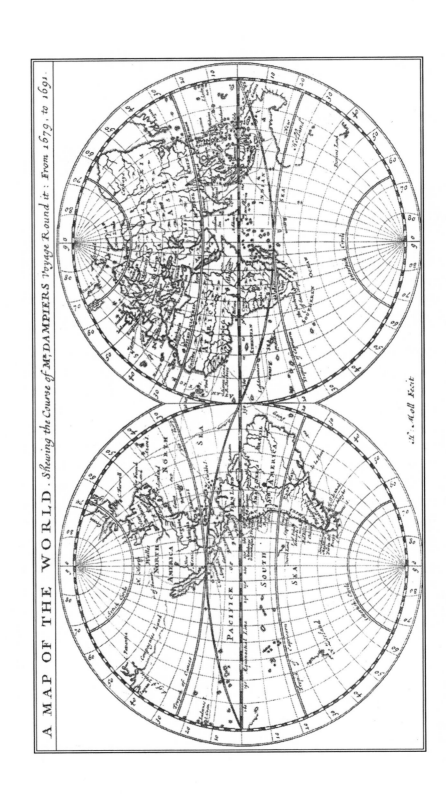

A MAP OF THE WORLD. *Shewing the Course of* M^r. DAMPIERS *Voyage Round it : From 1679, to 1691.*

H. Moll Fecit

CHAPTER FOUR

Comleys or
Enchanted Island

WILLIAM AMBROSIA COWLEY, MARRINER

*We sailed away to the Westward to see if wee could
find those Ilands called the Galipoloes, which made the
Spaniards laugh at us, teling us they were enchanted
ilands. They were but shadows and no real ilands.*

in his journal, May 1684

AUGUST 1683. THE GOOD SHIP *REVENGE*, Captain John Cook,
set sail from Smith's Island, Virginia. At first glance the
departure might have looked like an outing of the Literary
Guild, for no less than three crew members eventually
wrote books about their experiences at sea. Actually, there
was a fourth author, who understandably signed himself
"The unfortunate James Kelly" after scratching out a few
barely literate paragraphs on the eve of his execution. If
he'd been a bit better at the writing game perhaps he too
would have received a book contract rather then a rope after
unsuccessfully defending himself at his trial for piracy.

As for the other three, we've already met one of them—
William Dampier. The ship's doctor, Lionel Wafer was
another, both recent arrivals in Virginia from a previous
Pacific voyage. A recent arrival from England was our third
literary buccaneer. William Ambrosia Cowley had barely
set foot in Virginia when he joined the ship's company as
Master, charged—or so he thought—to bring the *Revenge*
safely to Petit Guâve in Haiti. He does not explain why
such an experienced ship's company would suddenly
need assistance getting to an area already known to them

all. Nevertheless, with that destination in mind and the Virginia horizon slipping below the stern, Cowley shaped his course for the West Indies.

And then something quite unexpected happened. The ship's company told their navigator that he was mistaken; they were in fact bound for the Great South Sea in search of gold and silver, and it would be his job to get them there. He protested and pointed to his paperwork: "It was not my contract to go anywhere else but where I was shipped for." The captain and crew were not impressed and Cowley got the message: "I found the contract was of no effect. I was to carry the ship wherever they pleased to command me." And so the reluctant navigator set out on a voyage that would carry the *Revenge* and himself to West Africa, then back across the Atlantic and down to the Horn in a new ship, on to Galápagos and later to another ship, and finally back to England in yet another, where he would write about his voyage. And he'd whine about it too:

> Thus was I forced to be out three years and
> four months, whereas I expected to be out
> but four months.

But what do we know of this man? Other than his name, not much—and even that is a puzzle. William *Ambrosia* Cowley? It's an uncommon name for a man, and all the more uncommon in 17th century England when any middle name at all was quite unusual. Nor did he need to distinguish himself from some other William Cowley of his day. In fact, the only other Cowley who comes to mind is the poet Abraham, who got along quite nicely with no middle name to call his own. And in buccaneering circles, Henry Morgan himself required no more than a first and last name to stand out from the motley mob. Why then did William carry around a middle name at a time when poets and pirates were quite content to do without? We'll probably never know.

What we do know — or what we can strongly suspect — about his little contract dispute is that our man Ambrosia doth protest too much. Either that, or he made a remarkably swift adjustment to his new life as a buccaneer, for before the year was out he's telling us of how he masterminded the capture of two vessels along the coast of West Africa. And in fact throughout his long voyage he fits in remarkably well with whatever schemes are devised to capture more vessels, to plunder more towns or to take more shots at uncooperative villagers, as required. His shipmate William Dampier says little or nothing about such unsavory actions, but Cowley does not hesitate to report all the dastardly details, which come to us in one letter, six manuscript journals and later on, a book.

The letter is addressed to a "Your Grace" who must have been a person of some consequence to William, for he wasted no time in writing: the six-page missive was dispatched on the 25th of October, 1686 — within two weeks of his arrival in London at the end of the voyage, and before he had received all his belongings from that voyage. He begins with a request:

> May it please your Grase To Except of A Short
> Acount of My Voyage Round this terestiall
> Globe of the world from Virginia to England
> and through the Great South Sea.

Whoever he was, why would Cowley address such an account to His Grace? Perhaps he hoped he would be sufficiently impressed with the adventure to open a few doors that would otherwise remain closed to a lowly seaman such as himself. Or perhaps there might be a little something from a well-filled pocket to comfort the poor voyager home at last from the sea. But whatever the reason for the letter, Cowley does not trouble His Grace with the less-savory aspects of his voyage. There's not a word about those captured ships, those plundered towns, nor any other incident that might raise a noble eyebrow. In fact, His Grace might very well have thought—if he didn't know his man well enough to read between the lines—that William had just returned from a harmless voyage of exploration.

Compared to the letter, Cowley's manuscript journals tell a rather different tale and describe a rather different traveler. In fact we soon learn that his description of himself as a "jackdaw among the rooks" is not quite on the mark, for here is a bird of no different feather than the rest of the flock. If dirty deeds were to be done, Ambrosia does not hesitate to report his role in the doing. He also took an active role in more routine activities, such as acquiring supplies along the African coast. Suitably armed with a cask, he and one of the ship's doctors dropped in on a local king, who kindly received the visitors—actually, the visitors' cask, which contained a bit of brandy to refresh a parched royal palette. His Majesty was no ungracious host; Cowley writes that he reciprocated by "presenting each of us one of his Black women to sleep by us so long as wee stayed there." But never one to keep an x-rated journal, he primly tells us "The Dr. stayed with his mistres but I went aboard, by Reason I did not like her Hide." And then he changes the subject. It turns out the good doctor may have lived to regret the dalliance, but not for long. Within a few weeks he was dead. Dampier observes in his own journal that the doctor's passing "was much lamented because wee had but one more for soe dangerous a voyage." The surviving doctor would have been Lionel Wafer. Cowley says nothing about the less-fortunate doctor's demise.

After taking leave of the African coast, the merry lads made their way back across the Atlantic and on to Cape Horn, where Cowley writes that

Wee came abreast of Cape Horn the 14th
day of February, 1684, when we chusing of
Valentines and discoursing of the intrigues of
women, there arose a prodigious storm.

The tempest lasted till the end of the month, and the merry lads got the message. Or at least William did: "We concluded that discoursing of women at sea was very unlucky." And so, women at sea are never mentioned again, and Cowley resumes his navigational narrative.

On clearing the Horn, the ship's company noticed that another vessel had followed them through the passage and was closing on their stern. Here might be their first opportunity at South Sea plunder. But no, it was the *Nicholas*, Captain John Eaton, out from London and also up to no good in these waters. The crews traded supplies—each ship had what the other lacked—and the captains agreed to travel in consort. The arrangement was most agreeable to Cowley, who was well-acquainted with Eaton, for the two had served as commanders in the past. Cowley tells us neither where they were nor what they were commanding.

This rendezvous does little to strengthen Cowley's assertion that he was an unwilling participant in the present caper. Eaton and Cowley had been engaged in some business in the past. The likelihood that the business was on one side of the law, and now they were both on the other, seems remote. So does the likelihood that these two ships would arrive at the same place, at the same time, and for the same purpose just by coincidence. Did the two make some sort of "arrangement" in London prior to Cowley's departure for Virginia? There's no evidence one way or the other, but Cape Horn is not the sort of neighborhood where one meets old acquaintances quite by accident.

But whatever was really behind the rendezvous, the two ships made their way northward, seizing a few Spanish vessels along the way, and in early June Cowley described their arrival in Galápagos, where "There being in number 15 ilands that I have seen: I have named 8 of them." Or at least that's what he did at first. But when his voyage was published at the end of the 17th century, we learn that "I being the first that came to an Anchor there, did give them all distinct Names." And indeed the accompanying map in his published account shows names for all fifteen islands that he saw. But as we shall see later, the new names may have been the work of someone else.

As for islands named or unnamed, of course Ambrosia knew very well that he was not the first that came to an anchor there. For even before he arrived he referred to them collectively by a name that had been applied more than a century earlier. In fact, even his countryman Sir Richard Hawkins knew the name, though he did not actually see the islands on his own 1593 voyage into the great South Sea. He later wrote that they were nothing but "... a heape of Ilands, the Spaniards call *Illas de los Galapagos*; They are desert and beare no fruite." Cowley may not have known Sir Richard's name, but since he knew the islands' name, then he also knew that others had not only come to an anchor there long ago, but they had gone ashore and later returned to the mainland to tell a tale of the inhabitants— *los galápagos*—for whom the islands were named. But as the early visitors had not taken the trouble to name the islands individually, Cowley attended to that little detail by first honoring his king, and next His Majesty's brother, then assorted gentlemen of quality, and finally, himself.

Of the first island, Cowley tells us that because of a wind from the south, "we could not sail to get to it, to discover what was upon it." Yet Dampier reports going ashore on that first island and finding "the largest land turtle that ever I saw." He also offers a clue to help resolve the conflict in their accounts: "One of the prizes got to anchor at the north end of the island, but the other two could not fetch in." These three "prizes" were ships captured a few weeks earlier, now under the command of buccaneers placed on each of them. Chances are that Cowley was on one of the two that could not fetch in. And so, from off shore he noted that "This island maketh high land, the which I called *King Charles's Island*."

The convoy sailed on. Says Cowley, "Standing still to the westward, I saw several islands, but that which I liked best I came to anchor under in a good bay." And later, "This island I named the Duke of York's Island, but now by the grace of God King James the Second's Island." But why the name change? Still in the Pacific more than a year after leaving Galápagos, the news reached Cowley that Charles was dead. His younger brother the duke was now king, and so it was more than appropriate to rename his island accordingly. It's clear then, that Cowley recorded the island names long after he saw the islands. What's not clear is why he went to the bother of recounting the naming transition, because by the time he got around to putting it to paper, the news was old. Then why not just call it King James' Island and be done with it? He doesn't say. The island is still popularly known as James, although its official name is now San Salvador.

After attending to the Royals, Cowley honored the Duke of Albemarle with the biggest plot of real estate in the entire archipelago—the island known today as Isabela. It's understandable enough that the buccaneer would name his first landfall, regardless of size, after the reigning monarch. But why award Albemarle an island twice the size of that assigned to the king's brother, who was king himself by the time Cowley got home? Perhaps he thought this duke might be inclined to return the compliment in some manner favorable to himself.

Moving on to the lesser nobility, the Baron Norris, James Bertie, was created First Earl of Abingdon in 1682, less than a year before William left England. Perhaps that news had not reached him before leaving, nor did he learn of it immediately after his return. That would explain why Cowley's letter to "Your Grace" refers to a "My Lord Nories" Island. But in his later manuscript journals and the printed book, the island is renamed to acknowledge His Lordship as Earl of Abingdon. Cowley himself may have done this on hearing the news, or his editors may have attended to it for him. But no matter: Abingdon is Isla Pinta today, celebrated as the ancestral home of "Lonesome George," sole survivor of the *Geochelone nigra abingdoni* tortoise species. The lonesome one now receives visitors at his new residence at the Charles Darwin Research Station on Isla Santa Cruz, the island Cowley named after the Duke of Norfolk.

> Perhaps erring on the side of caution, William Hacke has written "Nories Island" *and* "Earle of Abingdons Island" on his 1687 chart.

Did William honor the recipient of his "Your Grace" letter by affixing his name to one of the islands? Apparently not. He lists each notable name, but in context its clear that he's passing on information to someone not included on that list. How odd, but perhaps there was reason for it. Perhaps there would be some cause for embarrassment (or worse?) if he were to publicly associate himself with this noble personage. But unless some clue comes to the surface, we'll just have to be content with "Your Grace" and know that he lacks an island of his own in Galápagos.

But Cowley himself suffers no such lack. After describing a handful of islands in some detail he concluded with a note—an afterthought, almost—that he saw two others;

"Ld. Culpeppers Island & Cowlys Iland." In another version of the manuscript journal, it's "Cowlyes." Apparently the copyists of the day did not know how to spell Ambrosia's last name.

Cowley's island got a bit more attention when his work was eventually brought to press in 1699, as "Cowley's Voyage Round the Globe," one of four accounts in *A Collection of Original Voyages*—a small volume published by James Knapton. The attention may not have been that of the author himself, who was unavailable. His editor, William Hacke, explains all:

> I have published with very little alteration from the
> Original Journal, given to me by Cap. Cowley, but
> for the ease of the Reader, I have contracted it in
> such places as contained nothing but plain Sailing.
> The Descriptions are as the Author left them
> with me at his going abroad again, and had he
> been here, I doubt not but I could have had them
> considerably enlarged by him, but the Reader has
> them in their own Simplicity and Brevity.

Hacke's "very little alteration" consisted of reducing Cowley's lengthy manuscript to just 45 printed pages. As Hacke "contracted it" for the press, perhaps he took note of this rather fanciful entry in February of 1684, in which Cowley described his course around the southern tip of South America:

> About the 7th of this month I was at the east end
> of Staten Island, which made so rich to sight at a
> distance, like towers and castles and spire steeples,
> all white rocks running a great height in the air like
> a famous city.

This remarkable description—doubly remarkable from the pen of a buccaneer—did not make it into print, or at least not at the point where Cowley had written it. But four months later, when William was busy naming the islands of Galápagos, we now read of his own island that:

> My fancy led me to call it Cowley's Enchanted Island, for we having had a sight of it upon several points of the compass, it appeared always in as many different forms; sometimes like a ruined fortification; upon another point like a great city, &c.

There's little at the actual Cowley's Island to suggest a ruined fortification or a great city, &c.

Did he *really* say that? Probably not, for on all points of the compass this unassuming little island looks like your standard little island. No doubt Cowley would have agreed with that assessment back in 1684, for it was then—as it is now—nothing to conjure visions of a ruined fortification, or of a city great or famous. It's just the partial remains of a volcanic crater, a small reminder of its former self, barely able to keep its head above water. Cowley saw it for what it was, gave it his name, and then went on to other things. But when his editor trimmed those February towers and castles he may have decided to burnish his author's image by transforming his island into something it was not. But who would know that in 1699? Or was the editor—with or without William's knowledge—just poking a bit of fun at Spaniards who spoke of enchanted islands that were but shadows?

Cowley offers no explanation for an additional ten island names that appear in his book, some in the text, others on an inserted map drawn by Herman Moll. But his silence could very well be because these islands were named by someone else in his absence. William Hacke has already told us that the author left his notes behind "… at his going abroad again." And without names enough in those notes to go around, perhaps Hacke or Moll (or both) decided to honor Sir John Narborough, the Duke of Albany, and a few others. There's a bit of a clue that they did indeed put a few words in Cowley's pen, naming two "unknown" islands in the South Atlantic in honor of Samuel Pepys. Cowley himself knew the actual identity of these islands, which he called Sibbel de Waards in his journal, after the Dutch Captain Sebald de Weert. We know them today as the Falkland Islands, or Islas Malvinas for those living in — or sympathetic to — Argentina.

Pepys Island, which is actually two islands, as seen in the published *Cowley's Voyage Round the Globe*. Was it placed there without the author's consent?

And what has this to do with Galápagos? Almost nothing, except for a tie-in with a new pair of names that appear in Cowley's book: Galápagos islands named Dean's and Eures's. The former, Sir Anthony Deane, shared lodgings with Pepys in the Tower of London when both were temporarily out of favor. The latter is most likely Pepys' long-time clerk and friend Will. Depending on which page of Pepys' diary you read, his last name was Eure, Ewre or Hewers.

Now, how came these people to Galápagos? Probably the same way Pepys came to the South Atlantic — brought in by someone other than Cowley. Since it is known that he did not choose to honor Pepys with an island, it's unlikely that he would have dubbed two of his Galápagos discoveries after the great man's lesser associates. And there are several other islands that may be more shadows of a map-maker's art than real islands—or, if real, not the islands one thinks they are today. The modern Brattle and Crossman, for example, are tiny little specks barely seen against the mountainous backdrop of Isla Isabela. In fact, they exist in an area that Cowley tells us he did not visit. Their names do not appear in his "Your Grace" letter, nor in the first four versions of his manuscript journal. They show up only in the manuscript written just as his book was going to press. And on his map, both are in open water to the east of King James Island, and south of the Duke of Norfolk's Island. The present islets are west of King James Island and quite close to Isabela. Where then, are Cowley's Brattle and Crossman today? Chances are, his Brattle is the present Isla Santa Fe, and the larger Crossman is now the larger Floreana.

In addition to editing Cowley's manuscript, William Hacke prepared an oversized *Description of the Islands of Gallapagos, delineated exactly according to the prescription of Mr. William Ambrose Cowley,* and this was done some dozen years before the book was published. The chart shows "Cowleys or Enchanted Island" as a little group of three mountains sitting in the "Enchanted Bay" between the Duke of Albemarle and King James Islands.

The little bit of enchantment bears no resemblance to reality, with contours no doubt inspired by that fanciful description (also by Hacke?) of an island looking "… sometimes like a ruined fortification; upon another point like a great city."

Next came a series of 16 smaller charts, the first "A general draught of the Islands of Gallapagos," followed by 14 charts of individual islands, including those named for Sir Anthony Deane and Mr. William Ewre. The last is "A description of Mr. Secretarie Pepyses Island: discovered by Wm. Ambrose Cowley." This is the only chart in the series where Hacke appends the name of its discoverer, even if he knew that the information was false. And there was nothing that Cowley—having gone abroad again—could do about all this, nor about the spelling of his middle name.

Wiliam Hacke's depiction of "Cowleys or Enchanted Island" has more to do with the cartographer's imagination than the author's description. Albemarle (Isabela) Island is on the left, and James (San Salvador) on the right.

And then, a dozen years after Cowley's account finally came off the press, Herman Moll, the cartographer who prepared the Galápagos chart found in that account, further clouds the island-naming issue. Moll wrote his own *A View of the Coasts, Countries and Islands Within the Limits of the South-Sea-Company,* and in this he offers his version of what Cowley actually wrote. He concludes with:

> 'Twas the Voyager who gave name to *Pepys Island,* he having it seems a particular fancy to christen the Places he came to, as Seamen generally affect to do, by which means they are oft confounded, Charts render'd different one from another, to the puzling those that use 'em; tho every Nation wou'd chuse that Appellation which was given by one of themselves, yet when a Name has prevail'd, 'twill always stand. The vanity of *Sharp,* to call

> *John Fernando* Queen *Catherine's Island*, has not
> lost the old name; and 'tis likely all the fine
> Denominations given the *Gallapagos* by *Cowley*
> will not be found any where but in his own
> Chart and Voyage, whatever the Fame of those
> Persons may deserve.

Moll's disingenuous remark about "the Voyager who gave name to Pepys Island" may have been a clumsy attempt to extricate himself from a cartographic *faux pas*. With Pepys now dead for almost a decade, perhaps he had second thoughts about whatever role he had played in placing the diarist's name on the map. With Cowley still not around to defend himself, Moll could publicly "credit" him with the naming, then follow it up with a Moll specialty: a criticism of anyone other than himself who had a hand in the fine art of island naming.

He did guess wrong though, in predicting that "… the fine Denominations given the Gallapagos by Cowley" would not survive. Many of Cowley's names enjoy a permanent place in the scientific literature, and some remain in popular usage to this day. But further commentary on such matters is best put off for another chapter, which can be skipped by those with more important things to do than sort out islands real from islands imaginary.

His signature in a letter to "Your
Grace" dated 25 October, 1686.

Cowley the man follows Dampier's example and doesn't say much about himself. Where did he come from? How old was he? Did he share his shipmate's interest in natural history? And what did he do after leaving England again for parts unknown? He leaves no direct answers, but here and there we find clues, such as one in that letter to His Grace telling of an unsuccessful search for a precious Galápagos resource:

"...But we found
noe water thare
but ware sartaine
thare ware water
about the island."

The distinctive spellings in this phrase are found throughout the letter, and if William wrote the way he spoke, then his accent suggests he grew up in the North country.

All but one of the surviving manuscript journals offer nothing to hint at Cowley's age. The exception is a document now at the Lambeth Palace Library in London, in which he describes the Galápagos terrain:

> Those Islands formerly burnt as Strombolo
> and Ætna doth, for the land in some places
> is burnt like to a Sinder and in other places
> there having been some cumbustable matter
> as salt Peter which hath blown up the very
> Rocks, that they lie as the ruines of the Citty of
> London did after it's being burnt.

Cowley refers to the great London fire of 1666, so it would seem he was old enough in that year to have seen, and later remembered, the damage done. There was a William Cowley christened in the little village of Crick in 1637, who would have been 29 in 1666 and 46 at the beginning of the voyage from Virginia—old enough to have gained some previous experience, perhaps as a fellow commander with John Eaton. Such a man might have cruised the Mediterranean and seen the volcanoes Stromboli and Aetna before joining the *Revenge*. Yet Crick is not a North country town, so our contradictory "evidence"—such as it is—leaves the question of his origin unanswered.

As for the manuscript at Lambeth Palace, how it got there
is anyone's guess but there it is, some 40 pages bound into
a volume of unrelated documents. Written across the top of
the first page in the hand of Thomas Tenison, Archbishop of
Canterbury is "The Voyage of Capt. Cowley. Papist." Alas,
His Grace (surely not the recipient of that "Your Grace"
letter?) offers no explanation for branding Cowley a Papist.
In fact, there is nothing in any of the Cowley manuscripts to
hint at his religion, although there is a little something that
reveals he held some belief in Christian teachings, which he
may have learned from the Church of England or of Rome.

While at Galápagos, Cowley and a few men went ashore
and he killed a tortoise. Left in charge of preparing dinner
while the others went off to search, unsuccessfully, for
water, he reflected on the life he had lived:

> I being alone dressing of the turtle & having
> made a great fire to roast him near the seaside,
> & having within my self some serious thoughts,
> thinking with my self that I had not long to live
> without water, & seeing that great fire I had
> made & thinking if I were burning within that
> fire how terrible it would be, and thinking of
> my loose life I had lived, how dreadful the fire
> of Hell would be, should I at last go thither,
> which would be aggravated with the fearful
> sight of those deformed fiends that were there.

And just then, one of those fiends paid him a visit. But for
Ambrosia the Day of Judgment was not yet at hand:

> Whilst I had those melancholy thoughts in my
> mind, I espied a great hollow place in the earth
> within one yard of the fire over against where I
> stood, there came out of the mouth of this cave
> a large sea dog or bear as they may be termed,

much like a bear, roaring like a bear against me.
I was for the present surprised with the sudden
sight & noise of him. I having a long pole in my
hand, I began to lay on with violence upon the
supposed devil, which made him run away as
fast as he could, & I after him till I had chased
him into the sea. This island has very many of
these fish, which are enemies to mankind.

Although Cowley was no naturalist on the level of William
Dampier, he did take some notice of the animals he saw on
King James' Island:

There being upon this island land turtle almost
200 pounds weight apiece. I sat upon the back
of one of them when they came aboard to try
his strength. He would have carried me had I
been much heavier. The flesh of them to many
of our judgements exceeded the sea turtle,
although the sea turtle there is as good as ever
I eat in any part of the world where they been
accounted most rare.

And later on, notwithstanding thoughts of hellfire, devils
and no water on the Duke of Albemarle's Island ("We
would have given a pint of blood out of our bodies for a
pint of water."), he found time to observe the habits of the
avian world:

Hawks would come & light upon our arms &
heads, one of which I took off of one of our
men's heads & fastened him with a string &
gave him meal. He eating very freely with us,
I let him loose. He would fly from place to
place, & come to us again. He stayed with us
as long as we stayed in that part of the island.

Little is known about the subsequent career of William Ambrosia Cowley. British Admiralty records lend some support to William Hacke's editorial comment about him going abroad again, perhaps to lead a respectable life at sea after the buccaneering days were done. In 1687, there was an Ambrose Cowley, gunner, on H. M. S. *Kingfisher*, and later the same year the name of William Ambrose Cowley is recorded as gunner on the *St. Paul* prize. Perhaps "His Grace" pulled a few strings to secure him a place in the Royal Navy, where a man might be shot at but surely not hanged for a pirate. But wherever his post-Galápagos voyages took him, William Ambrosia Cowley wrote no more.

Facing page: The Herman Moll chart inserted in Cowley's *Voyage Round the Globe* was redrawn by Emanuel Bowen for John Harris' Atlas, *Navigantium atque Itinerantium Bibliotheca*, with editorial commentary from Woodes Rogers added at the bottom:

> *These Islands derive their Name from the Resort of* Tortoiſes *to them in order to lay their Eggs; for in Spanish* Gallapagos *signifies a* Tortoiſe. *The* Buccaneers *who had frequent occasion for such Places sailed thither often and found them very convenient Retreats. Capt.* Woodes Rogers *who had a very indifferent opinion of Discoveries made by these sort of people, complains that he was deceived by one Capt. Davis's account of these Islands, and aſserts he could not find a drop of Fresh Water upon any of them, yet succeeding Navigators have found them Agreeable to this Description which is indeed the only good one we have.*

> *The Spaniards mention an Island in the Latitude of 1°20' or 30' S. which they call S^t. Maria de l'Aquada full of Wood, having plenty of Fresh Water and affording other Conveniences.*

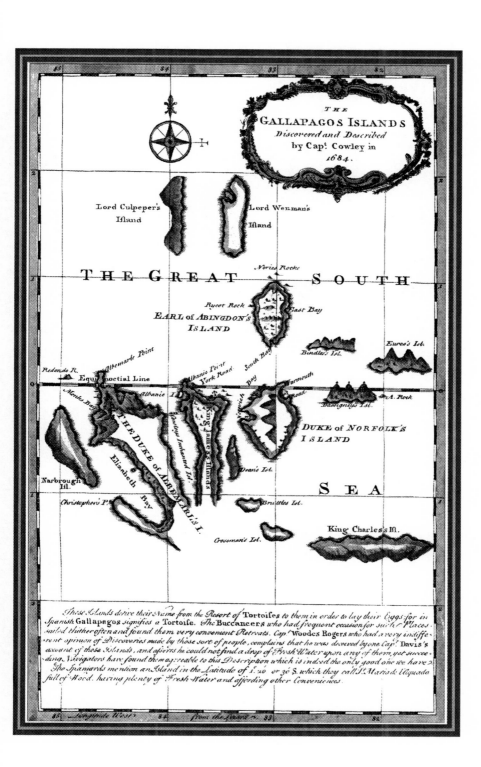

THE
GALLAPAGOS ISLANDS
Discovered and Described
by Cap.t Cowley in
1684.

Lord Culpeper's
Island

Lord Wenman's
Island

Nories Rocks

THE GREAT SOUTH

Rycot Rock

East Bay

EARL of ABINGDON'S
ISLAND

South Bay

Albemarle Point

Eures's Isl.

Redondo R.

Equinoctial Line

Bindloe's Isl.

Albanie Point

York Road

Yarmouth

Albanie Isld.

King James Bay

Yarmouth Road

A. Rock

Montis Bay

King James Islands

Dassignies Isl.

DUKE of NORFOLK'S
ISLAND

THE DUKE of ALBEMARLE'S I.

Crossley Inchanted Isl.

Deans Isl.

Elizabeth Bay

Narbrough
Isl.

SEA

Christopher's P.

Brattles Isl.

King Charles's Isl.

Crossmans Isl.

These Islands derive their Name from the Resort of **Tortoises** to them in order to lay their Eggs: for in Spanish **Gallapagos** signifies a Tortoise. The Buccaneers who had frequent occasion for such Places sailed thither often and found them very convenient Retreats. Cap.t **Woodes Rogers** who had a very indifferent opinion of Discoveries made by these sort of people, complains that he was deceived by one Cap.t **Davis's** account of these Islands, and asserts he could not find a drop of Fresh Water upon any of them, yet succeeding Navigators have found them agreeable to this Description which is indeed the only good one we have.
The Spaniards mention an Island in the Latitude of 1° 40ʹ or 3° S. which they call S.t Maria de Llguada full of Wood, having plenty of Fresh Water and affording other Conveniencies.

Longitude West from the Peak

A segment of William Hacke's 1687 Galápagos chart. The vertical scale of King James Island is grossly exaggerated.

CHAPTER FIVE

THE LEGEND OF IRISH PAT

*His appearance, from all accounts, was that of
the victim of some malignant sorceress; ... He
struck strangers much as if he were a volcanic
creature thrown up by the same convulsion which
exploded into sight the isle.*

Herman Melville's description
of a Galápagos resident

HERMAN MELVILLE WILL BE OUR GALÁPAGOS GUIDE in pages
to come, taking us on a tour unlike any of those offered
today. And as we shall see, the great American storyteller
was not above "borrowing" from previous guides, such as
Captain David Porter, whom we shall also meet in another
chapter. But before that, let's have a look at a very strange
Galápagos character who had come and gone before the
arrival of either visitor, yet was to be remembered by both.

This is the tale of Irish Pat Watkins, and it begins in a letter
written by a Captain John Macy. The Captain "mailed" his
letter at the Galápagos Post Office barrel (which at that time
was a box) on Charles Island. Lieutenant John Downes of
the American frigate *Essex* retrieved it, brought it back to the
ship and turned it over to Captain Porter, who thought that
since the letter was such "... a rare specimen of orthography,
I hope I shall be pardoned for giving an exact copy of it."

Ship Sukey John Macy 7½ Months out 150
Barrels 75 days from Lima No oil Since
Leaving that Port. Spanyards Very Savage Lost
on the Braziel Bank John Sealin Apprentice to
Capt Benjamin Worth Fell from the fore top
sail Yard in A Gale of Wind. Left Diana Capt
paddock 14 day Since 250 Barrels I Leave this
port this Day With 250 Turpen 8 Boat Load
Wood Yesterday Went Up to Patts Landing East
Side. to the Starboard hand of the Landing 1½
Miles Saw 100 Turpen 20 Rods A part Road
Very Bad

Yours Forevir

JOHN MACY

Macy was apparently better at whaling than at punctuation.
The Captain read his reference to a "Patts Landing" and
offered this explanation:

It may be seen by captain Macy's letter, that
on the east side of the island there is another
landing, which he calls Pat's landing; and this
place will probably immortalize an Irishman,
named Patrick Watkins, who some years since
left an English ship, and took up his abode
on this island, and built himself a miserable
hut, about a mile from the landing called after
him, in a valley containing about two acres of
ground capable of cultivation, and perhaps the
only spot on the island which affords sufficient
moisture for the purpose. Here he succeeded in
raising potatoes and pumpkins in considerable
quantities, which he generally exchanged for
rum, or sold for cash.

For several years this wretched being lived
by himself on this desolate spot, without any
apparent desire than that of procuring rum in

sufficient quantities to keep himself intoxicated, and, at such times, after an absence from his hut of several days, he would be found in a state of perfect insensibility, rolling among the rocks of the mountains. He appeared to be reduced to the lowest grade of which human nature is capable, and seemed to have no desire beyond the tortoises and other animals of the island, except that of getting drunk.

But this man, wretched and miserable as he may have appeared, was neither destitute of ambition, nor incapable of undertaking an enterprise that would have appalled the heart of any other man; nor was he devoid of the talent of rousing others to second his hardihood.

He by some means became possessed of an old musket, and a few charges of powder and ball; and the possession of this weapon probably first stimulated his ambition. He felt himself strong as the sovereign of the island, and was desirous of proving his strength on the first human being that fell in his way, which happened to be a negro, who was left in charge of a boat belonging to an American ship that had touched there for refreshments. Patrick came down to the beach where the boat lay, armed with his musket, now become his constant companion, directed the negro, in an authoritative manner, to follow him, and on his refusal, snapped his musket at him twice, which luckily missed fire. The negro, however, became intimidated, and followed him. Patrick now shouldered his musket, marched off before, and on his way

up the mountains exultingly informed the
negro he was henceforth to work for him, and
become his slave, and that his good or bad
treatment would depend on his future conduct.
On arriving at a narrow defile, and perceiving
Patrick off his guard, the negro seized the
moment, grasped him in his arms, threw him
down, tied his hands behind, shouldered him,
and carried him to his boat, and when the
crew had arrived he was taken on board the
ship.

An English smuggler was lying in the harbour
at the same time, the captain of which
sentenced Patrick to be severely whipped
on board both vessels, which was put in
execution, and he was afterwards taken on
shore handcuffed by the Englishmen, who
compelled him to make known where he had
concealed the few dollars he had been enabled
to accumulate from the sale of his potatoes
and pumpkins, which they took from him. But
while they were busy in destroying his hut and
garden, the wretched being made his escape,
and concealed himself among the rocks in the
interior of the island, until the ship had sailed,
when he ventured from his hiding-place, and
by means of an old file, which he drove into
a tree, freed himself from the handcuffs. He
now meditated a severe revenge, but concealed
his intentions. Vessels continued to touch
there, and Patrick, as usual, to furnish them
with vegetables; but from time to time he was
enabled, by administering potent draughts of
his darling liquor to some of the men of their
crews, and getting them so drunk that they
were rendered insensible, to conceal them until

the ship had sailed; when finding themselves
entirely dependent on him, they willingly
enlisted under his banner, became his slaves,
and he the most absolute of tyrants. By this
means he had augmented the number to five,
including himself, and every means was used
by him to endeavour to procure arms for them,
but without effect. It is supposed that his object
was to have surprised some vessel, massacred
her crew, and taken her off. While Patrick was
meditating his plans, two ships, an American
and an English vessel, touched there, and
applied to Patrick for vegetables. He promised
them the greatest abundance, provided they
would send their boats to his landing, and
their people to bring them from his garden,
informing them that his rascals had become
so indolent of late, that he could not get them
to work. This arrangement was agreed to; two
boats were sent from each vessel, and hauled
on the beach. Their crew all went to Patrick's
habitation, but neither he nor any of his people
were to be found; and, after waiting until
their patience was exhausted, they returned to
the beach, where they found only the wreck
of their boats, which were broken to pieces,
and the fourth one missing. They succeeded,
however, after much difficulty, in getting
around to the bay opposite to their ships,
where other boats were sent to their relief; and
the commanders of the ships, apprehensive of
some other trick, saw no security except in a
flight from the island, leaving Patrick and his
gang in quiet possession of the boat.

The two ships were the *Argo* and the *Cyrus*, the latter
commanded by Paul West, who made a few remarks about
the 1809 encounter in the ship's log.

May 14th ... Found the island inhabited by
the notorious Irishman ... & agreed to take a
number of pumpkins and a few potatoes at a
very high price. Found two men in company
with the Irishman and had reason to suspect
others being on the island.

And a few days later, ...

Manned two boats from the Argo and two
from the Cyrus, and according to agreement
with the inhabitant landed at his valley and
went up to his place of pumpkins, where he
delivered 120 pumpkins which we took down
to our boats at two turns. Then went up to
take another turn but not finding the villains or
anything else worth notice, made the best of
our way to the boats, where to our surprise we
found that the villain with his comrades had
taken away one of the Argo's boats and stove
both boats belonging to the Cyrus. He took or
destroyed all the oars except two steer-oars,
two boat-sails, an anchor-&-rode, two small
casks, & kegs with water, and every thing else
about the boats whether it could be of any
use to him or not. One sail that was under the
bushes was left, which together with two steer-
oars and four rowing oars that we found on
our passage enabled us to get on board. After
repairing one of my boats with canvas and
ceiling-nails, leaving one boat on the beach
with three holes in her bottom, and part of
our pumpkins at 4 PM reached the Ships with
two boats, then man'd and sent two armed
boats that patched and tarpaulined my other
boat and at 8 PM got her and the rest of the
pumpkins to the Ship.

Then with a light air got under way in
company with the Argo and left Charles Island
with 310 tortoises & 60 pumpkins. We did not
think it prudent to allow our crews to attempt
any kind of revenge on Paddy, since we are so
well convinced of his good supply of arms &
ammunition, knowing such a remedy would in
the end be worse than the disease.

And now the monarch of Charles Island, having grown
disenchanted with his kingdom, looked to the continent
for new opportunities, and the captured boat gave him the
means to his end. Watkins left the island with his small band
and eventually arrived on the mainland. But he arrived
alone. Porter continues the story:

Patrick arrived alone at Guyaquil in his open
boat, the rest who sailed with him having
perished for want of water, or, as is generally
supposed, were put to death by him on his
finding the water to grow scarce. From thence
he proceeded to Payta, where he wound
himself into the affection of a tawny damsel,
and prevailed on her to consent to accompany
him back to his enchanted island, the beauties
of which he no doubt painted in glowing
colours; but, from his savage appearance,
he was there considered by the police as a
suspicious person, and being found under
the keel of a small vessel then ready to be
launched, and suspected of some improper
intentions, he was confined in Payta gaol,
where he now remains; and probably owing to
this circumstance Charles' Island, as well as the
rest of the Gallipagos, may remain unpopulated
for many ages to come. This reflection may
naturally lead us to a consideration of the

question concerning the population of the other islands scattered about the Pacific ocean, respecting which so many conjectures have been hazarded. I shall only hazard one, which is briefly this: that former ages may have produced men equally as bold and as daring at Pat, and women as willing as his tender one to accompany them in their adventurous voyages. And when we consider the issue which might be produced from a union between a red-haired wild Irishman, and a copper-coloured mixt-blooded squaw, we need not be any longer surprised at the different varieties of human nature.

If Patrick should be liberated from durance, and should arrive with his love at this enchanting spot, perhaps (when neither Pat nor the Gallipagos are any longer remembered) some future navigator may surprise the world by discovery of them, and his accounts of the strange people with which they may probably be inhabited; and from the source from which they shall have sprung, it does not seem unlikely that they will have one trait in their character, which is common to the natives of all the islands in the Pacific, a disposition to appropriate to themselves the property of others; and from this circumstance future speculators may confound their origin with that of all the rest.

Since Irish Pat Watkins left Galápagos in 1809, several years before Porter's arrival, the description of his imprisonment is presumably based on information he received from others.

"Patrick Watkins reaches the mainland alone; 6 had started from Floreana." A 21st-century interpretation of the tale by Christy Gallardo. Puerto Ayora, Galápagos.

More than a quarter-century later, Monsieur Abel du Petit-Thouars, captain of the French frigate *Vénus*, anchored his ship at Black Beach, and later wrote about the same character—with a slight variation in his name:

> Around the time of the establishment of whale
> fishery in the Galapagos Islands, a man named
> Fitz-Patrick, Irish by birth, maltreated and
> unhappy on the ship where he was embarked,
> conceived a plan to remain in these islands
> and, modern Robinson, to live there alone
> and from his own industry. He hid while his
> vessel was anchored at Charles Island, up until
> the moment of departure. Then he worked to
> make a residence. In a little time, he managed
> to cultivate potatoes and some edible plants,
> which gave him the means to trade with the
> whalers, so that he could procure clothes,
> brandy and also, to his misfortune, money.
> Having been imprudent in letting others know

about his treasure, some seamen robbed him,
after having beaten and tied him up, and then
left him in that state. However, Fitz-Patrick
managed to untie himself and swore vengeance.

The occasion presented itself shortly when a
whaler came to anchor in the bay. The captain
asked him, as was customary, for provisions;
Fitz-Patrick was known to all the whalers, by
hearsay if not by face; one knew that with
his help it was possible to procure vegetables;
Fitz-Patrick asked that they send a whaler
to get them, and that the sailors come to
his cave to do so. He waited, hidden in the
rocks near the landing stage, for the whaler
to land on the beach and for the sailors to
leave. Then he left his retreat and broke up
the boat in a manner that it could not serve
to take them back. The sailors having found
no one at the cave, returned to the beach,
and saw the impossibility of returning to their
ship. They were at the mercy of Fitz-Patrick
for their survival. He, being armed, made
them work for him and thus became a type of
monarch. It is said that his companions grew
accustomed to their lot, or rather that, seduced
by his promises and the hope of sharing the
benefits of his establishment, they consented
to stay with him, from which soon followed
a new prosperity. However, Fitz-Patrick, often
tricked by the whalers, grew disgusted with
his position and formed a plan to go to the
continent. He took a boat from a whaler
and, followed by his men, in number six in
all, he left Galápagos without compass; but
guided by the sun he made towards the East,
and after endless struggle against winds and

currents which generally flow to the West, Fitz-
Patrick landed in the bay of Tumbez, at the
mouth of the Guayaquil river. From Tumbez,
he went to Payta, where soon his behavior
aroused suspicion. He had married an Indian
woman and talked of returning with her to
the Galápagos Islands. But the rumor spread
of his departure from Charles Island with five
sailors, none of whom arrived with him. He
was finally arrested and taken to the prison of
San-Miguel de Piùra; after this arrest, no one
knows what became of him: one has heard no
more of him.

And then a few years later, the Watkins legend is re-told by
Dr. John Coulter, ship's surgeon aboard the British whaler
Stratford, Captain Abijah Lock. The doctor had heard tales of
this character, and left us this description in his *Adventures
in the Pacific* published in 1845:

> To the eastward of the anchorage [at Charles
> Island] there is more level ground; which from
> the natural arrangement of the trees, looks like
> a well-laid-out park. There is also a fine beach
> for landing at, called and known well by the
> name of "Pat's Landing."

> This beach I have mentioned got its name from
> an Irishman who many years ago resided on
> this island for a long time, the sole inhabitant,
> except when a runaway sailor or two would
> join him. His history, as far as is known, was
> that of a very daring, reckless, and strange
> being. He belonged to several ships on the
> coast, and was in many of the revolutionary
> rows, so common in Chili, Peru, Colombia,
> &c. At last he formed one of the crew of a
> whale ship which was cruising round those

islands, the captain of her having a great
deal of trouble with him, he having formed
several plots to mutiny, and take the ship,
there being no feeling of security as long as he
was on board, he was landed on the southern
extremity of Albemarl Island.

Here water being extremely scarce, he was
nearly famishing, and would have died from
the want of it, but that he squeezed the juice
out of the prickly pear and cabbage tree. This
was a substitute, which saved his life. As to
food, he had plenty of doves and terapin, or
the land tortoise, which is excellent. After
some months the captain of an American
whale ship humanely took him off, and landed
him, at his own request, on Charles's Island,
with which he was familiar, and which he
knew possessed plenty of fine water from
springs.

He was landed on the beach in question,
from which there is a complete and naturally
beautiful avenue up to the mountains; and
nearly at the summit of one of them there is
a spot of excellent land, of four or five acres
in extent, nearly surrounded with high hills;
in fact, there is only one pass into it. On this
level he erected his house or hut, and had
a great deal of it under cultivation; so much
so that he had a quantity of vegetables, such
as sweet potatoes, pumpkins, Indian corn,
melons, with plenty of hogs and poultry; those
he sold for years to the shipping. He also dug
a well on his farm, and though in high land,
at a moderate depth obtained a good supply of
water.

I understood his chief dress consisted of a seal-
skin cap over his red bushy hair, a red flannel
shirt, and pair of flannel drawers, with seal-skin
mocasins on his feet. He never went without
his gun, particularly when he had those
runaways with him; neither did he sleep two
nights in the same place. He knew every cave
and secret spot on the island, and occasionally
used them for dormitories. Now, it is a strange
circumstance, and yet a fact, that this man,
whenever those runaway sailors resided on the
island, would enforce subjection, and actually
compelled them to work his farm for him.
They were soon glad to separate from him by
joining, on any terms, the first ship that came
in.

He was often greatly blamed, (though I believe
unjustly), for inducing sailors to leave their
ships, and in one case he suffered for it. An
American whale ship put in there, and two of
the crew, who had been severely treated on
board, took to the bush, and Pat was blamed
for harbouring them. Captain Bunker, of
Nantucket, who commanded the ship, invited
him on board, and in ignorance of what had
occurred, or the men leaving, he accepted the
invitation.

As soon as he came on board, he was tied
up and severely flogged, then handcuffed and
landed on the beach to die or live as he might,
with his hands fast, and no one to loose them.
It was a murdering, brutal [sic] act of this
ruffianly captain. The ship sailed the next day,
and left him to his fate.

Pat, however, was not to die in this manner; for in his seal-skin cap, which was, fortunately for him, not removed from his head, he had two files, one of which, with both hands, he drove firmly into a tree; he then patiently and perseveringly commenced and continued the operation of filing through the handcuffs, until he freed himself. He then for ever vowed vengeance against the captain who treated him so, if ever he should be in his power.

He had an iron frame, a strong and well cultivated mind. He had received a good education in his youth; this, to a character like him, made him doubly mischievous. A few months afterwards, as he was round at the other side of the island, after seal, in his boat, which he called the Black Prince, he fell in with an English whale ship. From the crew he learned that he would soon have visitors, as two or three American ships were to call at the island. One of them was that on board of which he had been so barbarously treated. He had at this time four men with him.

On hearing this news, he pulled directly round to his landing-place. In a few days after, the expected ships arrived. He determined not to appear, but watch them well, and keep his men out of sight. The three captains, one of whom was Bunker, pulled on shore, and in a bottle, made fast to a pole on the beach, they found a note written by Pat, stating that, from the bad treatment he often received, he had left the island for ever, and that whoever would arrive first would find plenty of everything in his garden. I may here remark, that this method generally forms a South Sea post-office, where one ship leaves a memorandum for the next.

The skippers concluded that all was right, and that there was no one on the island; and after walking about a little, they agreed to come on shore the next day to have a picnic dinner, and to send their men up and plunder the garden. Pat was concealed so near that he heard all, and made his arrangements accordingly. Next day they came on shore, and brought their cold meat and wines away up the valley to a pleasant green plot, where they had a view of the ships, but not of the landing-place they came to. They had four boats on shore, hauled well up on the beach. They enjoyed themselves for hours, when one went up to an eminence near, to have a look round. He no sooner got a view of the beach then he came back like a madman, and told them their boats were knocked about, and to come down at once.

These tyrannical rascals were now complete cowards; they left all and ran as quick as they could down to the beach, where they found the four boats, oars, and all in pieces; also a large slip of paper, with "remember the handcuffs" on it; also, "Bunker, I'll have you yet." There was an instant signal made to the ships to send a boat; fortunately for them, it was instantly answered. They were scarcely seated and shoved off, when a bullet from a gun on shore whistled among them and through the boat. In another instant three shots were fired after them; but they were safe, and out of reach of the guns. Pat then showed himself on the beach, gun in hand, and waved his cap over his head in triumph. No one came on shore to pick up the fragments. Those ships got under weigh in the evening, and disappeared. So much for barbarity on one side, and revenge on the other.

This wild and strange man lived, I believe, about eighteen or twenty years on this island, but did not die here. He went in his open boat, "the Black Prince," more than once, in on the coast a distance of six hundred miles; but the water is always smooth here, so it is not to be wondered at.

The last time he went to Guyaquil, and thinking he might as well have a queen for his beautiful island, of which he was the sole and daring monarch, after, I suppose, telling all manner of inducing stories, there was the wife of a Spaniard who agreed to accompany him. She was actually in the boat, and they about to shove off, when the Spaniard jumped in to bring back his wife. A struggle ensued; "Pat" was stabbed to the heart, and fell dead in the bottom of his "Black Prince."

Such was the termination of the career of this extraordinary man. He is reported to have been always warm-hearted and kind to those who were at all friendly to him, but implacably revengeful to those who ill-used or insulted him.

And such is the termination of a few accounts of the extraordinary Irish Pat Watkins. By the time du Petit-Thouars and Coulter wrote their versions, the tale been circulating about the islands for years. It had no doubt picked up a few embellishments as it passed from one mouth to another on its way to their ears, and perhaps Coulter added his own touches to the legend.

Porter's account, set down just a few years after Pat's departure, is no doubt a bit closer to the actual truth then the others. But perhaps there is something to all of them: Irish Pat Watkins may have been a guest at Payta Gaol for a time and then, liberated from durance, met his end on a blade of Spanish steel. But whatever happened to Pat, there is no further news of a tawny damsel, an angry Spaniard or an Indian wife. Chances are though, that they didn't sail out to Galápagos in the *Black Prince*.

Or did they? More than a half century after the departure of Irish Pat Watkins, he shows up again, this time in the pages of Boston's *Ballou's Monthly Magazine*. Apparently, William H. Macy—a frequent contributor of sea stories—had heard a little something about this character, who became "King Pat, the Crusoe of the Galápagos" in the June 1869 issue of the magazine. The writer tells of his uncle Malachi Worth, veteran whaler of the old school, who had made several voyages in days when ships were small and sperm whales numerous. Uncle Malachi was the best of company for the younger set, with an ample stock of yarns about places visited in years gone by.

> "The Galleypaguses," said the old gentleman, "is as far off shore as ever I saw any need to go. I was put ashore once there, and lived there some months."

> "Lived there!" I exclaimed, in astonishment. "That's the last place I should select for a hermitage."

But Malachi hadn't selected this place as his hermitage: it was selected for him after a falling out with the captain of the ship he was on, and he was left on Charles Island to live or to die. And presently he discovered that he was not alone:

> I saw a man, or, at any rate, something in
> human form, coming towards me. He had no
> covering on his body above the waist, and
> his skin was burnt and tanned from exposure
> to the sun. His long red hair and beard were
> matted and tangled together, and his face and
> body had a baked appearance, as if all the
> juices had been dried out of him.
>
> "What are you doing here?" he roared, with a
> strong Irish brogue.

Uncle Malachi explained his situation, and the red-haired Irishman introduced himself:

> "King Pat's my name, and I've two subjects
> now. There's one thing I want to put in my
> palace here."
>
> "What may that be?" I inquired.
>
> "A queen," said he. "As soon as I can get a
> boat, I'll go and get me one."

The yarn continues as Uncle Malachi helps His Majesty swipe a boat from a visiting whaler, then remains behind as sole proprietor of the island while King Pat and his young English servant Jake go to the mainland in search of a queen. Months pass, and then one day a small boat is seen approaching. It is the Irishman, and he is not alone.

> Pat, so far as I could judge at that distance,
> was much metamorphosed since he left me.
> His hair and beard were trimmed, and he was
> dressed in a decent suit of clothes, with a broad
> Panama hat, looking, for the first time since
> my knowledge of him, like a Christian being.
> This I attributed, of course, to the humanizing
> influence of the woman at his side.

But their Majesties' reign would be short: both would be dead before the sun had set. In pursuit of the royal couple was a fore-and-aft schooner, and as Pat and his lady hid themselves in a convenient nearby cave, the schooner put off its own small boat with four armed men and a boy. It should come as no surprise that the boy was Jake, and he explained why they were in pursuit of King Pat:

> He has run away with Catalina, the niece
> of old Don Whon, and killed a soldier in
> Guayaquil, and they are after him now and
> bound to have him.

Of course Jake knew just where Pat would be hiding, and led the men to the cave. A shot rang out, the boy was wounded and the men paused while his arm was bandaged. And then fate intervened. Rumbling noises were heard from below.

> The swarthy Spaniards turned pale with
> affright, as the dreadful, whispered word,
> "terremoto!" passed from mouth to mouth.
> ... The whole air about us became thickened
> and filled with choking vapors, and a sudden
> blast from the narrow passage in the cape-
> rock fairly drove us to seek safety by flight. ...
> Then a sound was heard like the explosion of a
> steam boiler, and the fierce after-escape of the
> confined vapors, combined with a noise like
> the crashing and splitting of massive rocks.

Uncle Malachi and the Spaniards were none the worse for the wear, and Jake's bullet wound was not that serious either. But what of the pair hiding in the cave?

> The outlaw and his innocent but too credulous
> companion were entombed, far beyond the
> reach of mortal quest, but not before they
> had been mercifully suffocated by the noxious
> vapors in the rocky vault.

The author tells us he was inclined to think of Uncle Malachi's yarn as "rather apocryphal" and he says as much to the old man.

> "I have been to 'Pat's Landing' myself, Uncle Worth," said I, "and I have heard that he went up to the coast in a whaleboat, but I have never heard that he returned to the islands."

> "His fate was just as I have told you," answered the old seaman. "You may take your old uncle's word for it, for no other one could tell you as much about it, except the English boy Jake, and I've never seen or heard of him since I left him at Guayaquil."

CHAPTER SIX

JOURNAL OF A CRUISE

*I have indulged many of my friends by
permitting them to peruse my Journal,
and all have requested me to publish it.*

David Porter: Introduction to his *Journal of a Cruise*

October 6ᵗʰ, 1812. I received orders from
commodore William Bainbridge to prepare
the Essex for a long cruize, and on the day
following received his final instructions,
appointing places of rendezvous, and the next
day a copy of his orders from the honourable
secretary of the navy.

SO BEGINS THE *JOURNAL* OF DAVID PORTER, Captain of the
Salem frigate *Essex*. The Commodore on the frigate
Constitution expected the Captain of the *Essex* to join him
shortly at one of several meeting places in the Atlantic, as
specified in his orders to Porter. It's unlikely he would have
expected Porter to instead make his way into the Pacific
and onward to Galápagos, there to do whatever he could
to annoy the British enemy. But that's just what happened
on this, the second voyage of the *Essex* under Porter's
command.

Among the crew was Porter's foster son, a midshipman who in time would achieve some fame as David "Damn the torpedoes!" Farragut, the United States Navy's first Admiral. Porter's natural son, David Dixon Porter, would be the second. But that would be years from now. At this moment, David Dixon was not yet born. And Farragut was only eleven.

Porter worked his ship southward, searching as instructed for Bainbridge's ship, but without success. He eventually learned that the *Constitution* had successfully engaged H. M. S. *Java*, although the ship's present whereabouts remained unknown.

By January of the new year, supplies on the *Essex* were running low, there was the imminent danger of falling into the hands of superior British forces, and there were no friendly ports nearby. That left Porter with only one possibility: "It became absolutely necessary to depart from the letter of my instructions." Those instructions were to proceed to a final rendezvous point off the island of St. Helena. But Porter concluded that by now the *Constitution* might very well be homeward bound for refitting after the encounter with H. M. S. *Java*. If that were so, there would be no point in looking for her at St. Helena, and that would leave him free to plot his own course, according to a further instruction that Bainbridge had included in the orders:

> Should any unforeseen cause or accident
> prevent our meeting by the 1st April next, you
> must then act according to your best judgment
> for the good of the Service on which we are
> engaged.

Never mind that April was still several months off; Porter hit upon the plan of venturing into the Pacific, there to do whatever he might to annoy the enemy. In his eyes, the only other alternatives were "… capture, starvation, or blockade."

But the decision to try his luck on the other side of South America was not quite a spur-of-the-moment whim:

> It accorded with the views of the honourable secretary of the navy, as well as those of my immediate commander. Before the declaration of war, I wrote a letter to the former, containing a plan for annoying the enemy's commerce in the Pacific ocean, which was approved of by him; and prior to my sailing, com. Bainbridge requested my opinion, as to the best mode of annoying the enemy. I laid before him the same plan, and received his answer approving of the same, and signifying his intentions to pursue it, provided we could get supplies of provisions.

In short, Porter had set his mind on the Pacific even before he left home port, and may not have been terribly disappointed at failing to meet up with Bainbridge in the Atlantic. His conclusion that the *Constitution* might be making its way back home conflicts with Porter's claim that his superior officer also intended to pursue the British on the other side of the South American continent. If so, Porter might have spent a bit more time searching for the *Constitution*, so that they might sail to the Pacific in consort. But perhaps he feared Bainbridge would direct him back to the United States too, thus putting an end to his own plans. And apparently he did have his own plans: his *Journal* makes frequent references to James Colnett's *Voyage to the South Atlantic and Round Cape Horn into the Pacific Ocean*. It would seem he had the volume close at hand as he plotted his own course. Now why would the work of a British whaling captain be on an American warship's bookshelf, unless its own captain anticipated some need for a convenient reference work?

Or maybe it was just a coincidence that Porter had Colnett along. But in any case, all sail was set and some weeks later David Porter duplicated something done by those two Williams—Dampier and Ambrosia Cowley. They all rounded Cape Horn on Valentine's Day; the British buccaneers in 1683, the American Navy 130 years later. If Porter's crew followed their predecessor's example of choosing valentines, he neglected to mention it.

Porter and the *Essex* eventually found their way into Galápagos waters, where he and it became a general nuisance to whaling vessels sailing under the flag of His Britannic Majesty. As the Captain saw it, his duty was to capture as many as he might, and so the first order of business was to put in at Post Office Bay, there to examine the contents of the Galápagos Post Office for letters that would reveal the whereabouts of his prey. In addition to the note from Captain Macy described in the previous chapter, Porter found evidence of several British ships that had arrived almost a year earlier. He also discovered a barrel of bread and a cask of water left by an unknown benefactor for the relief of anyone who might pass by in distress. At the moment the cask was not needed, for within a very few paces a torrential stream of fresh water flowed to the sea, the result of recent rains. Porter realized he was witness to a temporary phenomenon though, for he noted that "...every tree on the island, at least all that could be approached by the boat's crew on shore, and such as we could perceive by means of our perspectives, were dead and withered."

Before setting out in search of the British whalers, which he hoped were still about their business in the island group, he followed the William Ambrosia Cowley naming tradition, on passing "... a remarkable high, black, ragged rock, which from its appearance, I have been induced to call *Rock Dismal.*" The name didn't stick, and today the offshore collapsed crater near Post Office Bay is known as Corona del Diablo (Devil's Crown).

The *Essex* proceeded to Albemarle Island, and on approaching their first anchorage, Porter gave it a name. This time the name stuck, and Point Essex may still be found on modern Galápagos maps. Then, following William Dampier's example, Porter presented his own pre-Darwinian observation on variation of species.

> We went on shore, and, to our great surprize, and no little alarm, on entering the bushes, found myriads of guanas, of an enormous size and the most hideous appearance imaginable; the rocks forming the cove were also covered with them, and, from their taking to the water very readily, we were induced to believe them a distinct species from those found among the keys of the West Indies.

The first thought was that the iguanas might attack the men, but it was soon enough realized there was nothing to fear, and so instead the men attacked the iguanas. Some of the victims were brought back to the ship, where they were "…found to be excellent eating, and many preferred them greatly to the turtle."

Something isn't quite right here. As Darwin discovered some years later, marine iguanas don't take to the water very readily at all, except at feeding time. And of course land iguanas don't take to it, period. Nor would anyone willingly dine on marine iguana, unless it were that or starvation. Perhaps the ship's cook served up some land iguana and the Captain mistakenly thought he was dining on the marine iguanas he'd seen on shore.

Porter noted the sea lions and remarked on their behavior:

> Nothing can be more sluggish or more inactive
> than this animal while on the sand; it appears
> incapable of making any exertions whatever to
> escape those in pursuit of it, ... but when they
> are in the water, or even on the rocks, nothing
> can exceed their activity: they seem then to
> be a different animal altogether; shy, cunning,
> and very alert in pursuit of their prey, and in
> avoiding pursuit, they are then very difficult to
> take.

Other members of the Galápagos menagerie did not escape
notice either as he examined the shores of the island:

> The rocks were every where covered with
> seals, penguins, guanas, and pelicans, and
> the sea filled with green turtle. ... Multitudes
> of enormous sharks were swimming about
> us, and from time to time caused us no little
> uneasiness, from the ferocious manner in which
> they came at the boat and snapped at our oars.

How did these creatures get here? Porter attempts no
explanation and contents himself with a simple report of
what he saw.

> I shall leave others to account for the manner
> in which all those islands obtained their supply
> of tortoises and guanas, and other animals of
> the reptile kind; it is not my business even to
> conjecture as to the cause. I shall merely state,
> that those islands have every appearance of
> being newly created, and that those perhaps
> are the only part of the animal creation that
> could subsist on them.

But Porter was not here in the interests of science. "Perceiving
a breeze springing up, I hastened on board (for I had objects

in view of more importance then examining the rocky coast of this dreary place, or catching guanas and seals)." Those objects were of course vessels of the British whaling fleet, which he hoped to find farther north, in the vicinity of Tagus Cove. The cove was devoid of prey, but before moving on Porter went off in search of another object—fresh water—and discovered traces of earlier visitors on a flat rock just outside the mouth of the Cove.

> In this rock I found four holes, each about 14 inches square, and from 6 to 7 deep, which had apparently been cut by some person with a pick-axe, for the purpose of catching the water as it dripped from the rocks above. ... And but a short distance from thence was erected a hut, built of loose stones, but destitute of a roof. This I afterwards understood was the work of a wretched English sailor, who had been landed there by his captain, destitute of every thing, for having used some insulting language to him.

Above: The remains of a stone enclosure found on Isla Isabela. Is this the first abode of Irish Pat Watkins?

The unfortunate sailor eventually prepared a float of inflated seal skins and set out for Banks Bay, fighting off sharks with a stick that also served for a paddle.

> He succeeded at length in getting along side an American ship early in the morning, where his unexpected arrival not only surprised but alarmed the crew; for his appearance was scarcely human; clothed in the skins of seals, his countenance haggard, thin, and emaciated,

his beard and hair long and matted, they
supposed him a being from another world.
The commander of the vessel where he
arrived felt a great sympathy for his sufferings,
and determined for the moment to bring to
punishment the villain who had, by thus
cruelly exposing the life of a fellow-being,
violated every principle of humanity; but from
some cause or other he was prevented from
carrying into effect his laudable intentions, and
to this day the poor sailor has not had justice
done to him.

In giving the account, Porter made no connection between
this wretched English sailor and the character we met on a
different island in the previous chapter—none other than
Irish Pat Watkins. Yet the two descriptions could easily be
applied to the same man, and Dr. John Coulter in the same
chapter added something that suggests this might indeed
be so. The doctor mentioned that Watkins had been left at
first on Albemarle Island, but later "… the captain of an
American whale ship humanely took him off, and landed
him, at his own request, on Charles's Island."

So, was the stone hut on Albemarle Island the first abode of
Fatherless Oberlus? Perhaps it was.

But now, to business: after a sleepless night fretting over
the emptiness of the Galápagos waters, the cry of "sail ho"
roused Porter from his bed. Three British whale ships had
been sighted, and soon the *Montezuma, Georgiana* and *Policy*
were his. He estimated their worth at some half-million
dollars, no small sum in those days, and with stores that
supplied all his wants, except water. The ships had recently
called at James Island, where they supplied themselves
abundantly with what Porter felt deserved the name
of the "elephant tortoise." He offers a description of the
creatures:

Nothing, perhaps, can be more disagreeable
or clumsy than they are in their external
appearance. Their motion resembles strongly
that of the elephant; their steps slow, regular,
and heavy; they carry their body about a foot
from the ground, and their legs and feet bear
no slight resemblance to the animal to which
I have likened them; their neck is from 18
inches to 2 feet in length,
and very slender; their head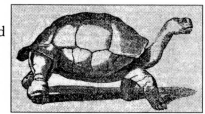
is proportioned to it, and
strongly resembles that of
a serpent; but, hideous
and disgusting as is their
appearance, no animal can possibly afford a
more wholesome, luscious, and delicate food
than they do; the finest green turtle is no more
to be compared to them, in point of excellence,
than the coarsest beef is to the finest veal;
and after once tasting the Gallapagos tortoises,
every other animal food fell greatly in our
estimation.

Above: A "Gallapagos turtle" from Porter's *Journal*.

Porter's enthusiasm for tortoise as main course continues,
and then he returns to the work at hand, putting midshipman
Cowan in command of the *Policy*. That ship's ten guns were
placed aboard the *Georgiana* to supplement her own six,
making her well-equipped for the business of war.

The tiny fleet made its way around the north head of
Albemarle Island, bound for James Island and water. But
currents drove them far to the north. Then a few days
later they were able to make their way southward and one
morning found themselves within a dozen miles of a large
island. But which island was it? Porter at first thought it was
James, and some of his prisoners agreed. But none could

account for sandy beaches and fine bays which suggested this was not the island they were seeking.

Porter consulted his handy reference—James Colnett's *Voyage*—which contained a chart drawn by Aaron Arrowsmith.

> As I could not find any correspondence
> between the position of this and other islands
> in sight, with those laid down on Colnett's
> chart, the only one which has been drawn of
> the Gallapagos, I felt myself much staggered in
> the belief of this being James.'

And indeed it was not. He thought it might be Barrington, while others assured him it was Norfolk. A fine breeze from the northward put the matter to rest: "I determined to give up the idea of making any further examination, ... hoping to reach Hood's Island, to get on board some tarrapins, as a refreshment for the crew." As the *Essex* put the unknown island astern, Porter seized the opportunity to begin a critique of both Colnett and his chart, which he found "...full of errors, none of the islands being laid down agreeable to their true position; nor are the shores of any of them correctly traced."

But instead of reaching Hood's Island, Porter was astonished to find himself approaching Charles Island, where he anchored in Post Office Bay and continued complaining about his predecessor.

> We were now convinced that no reliance
> whatsoever should be placed on Colnett's
> survey, which has been drawn only from fancy
> or the incorrect information of others; for
> no such islands as Duncan's and James' exist
> where he has placed them, nor has he any
> where traced an island bearing the slightest
> resemblance to the one in question.

Porter seized the opportunity of his return to Charles Island to re-examine the Galápagos Post Office, but found no new information there. However, the barrel of bread and cask of water were gone. And by now the rains had ceased, so there was no stream of water at which they could refresh themselves. The *Essex* repositioned itself to Black Beach, where some of the crew began the laborious task of fetching water from a spring some few miles inland. Others loaded the ship with tortoises, now affectionately known to the men as "Gallapagos mutton."

The mystery of the large island to the north remained, and Porter proposed to ship's chaplain David P. Adams that he proceed there to make a survey. The Reverend Mr. Adams was delighted with the assignment, returning some days later with his report.

> From this island, James', Albemarle, Norfolk,
> Barrington, Crossman's, Charles', and many
> others were to be seen; but he could perceive
> none that bore the slightest resemblance, in
> position or appearance, to those called by
> captain Colnett Duncan's and Jarvis' islands;
> and as this island was now destitute of a name,
> and he could perceive no traces of its having
> been visited before, he highly complimented
> me, by giving it the name of Porter's Island.

And here we have yet another Galápagos mystery. The unknown island was of course Norfolk—the present Isla Santa Cruz—and Chaplain Adams was standing on it when he made his observations, including that he could see Norfolk. Well of *course* he could see Norfolk; it was after all directly beneath his feet. Perhaps he meant Colnett's Norfolk, marked on his chart about 60 miles due east. But there is no island in that location, nor was there a Norfolk placed on Porter's own chart when his *Journal of a Cruise* was published a few years later. Maybe the Chaplain (or the Captain?) knew very well that the island was Norfolk itself, but given the cartographic confusions of the day, saw little harm done by adding to the confusion.

For a time, the name stuck. The logs of American whalers often referred to the island by Porter's name, and even the enemy—British Captain John Fyffe—placed "Porters Isle" on a chart he prepared during his 1815 visit. And then a year or so later, Aaron Arrowsmith published an updated version of Colnett's chart. He consulted Captain Fyffe, copied his sketch of the island, but not the name. Arrowsmith re-named it in honor of Fyffe's vessel, H. M. S. *Indefatigable*.

Although his name did not last long on the island where Chaplain Adams placed it, that is not to say "Porter" is unknown there: Up in the highlands of Isla Santa Cruz dwells a sub-species of the Galápagos tortoise. In scientific circles, it is known today as *Geochelone elephantopus porteri*.

Although Captain David Porter did not visit Isla Santa Cruz, one of its distinguished highland residents, *Geochelone elephantopus porteri*, bears his name.

Porter was now ready to quit Charles Island, but after an unsuccessful attempt to sail eastward, he altered his course back to Charles and then to Albemarle again, where he captured two more ships, the *Atlantic* and *Greenwich*, placing Lieutenant Gamble of the *Essex* Marine detachment in charge of the latter. Several more ships were taken, and eventually the little navy made its way to James Island. Tortoises were brought aboard, left on deck for a few days—allowing them sufficient time "...to discharge the contents of their stomachs" as he delicately put it—then stowed below decks.

Norfolk Isle (inset) appeared as a tiny fragment on the Colnett chart seen by Porter. On a later version of the same chart, cartographer Aaron Arrowsmith referred to new information from Captain John Fyffe. The old Norfolk became Indefatigable, in honor of Fyffe's ship.

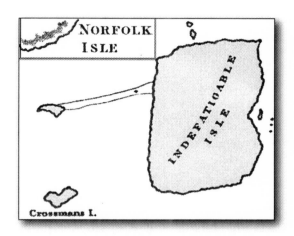

Porter made some notes about the tortoises and other creatures that he'd seen.

> The shells of those of James' Island are
> sometimes remarkably thin and easily
> broken, but more particularly so as they
> become advanced in age; for then, whether
> owing to the injuries they receive from their
> repeated falls in ascending and descending
> the mountains, or from injuries received
> otherwise, or from the course of nature, their
> shells become very rough, and peal off in large
> scales, which renders them very thin and easily
> broken. Those of James' Island appear to be a
> species entirely distinct from those of Hood's
> and Charles' Islands. The form of the shell of
> the latter is elongated, turning up forward, in
> the manner of a Spanish saddle, of a brown

colour, and of considerable thickness; they are
very disagreeable to the sight, but far superior
to those of James' Island in point of fatness,
and their livers are considered the greatest
delicacy. Those of James' Island are round,
plump, and black as ebony, some of them
handsome to the eye; but their liver is black,
hard when cooked, and the flesh altogether not
so highly esteemed as the others.

Among the whole only three were male,
which may be easily known by their great size,
and from the length of their tails, which are
much longer than those of the females. As
the females were found in low sandy bottoms,
and all without exception were full of eggs, of
which generally from 10 to 14 were hard, it
is presumable that they come down from the
mountains for the express purpose of laying;
and this opinion seems strengthened from the
circumstance of there being no male tortoises
among them, the few we found having been
taken a considerable distance up the mountain.
One remarkable peculiarity in this animal
is, that the blood is cold. I shall leave it to
those better acquainted with natural history
to investigate the cause of a circumstance so
extraordinary; my business is to state facts, not
to reason on them.

Facing page: "Gallapagos Turtle" — An engraving in the
July 1859 edition of *Harper's New Monthly Magazine* accompanied a lengthy feature about the Cruise of the *Essex*.

Again, Porter complains about Colnett, who had written that of all the islands in the archipelago, "… the preference must be given to James' isle, as it is the only one we found sufficient fresh water at to supply a small ship." After a fruitless search for Colnett's water supply, the Captain of the *Essex* cannot conceal his annoyance:

> Where is the advantage of James' Island furnishing fresh water "sufficient to supply a small ship," if we are ignorant where it is to be found? … However, he has committed so

many errors in his description of this island, as well as in the chart he has drawn of the whole group, that in their multiplicity this single one might be passed over in silence, were it not for the deplorable consequences that might result to a whole ship's company, who, when short of water, should (relying on Colnett's statement) put into James' Island for a supply.

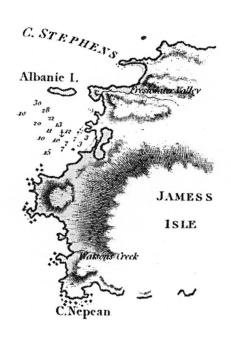

Aaron Arrowsmith's rendition of James Island appeared on a large fold-out map in Colnett's *Voyage.* Contrary to Porter's complaint, the map shows a "Freshwater Valley" just to the right of Albanie Island. But perhaps this source was dry during his visit.

Next came the task of reporting the unhappy results of a duel between two of his officers which we will return to later on. And then he writes of the accidental introduction of a species alien to Galápagos:

While we lay at the bay in James' Island, we put our goats on shore to graze, keeping a person to attend them through the day and give them water; and as they were all very tame, and kept about the landing-place, we every night left them on shore. There was one young male, and three females. ... One

morning, after they had been there several days
and nights, the person who attended them
went on shore, as usual, to give them their
water; but no goats were to be found; they
had all, as with one accord, disappeared. ...
They undoubtedly took to the mountains in the
interior, where unerring instinct led them to the
springs or reservoirs from whence the tortoises
obtain their supply. It is probable their increase
will be very rapid; and perhaps nature, whose
ways are mysterious, has embraced this first
opportunity of inhabiting this island with a race
of animals, who are, from their nature, almost
as well enabled to withstand the want of water
as the tortoises with which it now abounds.

The sudden disappearance of the goats led Porter to some
speculations on animal intelligence:

There was one fact, which was noticed by
myself and many others, the day preceding
the departure of the goats, and must lead us
to believe that something more than chance
directed their movements. It was observed that
they all drank an unusual quantity of water;
the old Welch goat particularly did not seem
satisfied until she had drunk upwards of half a
gallon (which for a goat, it must be admitted,
is an extraordinary quantity), and the others
a quantity not far short of it, which seems
as though they had determined to provide
themselves with a supply to enable them to
reach the mountains; and this fact, which (if
we take into consideration the extraordinary
sagacity of the goat) bears something the
appearance of the marvellous.

Before quitting Galápagos, Porter spent a bit more time observing the wildlife, noting among other things the feeding habits of sea lions. In his continuing commentary on the inaccuracies of James Colnett, Porter makes one of his own. He tells us that he went "...searching for M'Gowen's Reef in my route, and can now with safety declare, that M'Gowen's Reef does not exist but in the chart of captain Colnett." On that chart, the reef "... lies nearly half way between Hood's and Barrington Islands, and in the direct passage of vessels running down between Hood's and Chatham for Charles' Island."

That description closely fits the location of MacGowen Reef today, and it's fortunate that Porter didn't find it the hard way as he made his run to Charles Island.

David Porter: "M'Gowen's Reef does not exist. ..." It's not much to look at, but more than enough to do in the unsuspecting frigate whose captain thinks it's not really there.

After Galápagos, Porter eventually took the *Essex* back to the coast of South America, and the neutral port of Valparaiso, Chile. There he saw his old friend Captain James Hillyar, now commanding His Majesty's Ship *Phoebe*, travelling in consort with H. M. S. *Cherub,* and both sent out to find and destroy the *Essex*. But having met in a neutral port, the friendly adversaries were expected to observe that neutrality. And so they did, until Porter attempted to make his escape. Then the *Phoebe* and *Cherub* captains apparently put aside their sense of honor, attacked and all but destroyed Porter's ship. He and his surviving crew were released on parole and permitted to make their way home, on condition that they withdraw from hostilities until such time as they might be "exchanged" with British forces captured by Americans.

Porter did not draw his sword again, but he considered his pen exempt from the conditions of parole. Within a year the first edition of his *Journal of A Cruise Made to the Pacific Ocean* was published. It didn't take too long for Porter's *Journal* to make its own voyage across another ocean to London, and into the hands of William Gifford, editor of *The Quarterly Review* and dedicated hater of all things American, including authors. In his July 1815 issue, Gifford treated his readers to a 32-page "review" of Porter's work, which is more an *ad hominem* attack on the writer than a review of his work. After reading the first sentence, one may wonder why Gifford went to the bother of soiling so much paper. After all,

> It will be thought superfluous, perhaps, to put the
> English reader on his guard against a book which
> he may never have an opportunity of perusing;
> for we believe that ours is the only copy which
> has crossed, or is likely to cross, the Atlantic.

But Gifford had his reasons, some of which are revealed by Porter's biographer David F. Long, who notes that Gifford was "renowned both for his merciless reviews and his animus toward Americans." The poet Robert Southey wrote that "Gifford looked upon authors as 'worms'—something beyond the pale of human sympathy." Presumably Gifford made an exception for such authors as himself.

Washington Irving—who had published previews of Porter's *Journal* prior to its appearance in book form—later described Gifford as "a small shriveled, deformed man of about sixty, with something of a humped back, eyes that diverge, and a large mouth." Irving said nothing about the man's writing style, or lack thereof.

The shriveled deformed man's diatribe made its own voyage back across the Atlantic, and some eight years later Porter had the last word. When the second edition of his *Journal* was published in 1822, he devoted a preface (of 74 pages!) to a point-by-point refutation of his mean-spirited critic. Porter's review of his reviewer is no doubt the highlight of the second edition, and of course both the author and the critic have plenty to say about the Galápagos Islands.

Gifford had attacked Porter's assertion that Galápagos tortoises can weigh as much as 400 pounds, citing the authority of William Dampier who reported "one of the largest of these creatures to weigh one hundred or two hundred pounds, and some of them to measure two feet, or two feet six inches." Gifford speculates that "They have grown, no doubt, since honest Dampier's time." To which Porter retorts

> If it were not too presuming, the author would here take
> the freedom of hinting to the critic, that it is necessary
> to read a little in order to be able to detect either
> mistakes or misrepresentations in the writings of others.

He proposes that "Honest Dampier is not exclusive authority, even for the magnitude of a turtle" and draws Gifford's attention to the words of another seafarer with whom, as we have seen, Porter was quite familiar. And Gifford was not. This was Captain—that is, *British* Captain—James Colnett, who wrote of tortoises weighing some 300 pounds and measuring about three feet in length.

Next, Gifford instructs his readers that the islands are "all volcanic, and in a state of activity" and these volcanoes are "fed by a constant indraught of the sea." But alas, "matters of this kind are beneath the observation of Mr. Porter." Mr. Porter reminds Mr. Gifford that the islands are in fact *not* all in a state of activity, and that the indraught of the sea theory had been opposed by many prominent scientists and recently ridiculed in the *Edinburgh Review*.

Gifford's review may have produced a result that he had not anticipated, for shortly after Porter's attack on his attacker appeared in his second edition, yet another edition was published, and this, in London. The flap had apparently created sufficient interest to warrant the publication of *A Voyage in the South Seas, in the years 1812, 1813, and 1814. With particular details of the Gallipagos and Washington Islands. By Captain David Porter, of the American Frigate, the Essex.* The edition was heavily abridged, omitting much of what was uncomplimentary to His Majesty's Navy.

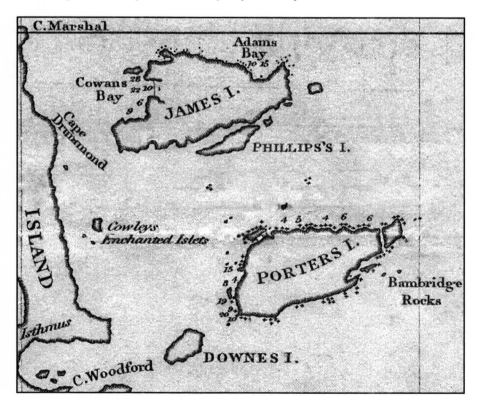

Published in London by Sir Richard Phillips & Co., the heavily abridged edition of Porter's *Journal* adds "Phillips's I." to an island left unnamed by the author. Bambridge [*sic*, Bainbridge] Rocks (now, Gordon Rocks) are in the location specified by Porter. Today, rocks of the same name are off James Island.

The American Frigate Essex, from a watercolor by Commander Edward Tufnell, Royal Navy.

There are numerous portraits whose subject is said to be Captain David Porter, and in fact the United States Naval Academy Museum has evidence of more than twenty. One of the most famous may be of someone else though, for it bears no resemblance at all to what we know of the Captain.

In the July 1814 issue of *The Analectic Magazine,* editor Washington Irving published an engraving of David Porter by Edwin David. The likeness suggests the subject was of short stature, and that agrees with a remark in the accompanying biography. On learning that young David was about to go to sea with his father, his constitution "... being feeble and delicate excited all the apprehensions of a tender mother, against exposing the puny stripling to the dangers and hardships of so rude a life." But, to sea he went, and later on was twice captured by—and twice escaped from—the British. Porter eventually worked his passage home during a winter season with no protective clothing. Washington Irving observed that "It would appear almost incredible that his feeble frame, little inured to hardship, could have sustained so much." The Captain's son and biographer Admiral David Dixon Porter also mentions the fragile frame of his father. And in *Nothing to Daring*, biographer David Long notes that "... one nineteenth century historian (unidentified by Long) described him as 'a small, slight, and rather ill-favored New England man.' "

In 1825, the sculptor John Henri Isaac Browere created a life mask of the Captain, and Porter himself stated that "Nothing can be more accurate and expressive." Both the engraving and the life mask display a distinctive tuft of hair at the top of the subject's head and extended sideburns. And the mask, when compared to others created by the same artist, also suggests that the subject was small in frame.

A portrait in oil was created about midway between these two works by the famous American artist Charles Willson Peale. It is on display in Philadelphia's Independence Hall. But the sitter's demeanor does not agree with Peale's own description of a man " ... seldom a minute in the same position, for when anyone speaks he turns toward them and never thinks that it is necessary to keep himself in the same view to the painter. In fact, for the sitter to be Porter, he would have had to change his hair style, shave his sideburns, alter his facial characteristics, and acquire the more robust physique suggested by the Peale portrait. And then he would have to revert to his former appearance before Browere created his life mask. Since this seems unlikely (to say the least), there's a possibility that the actual portrait of David Porter has gone missing over the years, and the subject of the Peale portrait is someone else. But who? And where is David Porter?

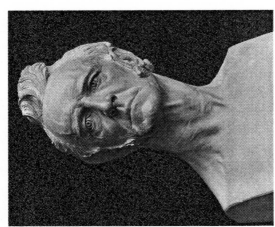

Three images of Captain David Porter. Left: An 1814 engraving in *Analectic Magazine* suggests the subject was of short stature, and in the accompanying biography, Porter's friend Washington Irving refers to his "feeble frame." Right: Of John Henri Isaac Browere's 1825 life mask, Porter himself remarked, "Nothing can be more accurate and expressive." Center: For Charles Willson Peale's 1818-19 subject to be Porter, he would have had to change his hair style, shave his sideburns, alter his facial characteristics and acquire the robust physique suggested by the portrait. And then he would have had to revert to his former appearance before Browere created his life mask. In all, an unlikely scenario, and one which suggests the Peale portrait is of someone else.

CHAPTER SEVEN

THE SEARCH FOR LIEUTENANT COWAN

Here, in 1813, fell in a daybreak duel, a
Lieutenant of the U. S. frigate Essex, aged
twenty-one: attaining his majority in death.

—Herman Melville: *The Encantadas*

A score NEEDED TO BE SETTLED. And so of an early morning in Galápagos, two of Captain David Porter's trusted subordinates went ashore at the customary hour for such unpleasantness. One of them was Acting 4th Lieutenant John S. Cowan, whom Porter had recently advanced from his rank of Midshipman. While awaiting approval of the promotion from the Secretary of the Navy, at which time the advancement would be permanent, Cowan was placed in temporary command of the captured British ship *Policy*. And then he and a fellow officer had a falling out, and a serious one at that, although no details have survived. But whatever the reason for their feud, one of them demanded satisfaction, and one of them got it. The score was settled shortly after dawn on August 10th, 1813. Captain Porter claims he knew nothing of the matter until it was too late, and then all that remained was to record the unhappy news in his *Journal*.

I have now the painful task of mentioning an occurrence which gave me the utmost pain, as it was attended by the premature death of a promising young officer, whereby the service at this time has received an irreparable injury, and by a practice which disgraces human nature. I shall, however, throw a veil over the whole previous proceedings, and merely state, that without my knowledge the parties met on shore at day-light, and at the third fire Mr. Cowan fell dead. His remains were buried the same day in the spot where he fell, with the following inscription placed over his tomb:

Sacred to the memory
OF LIEUT. JOHN S. COWAN,
of the U. S. Frigate Essex,
Who died here anno 1813,
Aged 21 years.

His loss is ever to be regretted
By his country;
And mourned by his friends
And brother officers.

And then, Porter writes about repairing his ship. Ten days later the *Essex* prepares for departure and he leaves a message behind:

Prior to my leaving the place, I buried a letter for lieutenant Downes, in a bottle at the head of Mr. Cowan's grave, and a duplicate of the same at the foot of a finger-post, erected by me, for the purpose of pointing out to such as may hereafter visit the island the grave of Mr. Cowan.

Porter names the anchorage Cowan Bay, the *Essex* sails off, and we hear nothing more about the late Acting 4th Lieutenant Cowan. Nor does Porter reveal the identity of the other duelist. But the news eventually reaches Hezikiah Niles, editor of the *Niles Weekly Register* in Baltimore, and an obituary notice appears in the *Register's* 1815 "Supplement to Volume Seven."

NILES' WEEKLY REGISTER.

SUPPLEMENT TO VOLUME SEVEN.

Midshipman Cowan.

On James' Island, in the South Pacific Ocean, on the 10th of August, 1813, Midshipman JOHN S. COWAN, late of the United States' Navy. At the time of his decease, he was acting Lieutenant on board the United States' frigate *Essex*, to which post he had been temporarily appointed by his gallant commander, in consideration of his high professional merit, and his enthusiastic devotion to the service of his country.—He possesed in an eminent degree the esteem and confidence of his commander, and of his brother Officers generally, and gave the strongest indications of future greatness; in his profession, promising at once to become an honor to his country and his family; but, alas! his destiny was otherwise ordered. An unhappy dispute with a brother officer, (lieut. Gambel of the marines) led on to a duel, in which fell the subject of this article. The intelligence of this distressing event occasioned the deepest regret in Captain Porter; no previous intimation of any misunderstanding between the parties had been received by him, or he would at once prevented the catastrophe that ensued. All that remained for him was to lament, what it was now too late to remedy, and to pay every mark of respect to his remains, which were entombed with the honors of war, on the Island before mentioned. In a strange and remote part of the world he fell; far, far from his kindred and his native soil; but his grave was hallowed by the tears of his countrymen, and his brave associates in arms. A neat and simple structure was raised to point out to the stanger who might visit the Island, the spot of earth where his remains rested; and on it were inscribed, by his friend, Lieutenant M'Knight, the following monumental lines:—

Sacred to the Memory
Of Lieutenant JOHN S. COWAN,
Of the U. S. frigate *Essex*,
Who died here, Anno. 1813,
Aged 21 years.
His loss is ever to be regretted
By his Country,
And mourned by his Friends
And Brother Officers,

Niles may have learned of the gallant commander's deepest regret—and perhaps even the identity of Cowan's foe—from the gallant commander himself. Porter had returned home a few months before the obituary appeared and in the intervening years since the duel may have decided to lift the veil enough to reveal the assailant's name, if not the reason for the dispute. By placing his name in the *Weekly Register* but not in Porter's own book, the public interest might be served without putting an undue strain on the Captain's cordial relationship with the surviving duelist, who was in fact Lieutenant John Gamble, commanding officer of the Marine detachment aboard the *Essex*. Porter had put him in charge of the captured British ship *Greenwich* at about the same time that he awarded Cowan his all-too temporary advancement in rank.

Was Cowan really back on the *Essex*, as the obituary states? Or had Porter moved him over to the *Greenwich* to serve under Lieutenant Gamble when the *Policy* was sent to the mainland? If so, did the Marine commander offend the junior officer? Or did the subordinate, accustomed to having his own command, fail to show proper respect to his superior? And how extraordinary that Porter—who permitted no detail to escape his notice—would know nothing of all this until it was too late. Or at least, he would *claim* to know nothing.

Above: Model 1811 flintlock pistol made by Simeon North in Berlin, Connecticut. Although the actual dueling weapons are unknown, this 69 caliber smoothbore model is typical of pistols often used by American Naval officers.

Yet even if he truly knew nothing prior to the duel, surely he would have questioned Gamble after the deed was done. But whatever he knew, and whenever he knew it, he kept his silence to the end. No doubt Lieutenant Stephen McKnight also knew something—as the author of the memorial tribute, he was presumably as close to Cowan as anyone might be. Perhaps he was even his second, and perhaps he would have been a good source of information for Hezikiah Niles's obituary.

But Lieutenant McKnight never reached home port.

After the defeat of the *Essex*, the victorious H. M. S. *Phoebe* brought him as far as Rio de Janeiro, where he transferred to the Swedish *Adonis* which was to take him to England. But then in mid-Atlantic he boarded another ship bound for the United States. He was never seen again. The ship was the American frigate *Wasp*, subsequently lost at sea with all hands.

Still later, the neat and simple structure mentioned in the *Niles' Weekly Register* obituary pointed a stranger to Cowan's grave. Less than a year after the duel, His Britannic Majesty's ship *Briton* called at James Island. And there on July 30th, 1814, Lieutenant John J. Shillibeer, R. M., discovered the finger-post. A few years later he recalled the event in his *Narrative of the Briton's Voyage to Pitcairn's Island.*

> Among some green bushes near the beach, is the tomb of Lieutenant Cowen [sic], of the United States Frigate, Essex, who fell in a duel with Mr. Gamble of that ship. That this unfortunate young man was much esteemed by his brother officers, is evident from the great respect they paid to his memory.

Lieutenant Shillibeer apparently read McKnight's tribute to his fallen comrade, although he doesn't say how he came by the intelligence that Cowan fell in a duel. Nor does he explain how he knew of Gamble's role. But some 40 pages later in his *Narrative* we have a clue: a few weeks after departing Galápagos, the *Briton* called at the Marquesas Islands.

> It was here one of Mr. Gamble's men, (Peter Swack,) joined us, who complained greatly of that gentleman's conduct, which he declared was the sole and only cause of his desertion. I do not imagine he entered on board the Briton with a view of serving against his country, but merely to ensure a passage back, his conduct during his stay on board was exemplary.

No doubt Swack—or Marine Private Peter C. Swook as he appears on the *Essex* crew list—was Shillibeer's source for details about the participants of the duel. But the Private may not have troubled Shillibeer with all the details of his recent change of accommodations. Swook was one of four crewmen who had robbed Gamble's ship of supplies and relieved several crewmen of their clothes. Gamble had recently treated one of the quartet, Isaac Coffin, to a severe flogging after an unsuccessful desertion attempt. And then there was John Robinson who, according to Porter, "had recently suffered severe punishment for theft." When they were all discovered missing, the Marine commander ordered out a search party, just as Swook and his companions had anticipated. Before fleeing the *Greenwich* in one of its two small boats, they scuttled the other.

Was Lieutenant Gamble such a man to provoke some men into duels and others into desertion? If so, his personality didn't interfere with his profession. A month before Shillibeer found Cowan's grave, Cowan's assailant found he'd been promoted to Captain. Some time later he advanced to Major, and eventually reached the rank of Lieutenant-Colonel, as we shall soon see.

In Gamble's days as a young Lieutenant, desertion and mutiny were not at all uncommon. In fact, in the paragraph after Shillibeer's Private Swook anecdote, the author notes that "Boyce, a boy 14 years old, deserted here." And then he gets on with the further travels of H. M. S. *Briton*, including the visit to Pitcairn Island and a meeting with the sole survivor of yet another shipboard dispute. Here lived the elderly John Adams, now leader of a small Pitcairn community but earlier a participant with Fletcher Christian in the mutiny on H. M. S. *Bounty*.

The meeting with Adams worked out rather nicely for Shillibeer the author, whose ship had actually been sent to the Pacific to join the hunt for Captain Porter. But they arrived at Valparaiso too late: Porter's *Essex* had already been captured by His Majesty's ships *Phoebe* and *Cherub*. That being the case, there was nothing much left for the *Briton* to do, and Shillibeer could hardly be expected to write a book about having nothing much to do. So he wrote about a visit to Pitcairn Island, as if that had been the reason for the voyage. But before reaching Pitcairn, the *Briton* visited Galápagos, where Shillibeer found Porter's finger post, and then the Marquesas, where he found Gamble's Private Swook.

Some 40 years later, another visitor passed by.

> Upon the beach of James's Isle for many years,
> was to be seen a rude finger-post pointing
> inland. And perhaps taking it for some signal
> of possible hospitality in this otherwise desolate
> spot—some good hermit living there with his
> maple dish—the stranger would follow on in
> the path thus indicated, till at last he would
> come out in a noiseless nook, and find his
> only welcome, a dead man; his sole greeting
> the inscription over a grave: "Here, in 1813,
> fell in a daybreak duel, a Lieutenant of the U.
> S. frigate Essex, aged twenty-one: attaining his
> majority in death."

The visitor says no more. In fact, he was probably no visitor at all. He was Herman Melville, who wrote about the grave in Sketch Tenth of his *The Encantadas*, but rearranged the details to suit his own story line. In his 1854 re-telling of the tale, Melville revises McKnight's tribute to omit Cowan's name, but to include notice of the duel. Although McKnight's verse didn't mention the latter detail, Porter's text did, and Melville was a frequent "visitor" to Porter's work, as we shall see in another chapter.

More than a century after the duel, two distinguished curators picked up the search for Lieutenant Cowan in an exchange of letters that continued for some twenty years. From the California Academy of Sciences' Department of Herpetology in San Francisco, Joseph Richard Slevin wrote to his counterpart in Washington, DC—Waldo Lasalle Schmitt of the Smithsonian Institution's Division of Marine Invertebrates. Both hoped to find the grave, but neither did. Their discussion begins in 1935 on a puzzling note from Slevin about Charles Darwin:

> It is strange to me that Darwin did not know
> of Porter's notes on Galápagos tortoises. As you
> know it was Porter who first called attention
> to the fact that the tortoises from the different
> islands were different. I should think the scientists
> would have known of these notes by 1835.

By return mail Schmitt offers a possible explanation:

> Darwin was perhaps too young a man to have
> known of Porter's account. In his "Voyage of
> the Beagle" he himself acknowledges having
> learned from Mr. Lawson for the first time that
> the tortoises differed on the different islands.

True enough, but Slevin returns to his earlier thought:

> I am still surprised that ... Darwin had not
> heard of Porter's activities seeing he was so
> vitally interested in the Galápagos. However,
> news no doubt traveled slowly in those days
> and Porter's account of his voyage might not
> have reached England by that time.

Schmitt's explanation was at least half right. Darwin wrote in his *Voyage* that Vice-Governor Nicholas Lawson informed him that "… the tortoises differed from the different islands, and that he could with certainty tell from which island any one was brought." And then in the next paragraph on the same page, Darwin mentions Captain Porter's own description of the tortoises. The puzzle is, how did Slevin *and* Schmitt miss this? It's too late now to know.

Moving on to the Cowan matter, Slevin encourages Schmitt to search for the grave:

> I think it would be quite a thing to discover
> this grave. Should you do so it would be nice
> to photograph it, or even see if there were any
> remains left of the casket made by the ship's
> carpenter. It would be a great event to bring
> the remains back to Arlington for interment.

Actually, Slevin didn't know if there was indeed a casket, but we know there was one available a few months earlier, and ironically it was made on the captured ship *Policy*, while that vessel was under the command of Lt. Cowan. In his *Journal*, Porter writes of "Doctor Miller, the surgeon of the ship, a very infirm man, who was in a deep consumption when he joined the ship." Miller had not been comfortable aboard the *Essex*, and requested that he be transferred to the *Barclay*, and later, to the *Policy*, where he passed away a few months before the duel. Porter wrote, "I directed a coffin to be made for him, with an intention of burying him on one of the islands, if it should be in my power." But then Porter changed his mind: "After the funeral service of the church had been read by Mr. Adams, the body of doctor Miller was committed to the deep." Presumably the coffin remained unoccupied, at least for the moment.

A few weeks later, Porter sent the *Policy* and other captured vessels to Valparaiso for disposal. The coffin may have gone along too, or like Cowan himself, it may have remained in Galápagos.

Returning to the Slevin/Schmitt correspondence, three years pass, and then in June of 1938 Slevin mentions the service record of David P. Adams, Ship's Chaplain on Porter's *Essex*, which he received from the Naval Museum "in relation to Acting Lieut. James Cowan." He means *John* Cowan of course, who fell on *James* Island. Slevin doesn't tell Schmitt what the service record contained, but apparently Cowan was still on his mind. He was certainly on Schmitt's mind too a month later, when he accompanied another visitor in search of John S. Cowan. The third presidential cruise of the U. S. S. *Houston* brought Waldo Lasalle Schmitt and Franklin Delano Roosevelt to Galápagos, and an onboard pamphlet noted each day's activities.

> July 29. At the request of the President, a searching party was organized and all preparations for a thorough search for Lieutenant Cowan's grave were made.

> July 30. During the morning hours the searching party made a futile effort to discover the grave of Lieutenant Cowan. James Bay was combed from end to end and inland about one-third of a mile. Evidently the passage of time—one hundred and twenty-five years of continuous erosion by wind and waters, had obliterated all evidence of the resting place of the Naval Lieutenant.

Had the search been successful as the President hoped it would be, Roosevelt (with the approval of the Ecuadorian Government) planned to take the remains to the United States Naval Academy for interment there with many of America's Naval Heroes.

Some 50 officers and men had covered about a mile and a half of ground in a 300-yard skirmish-line formation, on the same day of the same month that the *Briton* had anchored here more than a century earlier. They found nothing, but they may have come close: a typed log reports that "Ensign Johnson located a peculiar and uniform assemblage of rocks at the foot of a thirty-five foot spire of volcanic rock, which might possibly have indicated a grave. Further investigation of this area revealed nothing." But the further investigation wasn't very thorough—the search party had left the ship shortly after 9:00 am, they returned before noon, and within the hour the U. S. S. *Houston* was on its way again. That didn't give Ensign Johnson much opportunity to investigate his find. Perhaps it was fortunate the grave was undiscovered—as it remains to this day. If Cowan's final resting place is ever found, it will be fitting to leave him in it, and do as Porter did—put up another finger-post to mark the spot for future visitors.

Scarcely had Schmitt returned to his office when a letter arrived from California. Slevin had read newspaper reports of the cruise, and now that it's too late he tells Schmitt about what Lieutenant Shillibeer of the *Briton* had said, and also passes on a part of Herman Mellville's account. And then he concludes with a request:

> After you are able to catch your breath I'd be
> glad to hear just what you did about looking
> for the grave. I think it would be a great thing
> to locate it and am sure there would be some
> remains of the box made by the carpenter (I
> suppose there must have been one), and of
> the bottle planted by Porter at the head of
> the grave with the orders for Lieut. Downes,
> who was then absent on a prize [the captured
> British *Georgiana*]. If I am not mistaken,
> Downes did not get back to James Bay.
> Certainly the bottle would be intact.

Schmitt doesn't even try to conceal his exasperation when he replies a few days later:

> I don't know whether to kick you or myself,
> but certainly I never got any other information
> from you regarding Cowan's grave than what
> was in Porter's book. Won't you kindly give me
> all the references you have to that grave? You
> refer to some of them in your letter, but what
> I want is details—either copies, or title and
> page references. If I had only known that you
> had all that extra information up your sleeve, I
> would have come down on you for it long ago!
> With all that Navy crew available, it seems as
> though we missed the opportunity of a lifetime.

You sure did, Waldo. And now with opportunity come and gone, Slevin writes several pages of analysis. He takes Shillibeer's remark about "… the respect they paid to his [Cowan's] memory" to imply a mound of some size, no doubt assembled from lava fragments "…piling up a monument over the grave." Slevin even sends Schmitt a little sketch to show where he thinks the searchers should have looked, and a suggestion: "Look for a handmade pile of lava clinkers, of fair size, near which may be an outline of lava clinkers to mark the direction of the grave."

To this day the mound of clinkers has not been found, but there may be a good reason for that. There may not have been a mound of clinkers. Captain Porter said nothing about a mound of clinkers, and neither did Lieutenant Shillibeer. Even that deckhand Herman Melville—who wrote about another clinkered grave in Galápagos—did not use that expression to describe the resting place. Joseph Slevin imagined a mound of clinkers and recommended Schmitt look for it. If it had been there though, surely someone would have stumbled upon it by now. But to recall Ensign Johnson for a moment, perhaps someone did.

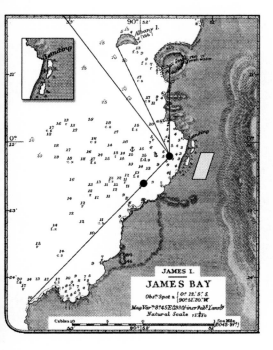

Joseph Slevin sketched an oblique rectangle in the area where he thought Cowan's grave would be found. The four compass bearings are taken from David Porter's *Journal of a Cruise....* The black circles indicate the anchorage of the *Essex* adjacent to the lagoons, and later on, the *Briton* slightly to the southwest. Inset shows lagoon detail.

Although neither scientist had any luck finding Cowan, Slevin did discover an unexpected link to Lieutenant Gamble. In a 1938 letter to his Smithsonian colleague, he recounts an incident from his youth. From time to time the youngster was put under the charge of a French lady who taught at a local boarding school, where Slevin would stay when his parents went out of town. While there he struck up an acquaintance with an artist who had a studio near the school, and now some 50 years later these details came back to him during an exchange of letters with a retired Marine Corps officer. In passing, the officer mentioned an exhibition held a few years previously at a local art museum. Slevin doesn't tell Schmitt the name of the retired officer, or of the museum, but does report there was a painting of another Marine officer on display there. The subject was Colonel John M. Gamble, and the painting was on loan from a relative—also named John M. Gamble. And then Slevin remembered the name of the artist of his childhood. John M. Gamble. In his day, Gamble was celebrated for his paintings of wildflowers, put to canvas with patterns so vivid they were known as "Gamble's Prairie Fires."

Marine Officer John Marshall Gamble, in a ca. 1816 portrait by Samuel Lovett Waldo.

Now in his 70s and living in Santa Barbara, he remembered young Slevin and the French lady, and confirmed that he was indeed the grandson of Lieutenant Cowan's murderer— although he probably didn't put it quite that way. He also wrote to Slevin that his grandfather kept a diary, but it would not be possible to see it. The San Francisco earthquake and fire of 1906 had taken the artist's home, and stored within it, his grandfather's diary.

Slevin hoped his old acquaintance would pay him a visit the next time the artist came to town. Maybe some details of his grandfather's life had been passed down to him, and surely he must have read the diary himself before it went up in smoke. Maybe there would be some clue. One year later there had still been no meeting, although Slevin did tell Schmitt about a recent phone chat. Gamble said that the old diary was in pretty rough shape even before the fire, and sorely regretted that no typewritten copy had been made, despite his best intentions—although of course that might have been destroyed in the same disaster that claimed the original work. As best he could recall though, there was nothing in it about either a duel or a grave. Slevin learned that much over the phone, and hoped there would be more when they finally met face to face. And at last, they did. In June 1941 Gamble, close to 80, now thought that "two or three lines told the story" and that his grandfather didn't even mention his own role in the duel. As near as he could recall, the diarist simply wrote that " 'Lieutenant Cowan was killed in a duel and buried near where he fell. He was very much beloved by his shipmates,' or words to that effect." No mention was made of what the duel was about, nor was anything said of a funeral. But was this anecdote reliable? In the phone chat a few years earlier, Gamble recalled nothing about Cowan in the diary. Now he remembered something that closely resembled Porter's own account of the tragedy. Perhaps he'd mixed up that account with his own recollection of the diary.

Slevin also commented on a search to be made by someone else. In March of 1941 he'd sent information about Cowan's grave site to this person, but didn't tell Schmitt who it was. He simply wrote that "I sent him everything I had on the subject and he is going to make a real effort to locate it on his trip to the islands this month." Of course Schmitt didn't have to guess the man's identity. He was Sherwood Picking, U. S. Navy, commanding officer of Submarine Squadron Three, and captain of submarine S-44. The S-44 paid a visit to Galápagos in April, along with three other subs and an accompanying tender. The latter was the U. S. S. *Mallard,* and onboard was Waldo Lasalle Schmitt, who wanted to scout around for a likely spot for a research center, while the Navy wanted to scout around for other reasons. And at one point Captain Picking took a break from other duties to scout around for Lieutenant Cowan.

Schmitt was back at his desk a few weeks later and wrote to Slevin about the trip: "Captain Picking ... is very grateful for the information that you furnished him. He did make a most earnest search and, as he expressed it to me, has almost convinced himself that he found something worthwhile."

Something worthwhile? From a 1942 U. S. Navy Intelligence report, a photo titled "Digging at possible site of grave of Lieutenant Cowan, U.S.N."

Next, Schmitt tosses out a confusing theory. Two years earlier, Slevin described a lagoon that had separated into two parts as the neck of water flowing between them receded over the years. At the time of the duel, the two were not quite apart yet, although some 20 years later the charts prepared by Captain FitzRoy of the *Beagle* showed dry land between them. But in 1813, this area would hardly have been a suitable spot for a grave. Yet Schmitt faults Captain Picking for searching the wrong area, and states that whatever he found, "It will be difficult to prove that it was Cowan's grave, I fear." And why not? "I felt that it [the grave] was in the narrow neck of land between the lagoons."

Slevin replies with another reminder that "in 1813 the narrow neck between the lagoons had shallow water over it, so the grave could not possibly be there." To add even more confusion, Picking sent a detailed search report to the Office of Naval Operations, written onboard the *Mallard* as it sailed from Galápagos to Coco Island. He included a sketch map showing that the search party *did* examine the narrow neck of land between the lagoons.

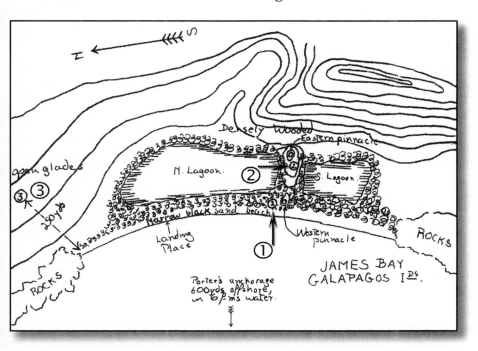

On Captain Picking's sketch map, three search areas are indicated by circled numbers. Enlarged numbers are added here for clarity.

So, what on earth was going through Schmitt's mind when he told Slevin that Picking searched the wrong area? And what was that mysterious "something worthwhile" that Picking found?

In his report, Picking included a sketch of a tree with a down-pointing arrow carved in its trunk. The search party cut it down, dug up the ground and found a lava bubble deep enough to hold a body, but empty. Was this the "something worthwhile" that Schmitt mentions? Or was it something else? And whatever it was, why doesn't Schmitt know about it? After all, he was right there. Or was he? From the correspondence with Slevin, one might think that he was off on another island doing something else while Picking made the search—and that they didn't compare notes afterwards. Unfortunately Slevin doesn't ask Schmitt for more details, and so the reason for his garbled account remains a mystery.

There is yet another mound mystery: Slevin apparently had known about a mound of rocks since his own Galápagos expedition in 1905. Yet he said nothing about it during all this exchange with Schmitt. In fact, he kept silent for another five years, and then finally, in a letter dated April 18, 1946 he offers Schmitt the following little tidbit: "My friend Mr. King, who was on our Galápagos expedition, saw a pile of rocks and wondered what it was doing out from the lava flow. I'm more than convinced now that the grave can be found." Why did it take forty years—the last ten spent discussing the grave site—to divulge this information? Slevin didn't say, and Schmitt didn't ask.

To return to another mystery: what was Captain Picking *really* up to in Galápagos in early 1941? Surely the Navy didn't send a submarine squadron down there just to look for a grave site. If Schmitt knew what the real business was, he kept it to himself. He did expect to see his Navy host again soon though, for in a July letter to Slevin he writes that "We are hoping to have a little get-together with Captain Picking." We don't know if that event ever happened, but if so it was the last time the curator saw the Captain. Within weeks Picking was dead, and we learn a bit more about him in a letter from Slevin.

Dear Dr. Schmitt:

On reading last night's paper I got an awful jolt when I saw that Captain Sherwood Picking was killed in a plane crash in England as he was enroute to be Assistant Naval Attaché. I doubt if we will ever get anyone as interested in the Cowan grave as he was. Too bad to lose such men.

Above: Midshipman Sherwood Picking, in his U. S. Naval Academy graduation photo, Class of 1911.

Captain Picking had spent much of his military career in the submarine service. In early 1941 he was on duty as Commander of the American submarine base at Coco Sola in the Panama Canal Zone, and that's where Slevin had sent him the information on Cowan's grave. The Captain had orders to visit Galápagos on business which we'll learn about in a later chapter, and took advantage of the opportunity to search for Lieutenant Cowan. Then he traveled to Washington, presumably to deliver his report on that other business, and then make his way to England. And then he was gone.

The two friends continued to chat about Cowan for more than another ten years, but there were no new leads. And then came some interesting news in an April 27, 1957 letter to Slevin from the United States Naval Academy. Midshipman F. W. Laing, Jr. had just looked through the Academy's own copy of Shillibeer's *Narrative*. The book had previously been the property of Lieutenant James Wilkie of H. M. S. *Briton*, who had jotted down some notes in the margin next to the description of Cowan's grave:

> On our arrival at this island, and before we
> anchored, a post was observed from the Briton
> on shore, with the form of an arm and hand
> at the top, the hand suspending a bottle, the
> finger pointing to the tomb of Lieut. Cowan.

> The bottle contained accounts of the fate of
> many of the American officers and men, with
> many letters from the survivors to their friends
> in America with a request to forward them to
> the United States which was faithfully executed
> by their inveterate enemies,
>
> The Britons

Laing wrote that the note

> ... seems to bear out your notion that the
> grave was inland, but it could be seen from
> the ship. Possibly, even probably, then, it was
> situated on a knoll or small hill, such as the
> triangulation point in back of the lagoons.

The writer hoped the information would be of interest. No doubt it would have been, but it arrived too late. Slevin was dead.

He passed away in his sleep a few weeks earlier, and the letter was eventually filed and forgotten in the Joseph Slevin Archives at the California Academy of Sciences.

But what of the midshipman's interest in the Cowan matter, and why did he write to Slevin about his discovery? It turns out he learned about the Cowan grave site from his father, Lieutenant Fred W. Laing, U. S. Navy. In April, 1941, the elder Laing was the captain of a submarine tender. It's name was the U. S. S. *Mallard,* and his squadron commanding officer was captain of the flagship submarine S-44, Sherwood Picking. Lt. Laing was part of Picking's search team and in later years told his son about the adventure. He also passed on some other information: back in his own midshipman days, one of his classmates was a lad named John Downes V, the fifth generation in his family to pursue a naval career. In 1813, the first John Downes served as a Lieutenant aboard an American ship. It was the United States frigate *Essex,*

Captain David Porter. And so there were two links between Lt. Fred Laing and Lt. John Cowan.

Continuing the link to the past, Midshipman Laing, Jr. contacted Slevin in connection with research to fulfill the requirements for graduation; his thesis "Midshipman Cowan's Grave" scored him a perfect 4.0.

It's doubtful Schmitt knew of Laing's letter to Slevin before his own passing some twenty years later. It's also doubtful that Porter's inveterate enemies the Britons realized that one of the notes in the bottle was intended for their eyes, for the *Essex* Captain had written…

> … with a design of misleading the enemy, I left in a bottle suspended at the finger-post, the following note:

> The United States frigate Essex arrived here on the 21st July, 1813, her crew much afflicted with the scurvy and ship-fever, which attacked them suddenly, out of which she lost the first lieutenant, surgeon, sailing-master, two midshipmen, gunner, carpenter, and thirty-six seamen and marines.

The note continued with a list of ships captured and the names of the "lost" crewmen, who really weren't lost at all. One can only hope this bit of mis-information did not find its way back to the families of the *Essex* crewmen whose names were on the list.

And now, almost another half century has passed since the last letter passed between Slevin and Schmitt. Lieutenant Cowan sleeps on undisturbed by the curious. Are his remains beneath a mound of clinkers? Is that what Slevin's colleague E. S. King saw almost 100 years ago? Did Ensign Jackson see the same thing? And what about the "something" reported by Captain Picking?

Perhaps it's time for another search.

Is this it? A recently-discovered rectangular arrangement of rocks might indicate the location at which something— or, someone—was buried.

Thanks to Lieutenant Wilkie of H. M. S. *Briton* we know a little something about the author of the *Narrative of the Briton's Voyage to Pitcairn's Island,* and also a bit more about the grave of Lieutenant Cowan. In addition to his marginal note about the grave site, and other remarks throughout the text, Wilkie penned the following comment about the author on the inside back cover:

> In fact, Jack Shillibeer, you have made a very strange account of the Briton's voyage, and only regret I did not produce to our friends a more perfect description of our very interesting Cruize of Pleasures. I think it was possible to have filled six times the paper you have made use of, with a smaller type.
>
> You are aware a considerable number of very interesting anecdotes are omitted.

As a hint of what anecdotes may have been omitted, on a page where Shillibeer writes of the arrival of a Tahitian, Wilkie writes "...who made a present of his lovely wife, a girl of 16, to Lieut. Shannon of the Briton." Shillibeer continues: "I am decidedly of opinion that the custom of having plurality of wives is confined to the chiefs alone." Wilkie also continues: "This was a privilege the author likewise indulged himself with!!!" The punctuation is Wilkie's. Surely this is the stuff of anecdotes, but Shillibeer says nothing more about the social habits of his hosts.

Later on, Shillibeer does favor us with an anecdote about a Lima dinner party at which the guests rampage the dessert table, carrying off everything in sight. Wilkie adds a note that

> This ceremony was never witnessed by anybody,
> but only in the author's own imagination; but
> distant travelers have wonderful stories to relate.

Poor old Jack Shillibeer can't please James Wilkie either way.

"The Kicker Rocks, del[ineated] & Etched by J. Shillibeer"

The famous Galápagos landmark in an engraving by Lieutenant John J. Shillibeer, Royal Marines. The illustration appeared in the author's *Narrative of the Briton's Voyage to Pitcairn's Island.*

CHAPTER EIGHT

CHARLES DARWIN SLEPT HERE

*You care for nothing but shooting, dogs
and rat-catching, and you will be a
disgrace to yourself and all your family.*

Dr. Robert Darwin, to his son Charles

"Oh my *God!!!*"

"What is it now, Charles? Surely not another
of your little creepy-crawly things?"

"Oh, bother creepy-crawly! I say, FitzRoy old
fellow, I have just discovered evolution!"

"I beg your pardon, Charles? Evil what?

". . . *lution. Evolution.* Men from apes, all that
sort of thing. Why, it's *just* as grandfather said."

"Do come in out of the sun, Charles."

P ERHAPS THAT'S NOT *EXACTLY* THE WAY THE LEGEND HAS COME DOWN TO US, yet it's reasonably close:

> Darwin is so impressed by the finches and their beaks
> that his theory of evolution leaps straight into his
> head. He sails away with impious visions, as if he has
> just tasted an apple from the Tree of Knowledge.

Jonathan Weiner thus summarizes the fable in his Pulitzer Prize winner, *The Beak of the Finch*, then gets down to the business of explaining what really happened, or rather, what really *didn't* happen in Galápagos. Darwin did indeed take casual notice of a tortoise or two and bagged a number of finches for future study, but neither creature made much of an impression on him at the time. In short, there was no *Eureka!* moment here, no blinding flash of insight into the mysteries of evolution. In fact it was not until somewhat later that it began to dawn on him that perhaps there might be an interesting theory in all of this.

The story really begins some years before the voyage of the *Beagle.* Darwinian evolution had gotten off to a bad start when young Charles failed to follow his father, and his father's father, into a career of medicine. Anesthesia had not yet come along when he was obliged to watch a child undergo the knife. Long before the youngster was wheeled off to (one hopes) recovery, the young med student fled the operating theater. Blood and gore were not to his taste, and in despair the elder Darwin prescribed a more pastoral setting. His son would become a clergyman—at that time a vocation thought appropriate for a young gentleman with possibly more income than intellect. Or, as one modern biographer put it, "the last resort of the family dullard."

Charles thought this would do quite nicely; why, he might even continue some of the small pleasures that so distressed his father. Shooting, dogs, an occasional rat-catching, surely these gentlemanly pastimes would be no disgrace for a combination country squire and parson, or squarson as some were called when out of earshot. But even then Darwin was not quite sure he believed all the Church dogmas, although much later he wrote "I did not then in the least doubt the strict and literal truth of every word in the Bible." Not then.

If it weren't for a letter, Darwin might have eventually come to terms with dogs and dogmas and settled into a comfortable parsonage and the twin callings of rat-catching and religion. In time, perhaps he might even reconsider which of the two were the more important. But then, the letter. It was from the Reverend John Stevens Henslow, Professor of Mineralogy and Botany at Cambridge. Described by Charles' elder brother as "a man who knows every branch of science," the professor and his student would take long walks almost daily, and Charles became known to the University dons as "the man who walks with Henslow." The professor suggested that Charles apply himself to a certain Captain FitzRoy, who sought a gentleman to accompany him on a voyage of survey and discovery. Henslow thought Darwin's interests in geology and nature made him the ideal candidate, and the hearty encouragement of Uncle Josiah Wedgewood helped persuade his unenthusiastic father to give consent. It was conceded that the voyage would be nothing more than an interlude, nothing more than a working vacation before the vocation. Nothing more than that.

H. M. S. *Beagle*, in the 1890 edition of Darwin's *Journal of Researches*.

Now, all that remained was to meet the Captain, who had already heard of Charles, described to him as a young man of promising ability, and the grandson of Dr. Darwin the poet. Although the distinguished physician-poet Erasmus Darwin died several years before his grandson was born, the doctor's reputation as a medical authority was still very much alive. In fact, he even turns up as such an authority in the preface to *Frankenstein:* "The event on which this fiction is founded has been supposed, by Dr. Darwin, and some of the physiological writers of Germany, as not of impossible occurrence." Mary Wollstonecraft Shelley wrote *Frankenstein* in 1818, when she was 19, as her entry in a four-way contest to see who could write the best ghost story. The other contestants—two poets and a physician— were Mary's husband Percy Bysshe Shelley, Lord Byron, and Byron's physician. Mary won. Her husband wrote the preface, no doubt taking advantage of his poetic license to revive the elder Darwin, dead for some 20 years before the birth of *Frankenstein.*

Perhaps FitzRoy had read of Frankenstein's monster during his youth. If he'd given the matter some thought, he might even have agreed that such a creation was not of impossible occurrence. But perhaps he had not read the elder Darwin. Otherwise, he might have had some premonition of another monster to come, and one which he would unwittingly help to unleash. In 1794, Erasmus Darwin wrote his *Zoonomia; or, The Laws of Organic Life,* in which he acquainted his readers with the heresy of natural adaptation:

> Some birds have acquired harder beaks to crack nuts, as the parrot. Others have acquired beaks adapted to break the harder seeds, as sparrows. Others for the softer seeds of flowers, or the buds of trees, as the finches.

And so there we have it—Darwin's Finches. Not *the* Darwin's Finches of course (which would come a bit later), but nevertheless a tentative beginning to Darwinian bird-watching. Years later, Charles would write that he had read his grandfather's work (twice, in fact), but that it produced no effect on him. Perhaps it didn't, for when he finally did find his own finches in Galápagos, it never occurred to him to take a closer look. In fact, he hardly looked at all. There is but one reference in his shipboard diary, and even that isn't much. On finding a sandstone pit with a few drops of water in it, he records that "Doves and finches swarmed round its margin." And that's all that the not-yet distinguished Charles Darwin has to say about finches. Two years post-Galápagos the ornithologist John Gould completed—at Darwin's request—a study of the birds he had collected, and told him that they were all separate species. Darwin was shocked—perhaps he should have been more attentive to Grandfather. Perhaps someone should have called the birds Gould's Finches. But someone didn't. Not even Darwin. In fact it took another hundred years until someone—the ornithologist Percy Lowe—coined the expression "Darwin's Finches." The label stuck.

Getting back to Grandfather, Doctor Erasmus also noted certain similarities among warm-blooded animals, which he explained:

> One is led to conclude, that they have alike been produced from a similar living filament. In some this filament has acquired hands and fingers, as in mankind. In others it has acquired claws or talons, as in tygers and eagles. In others, toes with an intervening web, as in seals and geese. In others it has acquired cloven hoofs, as in cows and swine; and whole hoofs in others, as in the horse. While in the bird kind this original living filament has put forth wings instead of arms or legs, and feathers instead of hair.

And then he drew another conclusion:

> Would it be too bold to imagine, that all
> warm-blooded animals have arisen from one
> living filament, which THE GREAT FIRST CAUSE
> endued with animality, with the power of
> acquiring new parts, attended with new
> propensities, directed by irritations, sensations,
> volitions, and associations; and thus possessing
> the faculty of continuing to improve by its own
> inherent activity, and of delivering down those
> improvements by generation to its posterity,
> world without end!

What on earth would Captain FitzRoy make of all this? His own grandfather had written against the infallibility of the Bible, and unlike Charles Darwin, the Captain was also unsure that he believed all of it. Yet, he was quite sure about creation. Did he know that his cabin mate's distinguished ancestor was not? If so, he might have chosen some other guest, one less likely to upset his own view of Genesis, one less likely to return home to create—or at least, to re-create—the monster of natural selection. In retrospect, Mary Shelley's creation might have seemed nothing more than an amusing little schoolgirl prank. If only he had known. But of course, he hadn't.

Charles almost missed the boat to Galápagos by a nose—his own. It seems the captain of the *Beagle* fancied himself something of a phrenologist—quite convinced, as Darwin recalled later, ". . . that he could judge a man's character by the outline of his features. He doubted whether any one with my nose could possess sufficient energy and determination for the voyage." To which Darwin added, "But I think he was afterwards well satisfied that my nose had spoken falsely." In time, perhaps Darwin's nose adapted itself to its shipboard environment, along with the rest of him. Years later, his grand-daughter Nora Barlow recalled what he said of the reunion with his father: "On first seeing me after the voyage, he turned round to my sisters, and exclaimed, 'Why, the shape of his head is quite altered.' "

One wonders what the Captain of the *Beagle* would have thought of an observation proffered many years later by a German psychological society. Darwin had sent them a photograph of himself, and one of the members "declared that I had the bump of reverence developed enough for ten priests." And but for a bump of fate in the form of that letter from Henslow, Charles might have been one of them, instead of shipmate—and later, theological thorn in the side—of Captain Robert FitzRoy.

In fact, FitzRoy and Darwin hit it off immediately. The Captain was assured that his guest would not mind the privations of a sailing trip, and the naturalist's only demand was that he be permitted to share the costs of the Captain's table.

And so the voyage of the *Beagle* began, with a young naturalist on board who fully expected to return by and by to a life of the cloth. In the meantime, he would quote the Bible to the ship's company as the unanswerable authority on morality. Evolution was not yet an issue.

> When I was on board the *Beagle* I believed in the
> permanence of species, but as far as I can remember,
> vague doubts occasionally flitted across my mind.

Vague doubts notwithstanding, he still rather liked the idea of becoming a country clergyman on his return to England. All in due course to be sure, but some months into the trip he wrote his sister Susan that "I find I steadily have a distant prospect of a very quiet parsonage, & I can see it even through a grove of Palms." This pleased Susan, who assured Charles that a "nice little wife" could surely be arranged, once the voyage was done. But first, there were oceans to cross, mountains to climb, priorities to sort out.

Hardly a month after his letter to Susan, Darwin's writing took a non-pastoral turn—he wrote to his cousin William Darwin Fox that "Geology carries the day: it is like the pleasure of gambling." And by the time the ship found its way to the western coast of South America, Charles was more than ready to bore his correspondents with matters geological rather than biblical. In another letter to sister Susan, "I do not suppose any of you can be much interested in geological details, but ... ." There followed a lengthy dissertation on geological details. Then a few months later, to cousin Fox again: "I look forward to the Galápagos with more interest than any other part of the voyage. They abound with volcanoes & I should hope contain Tertiary strata." And to his sister Caroline, "I am very anxious for the Galápagos Islands,—I think both the Geology & Zoology cannot fail to be very interesting."

The evolution of Charles Darwin had begun.

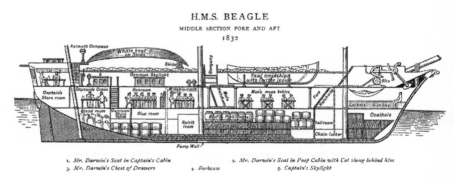

H. M. S. *Beagle* Deck Plan in the

As the *Beagle* worked its way along both sides of the South American continent, Charles spent his time collecting what he could, while the Captain attended to his charts. And then at last on September 7th, 1835, they were ready—for Charles perhaps, *more* than ready—to quit the new world and begin the long voyage home, with a brief stop in Galápagos. After having been away from England now for almost five years, surely Charles would have something to say about the occasion. But no—his Diary celebrates the event with a one-liner: "7ᵗʰ. The Beagle sailed for the Galápagos:" It would take a week to get there, during which the Diary sat unopened. Perhaps its owner was under the weather, as usually happened when the *Beagle* was in open water.

On arrival, Charles finishes the sentence: "on the 15ᵗʰ she was employed in surveying the outer coast of Chatham Island, the S. Eastern one of the Archipelago." The next day Charles goes ashore for an hour, but doesn't much care for the flora:

> The stunted trees show little signs of life. The black rocks heated by the rays of the vertical sun, like a stove, give to the air a close & sultry feeling. The plants also smell unpleasantly. The country was compared to what we might imagine the cultivated parts of the Infernal regions to be.

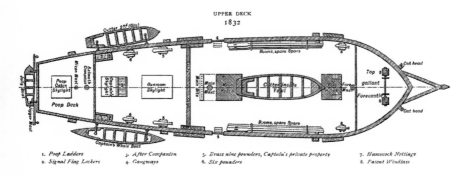

1890 edition of Darwin's *Journal of Researches*.

FitzRoy quite agreed:

> We landed upon black, dismal-looking heaps of broken lava, forming a shore fit for Pandemonium.

And, he might have added, "comfortable sneakers."

The fauna don't get high marks either.

> The black Lava rocks on the beach are frequented
> by large (2-3 ft.) most disgusting, clumsy Lizards.
> They are as black as the porous rocks over
> which they crawl & seek their prey from the Sea.
> Somebody calls them 'imps of darkness.' They
> assuredly well become the land they inhabit.

And then he returns to the flora, collecting "…10 different flowers; but such insignificant, ugly little flowers, as would better become an Arctic than a Tropical country." He spends a few pleasant moments molesting birds: "Mr. King killed one with his hat & I pushed off a branch with the end of my gun a large Hawk."

An overnight visit was arranged a few days later, and on September 21st Charles Darwin slept on Chatham Island in company with his servant Syms Covington. According to an entry in his Diary the next day, "The day was glowing hot, & was the first when our closeness to the Equator was very sensible." Charles met a large pair of Galápagos tortoises on that glowing hot day, but didn't give the beasts much thought. And then they were off to visit Charles Island, named after a King, not a naturalist.

> Here there is a settlement of only five to 6
> years' standing. An Englishman, Mr Lawson, is
> now acting as Governor. By chance, he came
> down to visit a whaling vessel & in the morning
> accompanied us to the Settlement.

The scenery improved:

> Passing round the side of the highest hill, the
> body is cooled by the fine Southerly trade wind
> & the eye refreshed by a plain green as England
> in the Spring time. Out of the wood extensive

patches have been cleared, in which sweet
Potatoes (convolvulus Batata) & Plantains grow
with luxuriance. The houses are scattered over the
cultivated ground & form what in Chili would be
called a "Pueblo". Since leaving Brazil we have not
seen so Tropical a Landscape, but there is a great
deficiency in the absence of the lofty, various & all-
beautiful trees of that country. It will not easily be
imagined how pleasant the change was from Peru &
Northern Chili, in walking in the pathways to find
black mud and on the trees to see mosses, ferns &
Lichens & parasitical plants adhering.

Lawson said that he could tell where each Galápagos
tortoise came from, just by looking at its shell. How mildly
uninteresting thought Charles—in fact, so uninteresting that
he didn't even record the remark in his Diary. Darwin's own
testudinal observations took quite a different direction:

The breast-plate roasted (as the Gauchos do carne
con cuero), with the flesh on it, is very good;
and the young tortoises make excellent soup; but
otherwise the meat to my taste is indifferent.

Later on Darwin realized that perhaps he had not paid
sufficient attention to what he'd been told in Galápagos.
He jotted down a note that "… the Spaniards can at once
pronounce from which Isd. any tortoise may have been
brought." There is no explanation why Spaniards are
credited for information he'd in fact received from an
Englishman. But in any case it was too late for a closer look
at the evidence. H. M. S. *Beagle* was near South Africa when
Charles entered this remark in his Ornithological Notebook.
The tortoises of Galápagos were now nothing more than a
memory. But why had he not been more attentive? A few
years after the voyage he explains:

> It never occurred to me, that the productions of
> islands only a few miles apart, and placed under
> the same physical conditions, would be dissimilar.
> I therefore did not attempt to make a series of
> specimens from the separate islands. It is the fate
> of every voyager, when he has just discovered what
> object in any place is more particularly worthy of
> his attention, to be hurried from it."

But that's not quite the way it was: Charles would spend an unhurried month in Galápagos after meeting Lawson, including 10 days ashore on James Island where he might have paid more attention to his growing collection, had he paid more attention to Mr. Lawson's observations on species variation in tortoises. However, he remained more concerned with their variation on the dinner plate, and more interested in geology than in natural history.

His third island visit was to Albemarle Island, where

> The Volcanic origin of all is but too plainly evident.
> Passed a point studded over with truncated cones
> or Spiracles as some Author calls them; the Craters
> were very perfect & generally red-coloured within.
> The whole had even a more work-shop appearance
> than that described at Chatham Island.

Here is another example of Charles' selective memory at work: he remembers what someone else had said, but "forgets" who said it. His source was probably Alexander von Humboldt, who described the Peak of Tenerife in his *Personal Narrative of Travels to the Equinoctial Regions of America*. "The acqueous vapours, discharged through great spiracles, do not contain alkaline solutions, like the waters of the Geyser, in Iceland."

The *Beagle* continued its way northward along the coast of the island, then anchored in Banks Cove, better known today as Tagus Cove. Of course, Charles went exploring:

> South of the Cove I found a most beautiful Crater,
> elliptic in form, less than a mile in its longer axis &
> about 500 feet deep. Its bottom was occupied by a lake,
> out of which a tiny Crater formed an Island. The day
> was overpoweringly hot; & the lake looked blue & clear.
> I hurried down the cindery side, choked with dust, to
> my disgust on tasting the water found it Salt as brine.

It's puzzling why Charles mentioned but a single island in his *Journal*, for there are several there. And in fact, he later on described the same "...lake of brine, out of which some little crateriform hills of tuff rise." Today, the half-dozen little islets rising from the briny water are in the place known as "Beagle Crater."

A century later, the explorer William Beebe arrived at Tagus Cove and found another lake. In Beebe's *Galápagos: World's End*, his colleague Ruth Rose describes

> ... a perfect little crater lake cupped in the hills. It
> was one of the most beautiful things we saw in the
> Galápagos, not only for the perfection of its setting, but
> also for the wild hope it roused in our parched souls.

Perhaps Miss Rose had not read her Darwin, or she might have known what to expect based on her predecessor's experience at the nearby crater. Her group rushed down the slope "... and in company with a small avalanche started by our tumultuous descent, we literally fell into the lake. It was as salt as the sea." The site is called "Lake Darwin" today. Although visitors who scramble ashore at Tagus Cove can hike up the hill for an overview of Darwin's lake, the crater to the south is not on the tourist circuit.

But to return to the adventures of Charles Darwin, it was here that he met another famous Galápagos resident; the land iguana: "We here have another large Reptile in great numbers; it is a great Lizard, from 10-15 lb. in weight & 2-4 feet in length." The great lizards may not have appreciated the attention of their visitor: "I opened the stomachs of several, and found them full of vegetable fibres, and leaves of different trees, especially of a species of acacia." And on a culinary note, "They are hideous animals; but are considered good food: this day forty were collected."

For the benefit of the 19th-century gourmet, Charles would expand on this observation when he prepared his journal for the press:

> The meat of these animals when cooked is
> white, and by those whose stomachs rise above
> all prejudices, it is relished as very good food.

Soon it was time to move on, and the next five days were "… most unpleasantly passed in struggling to get about 50 miles to Windward against a strong current." Charles may have unpleasantly passed much of this time in his hammock or at the rail being ill, for the Diary remains closed until

> At last we reached Jame's [sic] Island, the
> rendezvous of Mr Sulivan. Myself, Mr. Bynoe
> & three men were landed with provisions,
> there to wait till the ship returned from
> watering at Chatham Island.

Charles hiked up into the highlands to watch tortoises with necks outstretched come and go to a spring for refreshment; "The effect is very comical." He watched them "bury their heads above the eyes in the muddy water & greedily suck in great mouthfuls, quite regardless of lookers on." He watched, but he didn't see characteristics which would distinguish one sub-species from another. He seemed more interested in the land than in its inhabitants, and while examining another crater made a grim discovery:

> We crossed a bare & apparently recent stream
> of Lava which had flowed round an ancient
> but very perfect Crater. At the bottom of this
> Crater is a Lake, which is only 3 or 4 inches
> deep & lies on layers of pure & beautifully
> Crystallized Salt. The Lake is quite circular &
> fringed with bright green succulent plants; the
> sides of [the] Crater are steep & wooded, so
> that the whole has rather a pretty appearance.
> A few years since in this quiet spot the crew
> of a Sealing vessel murdered their Captain. We
> saw the skull lying in the bushes.

Darwin does not reveal how he came to know the identity of the unfortunate person whose skull was all that remained. Perhaps he heard about the incident from a visiting whaler. Charles apparently met several whalers, one in particular coming to his assistance after a rising surf spoiled the fresh water source on the island.

> We should have been distressed if an American
> Whaler had not very kindly given us three
> casks of water (& made us a present of a
> bucket of Onions). Several times during the
> Voyage Americans have showed themselves
> at least as obliging, if not more so, than any
> of our Countrymen would have been. Their
> liberality moreover has always been offered
> in the most hearty manner. If their prejudices
> against the English are as strong as ours against
> the Americans, they forget & smother them in
> an admirable manner.

At last, on the afternoon of October 17th the *Beagle* returned from her own watering expedition, Charles and the others were retrieved from the island, and they were ready, almost, to leave the archipelago. The next two days were spent surveying the outlying islands of Wenman and

Culpepper—one re-named later as Wolf and the other as Darwin. Theodor Wolf was a German geologist who did much work in Galápagos, and you don't need to be told about the other. And now with the last of the chart work out of the way, it was time to put Galápagos astern. Charles hardly noticed:

> After having surveyed these the Ship's head was put towards Otaheiti (Tahiti) & we commenced our long passage of 3,200 miles.

He closes the Diary and doesn't open it again for the rest of the month. Then a brief entry and nothing more for another week. On November 9th, the first of Polynesia is seen and Galápagos is forgotten. Another eleven months and he would at last be home again, ready to think about the places he'd been and the things that he'd seen.

A year or so later, Charles began to realize what he'd been witness to while on H. M. S. *Beagle.* In 1837, he wrote:

> In July opened first note-Book on 'Transmutation of Species'—Had been greatly struck from about month of previous March on character of S. American fossils—species on Galapagos Archipelago.—These facts origin (especially latter) of all my views.

Or to put it another way, the significance of what he saw on the voyage did not fully register until some time after it was over. And by then the opportunity for a second look was lost.

In Galápagos for example, Charles had busied himself between meals collecting samples of the local flora and fauna. But he hadn't taken care to label his specimens by island, and by the time he discovered his error after the voyage it was too late. Or it would have been, had not FitzRoy and others also done a bit of collecting. As non-scientists they didn't know that it was not important to record the location of each specimen. And so, they did. When Darwin realized later that his own collection lacked some vital information, he was able to consult the other collectors to supply what he lacked. Once again, FitzRoy unwittingly helped to advance the very theory that his Bible would have him renounce.

As the Captain moved ever-closer to holy scripture as the ultimate answer to everything, the naturalist sailed off in the opposite direction. Years later Darwin would confess that "It seems ludicrous that I once intended to be a clergyman. This intention ... died a natural death when I joined the *Beagle* as naturalist." But fortunately a new intention had been born early in the voyage, when the *Beagle* stopped at St. Jago in the Cape Verde Islands. He recalled the visit in his autobiography: "It then first dawned on me that I might perhaps write a book on the geology of the various countries visited, and this made me thrill with delight."

The thrill of authorship would obviously agree with Darwin, for he wrote his geology book and quite a few others. In fact he was rarely at a loss for words for the rest of his life. And when there was a momentary lapse, he was not above lifting a convenient turn of phrase from someone else's page, such as his "Somebody calls them 'imps of darkness'" comment on encountering the marine iguana. The unnamed Somebody was a colleague of the seventh Lord Byron, cousin of the late poet and Captain of His Majesty's ship *Blonde,* which visited Galápagos some years earlier. Byron's group awarded the resident marine iguanas the dubious honor of being "the ugliest living creatures we ever beheld." To put the phrase in context, someone in the Byron party noted that the beasts possessed a "hideous head and were of a dirty sooty black colour, and sat on the black lava rocks like so many imps of darkness."

Apparently Darwin read the Byron account closely, for his own diary continues: "The black Lava rocks on the beach are frequented by large, most disgusting, clumsy Lizards. They are as black as the porous rocks over which they crawl." He particularly enjoyed the impish allusion: less than two weeks later, the diary describes the Galápagos land iguana as "a great Lizard, closely allied to those 'imps of darkness' which frequent the seashore." And again in early October, "the 'imps of darkness' live entirely on sea weed." For whatever reason, Darwin did not pick up on another of the Byron party's Galápagos observations: "The place is like a new creation." Nor did the Byronic imps make it into Darwin's published work.

He did mention Byron by name though, but it was another Byron—His Lordship's grandfather "Foul-Weather Jack." Witness to murder in Tierra del Fuego, this Byron wrote that when a small boy dropped a basket of sea eggs, "... the father jumped out of the canoe, and catching the boy up in his arms, dashed him with the utmost violence against the stones." Some 40 years later, in *Descent of Man,* Darwin recalled "the man described by the old navigator Byron [an 18-year-old midshipman at the time], who dashed his child on the rocks for dropping a basket of sea-urchins."

Charles would of course give culinary credit when it was due. Some twenty years before he reached Galápagos, Captain David Porter did a comparative analysis of tortoise as a main course. The ship's company respectfully referred to the beasts as Galápagos mutton, and the Captain himself admired the Charles and Hood Island varieties:

> They are far superior to those of James' Island in
> point of fatness, and their livers are considered
> the greatest delicacy. Those of James' Island are
> round, plump, and black as ebony, but their
> liver is black, hard when cooked, and the flesh
> altogether not so highly esteemed as the others.

Charles would later miscredit the Captain as saying that "the tortoises from James Island are rounder, blacker, and have a better taste when cooked." It's tempting to ask why he took the trouble to acquaint his readers with Captain Porter's palette, and then, to offer a roundabout speculation on the answer.

The speculation begins in 1839—a few years after the celebrated voyage—when FitzRoy edited the three-volume *Narrative of the Surveying Voyages of his Majesty's ships Adventure and Beagle.* The first two volumes were by Philip Parker King of the *Adventure* and Robert FitzRoy of the *Beagle.* At his Captain's suggestion, Charles contributed the third. Drawn largely from his shipboard diary, it was simply titled *Journal and Remarks* and attracted immediate favorable notice, something that cannot be said for volumes I and II. Darwin's volume was also published as a separate edition with the longer title *Journal of Researches into the Geology and Natural History of the various countries visited by H. M. S. Beagle.* We know it today as *Voyage of the Beagle.*

The earliest editions of the *Journal* contained little to rock the evolutionary boat, although FitzRoy the editor was scandalized by Darwin's geological observations. By now the Captain had discarded all prior reservations and took the Bible—all of it—as his only truth. Darwin's geology was at odds with a seven-day creation, and there was nothing FitzRoy could do about that. Or, almost nothing: He appended "A Very Few Remarks with Reference to the Deluge" to his own volume, in which he explains away some old geological views not well-suited to a new creationist, and even confesses a former "disposition to doubt, if not disbelieve, the inspired History written by Moses." To give an example of his former error, FitzRoy remembers "one of my remarks to a friend" (guess who?). On treading high ground that gave convincing evidence of long submersion, the Captain announced that "this could never have been effected by a forty days' flood." But now that he had seen the biblical light, he hoped his "Few Remarks" would at once warn young men "against assenting hastily to new theories—while they induce a closer examination into the Record of truth." But alas, brevity was not the Captain's strong suit: his few remarks occupy 25 printed pages.

And there was nothing Darwin could do about that, except offer the observation that "Although I owe very much to FitzRoy, I for many reasons am anxious to avoid seeing much of him." On this point, perhaps the feeling was mutual.

But to return to Darwin alone, he much enjoyed the *Journal's* success, and welcomed publisher John Murray's suggestion that he prepare a revised edition a few years later. The first revision was on the outside: Darwin re-arranged the title's *Geology and Natural History* phrase to become *Natural History and Geology* instead, which tells us a bit about how the author's own priorities were evolving over time. Next, he unobtrusively introduced the observations of others into the new edition; observations that might show he was not alone in his thoughts. But still he kept certain of those thoughts to himself. His great-grandson, Richard Darwin Keynes, recalls what Charles wrote in his *Diary* in August of 1834. While near Valparaiso, Chile, he noted "there are very few quadrupeds, & birds are not very plentiful." And then he explained:

> It seems not a very improbable conjecture that the want of animals may be owing to none having been created since this country was raised from the sea.

Five years later, an observation that "few birds, or even insects, frequent these dry parched mountains" found its way into Darwin's published *Journal*. The explanation did not. He was not quite ready to reveal such ideas to the public. Instead, he incorporated more of Gould's work on those Galápagos finches and then found room to describe Captain Porter's preferences in tortoise steak.

Now at first reading, Porter's observations might not seem to do much to advance Darwin's own ideas, but it did introduce the American Naval Captain to his readers. And it was Porter who wrote what amounts to a splendid, if unintentional, introduction to Darwinian theory:

> I shall leave others to account for the manner in which all those islands obtained their supply of tortoises and guanas, and other animals of the reptile kind; it is not my business even to conjecture as to the cause. I shall merely state, that those islands have every appearance of being newly created, and that those perhaps are the only part of the animal creation that could subsist on them.

Porter was not the first to wonder how remote islands became populated by curious creatures. Almost two centuries earlier, Sir Thomas Browne's *Pseudodoxia epidemica: or, Enquiries into Very Many Received Tenents, and Commonly Preserved Truths* was published, in which the author raised many questions, which were not always answered. Among them, he observed that "... it will be no easie question to resolve, how several sorts of animals were first dispersed into Islands, and almost how any into *America*."

Sir Thomas took a closer look at America in *Religio Medici*:

> How *America* abounded with Beasts of prey, and noxious Animals, yet contained not in it that necessary Creature, a Horse, is very strange. By what passage those, not only Birds, but dangerous and unwelcome Beasts, came over: How there be Creatures there (which are not found in this Triple Continent): all which must needs be strange unto us, that hold but one Ark, and that the Creatures began their progress from the Mountains of *Ararat*.

What else might Sir Thomas have written if he'd known about Galápagos?

Darwin included nothing from Sir Thomas, nor did Porter's observations on introduced species find their way into his *Journal*. However, a few pages earlier in his description of the Galápagos tortoise, he did introduce another second-hand observation:

> Wood and Rogers, in 1708, say that it is the
> opinion of the Spaniards, that it is found
> nowhere else in this quarter of the world.

To possibly-hostile critics, Darwin might plead that he was merely following a line of thought already laid down by Wood, Rogers, assorted Spaniards, Porter, and of course, the party of the seventh Lord Byron. As to the identity of Wood and Rogers, the two were actually one: Woodes Rogers visited Galápagos and wrote his highly successful *Cruising Voyage Round the World* upon his return to England. Oddly enough, the mis-attribution has not been corrected to this day. (Remember, you read it here first.)

To come closer to his point, and move the discussion to a properly scientific level, Darwin did some more borrowing, but this time without credit. In a letter dated February 20, 1836, John Herschel wrote to Charles Lyell of "that mystery of mysteries the replacement of extinct species by others." Darwin worked this into his 1845 *Journal* revision, where he tells us that

> We seem to be brought somewhat
> near to that great fact—that mystery
> of mysteries—the first appearance of
> new beings on this earth.

He doesn't identify the writer, but he must have liked the writing—fourteen years later it shows up again, this time on the first page of his Introduction to *On the Origin of Species*. Of his observations in South America, Darwin writes that he was much struck with certain facts which "seemed to throw some light on the origin of species—that mystery of mysteries, as it has been called by one of our greatest philosophers." He still does not identify the great philosopher by name.

On the origin of Darwin's *Origin*, we know the species of Galápagos were a powerful influence on his views, and on his book of course, and both of these were a powerful influence—not for the better—on his former friend and companion Robert FitzRoy. Although the poor soul was now an Admiral, his Bible had gotten the best of him, to the point where he regarded evolution and its author as blasphemy and blasphemer, respectively. And which was the worse he was not quite sure. Under the circumstances it's no wonder that Darwin had mentioned that he was now anxious to avoid seeing much of his Captain.

The story is told of a meeting—the "Oxford Debate"—at which FitzRoy was present. Thomas Henry Huxley, later to be dubbed "Darwin's Bulldog," would find himself unexpectedly obliged to defend the views of his naturalist friend against a rather eloquent but rather empty-headed clergyman. At the debate, the Most Reverend Bishop of Oxford Samuel Wilberforce, known as "Soapy Sam" for his skill at emerging clean from dirty debates, played the part of a parrot, coached by Sir Richard Owen, a former Darwin friend now turned arch enemy, into publicly ridiculing the Darwinian view from the stage. At the end of his dissertation, the Bishop smiled at the Bulldog and posed a question: Was Mr. Huxley related to an ape on the side of his grandfather, or was it perhaps his grandmother? "The Lord," whispered Huxley to another, "hath delivered him into mine hands."

Caricatures of Darwin (left), Wilberforce (above) and Huxley (overleaf) by Carlo Pellegrini for *Vanity Fair* Magazine.

The Bulldog did not immediately snap at the proffered bone, but instead presented a reasoned argument on behalf of his friend's views. And then when all was done he turned his attention to the Bishop's insulting inquiry:

It would not have occurred to me to bring forward such a topic as that for discussion myself. But, if the question is put to me, would I rather have a miserable ape for a grandfather, or a *man* highly endowed by nature and possessed of great means and influence, and yet who employs these faculties and that influence for the mere purpose of introducing ridicule into a grave scientific discussion, I unhesitatingly affirm my preference. It is for the ape."

The day was Huxley's. It was said that a lady fainted while others applauded, and he won some sympathy from many in the audience, not including Robert FitzRoy. The Captain is reported to have wandered the aisles, waving the Bible overhead and shouting "The Book!, The Book!" Another account simply states that he implored the audience to believe God's holy word rather than that of a mere human on the question of creation." He was ignored. The theological tide was turning, and FitzRoy could either sink or swim. He chose the former: five years later he slit his throat.

So ended the life of the man who brought Darwin into the world of Galápagos, and Galápagos into the world of science. The aftershocks were not entirely what drove FitzRoy's hand, but no doubt they played some mischief in his tormented mind. "Charles was very sorry about FitzRoy—but not much surprised" said Emma, his wife. And according to Darwin biographer Janet Browne, "He did not feel nearly as sad as he ought to have done." Alas, Charles did not always feel, or act, as he ought to have done. He ought to have given more credit to those who helped him. He didn't.

The description of the debate at Oxford might seem a work of fiction. There is something almost too clever in the scene: at stage center, Wilberforce in the spotlight delivers a shocking (for the times) insult upon Huxley's mother. In a heartbeat—if not a stage whisper—Huxley invokes the Lord, then turns the tables on the Bishop. The crowd cheers, a lady faints, and FitzRoy stalks the audience with bible at the ready.

Did the players really deliver the lines attributed to them? Or has the script been "improved" over the years since the event? Perhaps it has. Contemporary press reports of the meeting make no mention of the verbal duel, which would surely have been worth a few words, directly under a suitably-phrased headline. Some witnesses thought Huxley said he would not object to a simian forebear, but would regret being descended from a gifted man (say, a Bishop) who used his talents to ridicule that which he did not understand. The gist is the same, but without the preference for ape as punch line. It has also been reported that whatever Huxley said, he couldn't be heard above the noise of the spectators.

But whatever the actual words, the meeting marked a turning point in Huxley's life. He had been a reluctant public speaker, but no longer. He now saw the value of addressing the masses, and from this day forward went at it with enthusiasm. But of course nothing from Huxley could move the Bishop from the creationist view of life, which for Wilberforce ended abruptly one day when he fell from his horse and struck his head on a rock.

Darwin's Bulldog didn't tread lightly in rendering his opinions about friends, about enemies, or even about himself. On the Bishop's demise, "For once, reality and his brains came into contact and the result was fatal." Earlier, after finishing Darwin's chapter on natural selection in *The Origin of Species*, he had this opinion of himself:

"How extremely stupid not to have thought of that!"

There is another source that Charles Darwin apparently did not mention, and perhaps for good reason. But since that source indirectly links the family of Captain David Porter with matters Darwinian, it is recounted here.

James Burnett, Lord Monboddo, is described in the *Dictionary of National Biography* as a man "...distinguished rather for profound than useful learning." His Lordship, who died in 1799, held "...that men were originally monkeys, and that a nation still existed with tails."

This was too much for Samuel Johnson, of dictionary fame, who had the following to say on the matter:

It is a pity to see Lord Monboddo publish such notions as he has done; a man of sense, and of so much elegant learning. There would be little in a fool doing it; we should only laugh: but when a wise man does it, we are sorry.

When James Boswell wrote his *Life of Samuel Johnson*, he recorded more of Johnson's opinions:

Other people have strange notions; but they conceal them. If they have tails, they hide them; but Monboddo is as jealous of his tail as a squirrel. ... When Sir Joseph Banks returned from Botany Bay, Monboddo inquired after the long-tailed men, and, according to Johnson, was not pleased that they had not been found in all his peregrinations.

And now to Captain David Porter. After the Civil War was done, Porter's son David Dixon Porter wrote a *Memoir of Commodore David Porter*, a biography of his father. In recounting the family history, the author mentioned his grandfather, and this re-telling of the tale is not helped a bit by the fact that the old man was also named David. But of grandfather, the author (who was our Navy's second Admiral) writes:

He was the author of some amusing works. ... His great work was on *The Origin of Man*, in which he showed conclusively that human beings were gradually developed from jelly fish into mermen and thence to their present form. This was a satire on the predecessors of Darwin, who were then promulgating their strange theories, but was particularly aimed at the famous Lord Monboddo, who had advanced the extraordinary idea that the human race are nothing but a lot of monkeys who had worn off their tails by sitting for so many ages on hard-bottomed chairs.

Above: Admiral and author David Dixon Porter.

The Admiral's grandfather was indeed an author, but this "great work" was written by someone else. It was in fact Benoît de Maillet's *Telliamed, or the World Explained,* with a complete title that occupies almost the entire page and contains the following except: "... containing Discourses ... on the Origin of Men & Animals. ..." The Porter connection comes at the bottom of the page:

Baltimore:
Printed by W. Pechin, No. 15, Market-Street
for D. Porter, at the Observatory,
Federal-Hill, 1797

So, old man Porter was selling books in Baltimore, and his grandson chose his words carefully to make it appear that grandfather was the author of a "great work" when in fact he was not. Although the Admiral did not exactly lie, he didn't exactly tell the truth either. But as one contemporary

observer wrote, David Dixon Porter reminded him of "…
one of those strange characters … who are never so happy
as when they are making mischief." The mischief here was
to send those who followed off on an author search for a
book he didn't write.

As for James Burnett's monkey men, anthropologist Richard
Milner wrote that "Lord Monboddo's writings paved
the way not only for the theories of Darwin, but also for
the *Tarzan* books of Edgar Rice Burroughs." Now, if only
Darwin had mentioned his profound predecessor, or His
Lordship had mentioned Galápagos, that would be reason
enough to include this tale here.

> Below: Darwin contemplates Huxley's ancestor
> (and vice versa).

The ominous prediction of an exasperated Dr. Darwin that
opened this chapter was made when Charles was about 20
years old, and recalled a half-century later:

> When I left the school I was for my age
> neither high nor low in it; and I believe that I
> was considered by all my masters and by my
> father as a very ordinary boy, rather below
> the common standard in intellect. To my deep
> mortification my father once
> said to me, "You care for
> nothing but shooting,
> dogs, and rat-catching,
> and you will be a disgrace
> to yourself and all your
> family." But my father, who was the
> kindest man I ever knew and whose
> memory I love with all my heart, must
> have been angry and somewhat unjust when he
> used such words.

Now, whatever gave him *that* idea?

CHAPTER NINE

THE GEOGRAPHY OF HERMAN MELVILLE

*Volcanic Narborough lies in the black
jaws of Albemarle like a wolf's red
tongue in his open mouth.*

—Herman Melville: *The Encantadas*

EVERYBODY KNOWS HERMAN MELVILLE wrote that whale of a tale, *Moby Dick*, yet few know of another work which is no less a masterpiece, though much less on word count. The shorter story takes its inspiration from Melville's visit to the Galápagos whaling ground aboard the *Acushnet*. Were it not for his presence on the ship's roster, both the vessel and its crew would have long since become just one more unwritten page in the history book of forgotten voyages. But thanks to Herman, the *Acushnet* lives on as that most famous whaler of them all, the *Pequod*. And some fifteen years after that little tale was told, the Galápagos Islands became the setting for a short story written in ten sketches which Melville called *The Encantadas, or, Enchanted Isles*. Its author does not get high marks as tour leader, for he has rearranged both the islands and their history, perhaps to suit his story line, perhaps because he didn't spend enough time there to get his facts straight. But no matter; he is neither first nor last to take artistic liberties with enchanted ground. We must leave such matters as dull geography to more-learned authorities and just depend on Melville to convey to us the mood of the place.

159

In setting that mood, many sketches begin with a few lines borrowed from Edmund Spenser, a sixteenth century poet who might have died wealthier if his *The Fairie Queene* had been retailed to the public by the pound. Melville is in fact one of those rare people who gives evidence of having actually read the damned thing in its entirety. Either that, or he had the extraordinary good fortune to stumble across just those passages that might have been written about Galápagos. For example, Sketch First begins with this from Spenser:

> That may not be, said the ferryman,
> Least we unweeting hap to be fordonne,
> For those same islands seeming now and than,
> Are not firme land, nor any certein wonne,
> But stragling plots which to and fro do ronne
> In the wide waters; therefore are they hight
> The Wandering Islands; therefore do them shonne;
> For they have oft drawne many a wandring wight
> Into most deadly daunger and distressed plight;
> For whosoever once hath fastened
> His foote thereon may never it secure
> But wandreth evermore uncertain and unsure.

It's rather doubtful that Spenser knew the Galápagos legend—of the enchanted place where landfalls "were but shadows and no Reall Ilands." That, according to the Spaniards, if we are to believe our old diarist and buccaneer friend Ambrosia Cowley. But when he wrote "shadows and no Reall Ilands" was he more under the influence of Spenser than of Spaniard? Perhaps. Melville reminds us that when the buccaneer named a little island after himself, he wrote that "My fancy led me to call it Cowley's Enchanted Island." Melville ignored the fanciful allusion to a great city served up by Cowley, or perhaps by the editor as his journal was prepared for the press, and seeks another explanation. Says Melville, "... as all the group is deemed enchanted, the reason must be given for the spell within a spell involved by this particular designation." And then he offers us the reason; that is, *his* reason for this particular designation:

> That Cowley linked his name with this self-
> transforming and bemocking isle, suggests
> the possibility that it conveyed to him some
> meditative image of himself. At least, as is not
> impossible, if he were any relative of the mildly
> thoughtful, and self-upbraiding poet Cowley
> who lived about this time, the conceit might
> seem not unwarranted; for that sort of thing
> runs in the blood, and may be seen in pirates
> as in poets.

If Ambrosia counted such a poetical personage as Abraham Cowley in his immediate family circle, then perhaps he had read *The Fairie Queene* (voluntarily?) in the days of his youth and before setting out on the long voyage into the great South Sea where—and again, just perhaps—a Spenserian influence insinuated itself into his journal. But Spenser or no, not all of Cowley's literary conceits made their way to the printed page, where shadows were replaced by simple description:

> Thereupon we stood away to the Westward,
> to try if we could find those Islands which
> the Spaniards calls Gallappagos or Enchanted
> Islands, when after 3 weeks we saw Land, ...

The journal's "shadows and no Reall Islands" treatment is certainly the more poetic, and we may wonder why Melville didn't pick up on it, especially since the tone further supports his speculation on a familial link between Abraham and Ambrosia. Probably, because he knew nothing of it. Melville did his work long before the day of the photocopy, and may have never seen anything but the book.

From Sketch First: "At one period, large fleets of whale-
men cruised for spermaceti upon what some seamen call
the Enchanted Ground. This was off the great outer isle of
Albemarle, away from the intricacies of the smaller isles."
Jules Huyot's 19th century engraving of Albemarle Island
shows whalers cruising upon Melville's enchanted ground.

The first two sketches continue the mood set by the
introductory verse, of a place held under a spell, where
desolation and despair are the order of the day, and of every
day. And we are to proceed with some caution through these
pages, for Melville warns us that "I know not whether I am
not the occasional victim of optical delusion concerning the
Galápagos." As we shall soon see, Melville was certainly
no occasional victim of geographical delusion within his
enchanted world. Yet the real world must wait—as it has
already waited for a century and a half—for someone to write
a better description of the place. Melville's own description
continues with two sketches devoted to one landmark—the
high stone tower known to all, both then and now, by the
title of Sketch Third: "Rock Redondo." Redondo rises from

its oceanic bed to a plateau some 250 feet above the surface. It is a cliff on all sides and there are no landing places. Yet for those willing to suspend belief, Melville escorts them to the summit, and, "How we got there, we alone know." But the view is good from atop this aviary of ocean, and our guide points out a few places of interest, both seen and unseen by those with lesser vision.

Nearby, "Volcanic Narborough lies in the black jaws of Albemarle like a wolf's red tongue in his open mouth." Next, he takes a census—perhaps having a bit of fun at the expense of a certain unnamed naturalist—and reports the population of Albemarle in excess of some 11 million generally unpleasant creatures. Then he repeats himself: "Albemarle opens his mouth towards the setting sun. His distended jaws form a great bay, which Narborough, his tongue, divides into halves." Modern visitors may wonder about black jaws and the red tongue of a wolf. These islands— better known today as Fernandina and Isabela—are of course neighbors, but it would take some imagination to see them through Melville's eyes.

Above: Did David Porter's chart give Melville the idea of a volcanic Narborough lying in the black jaws of Albemarle?

Our attention is now directed to the distant Abington Isle, where "I doubt whether two human beings ever touched upon that spot." Today, human beings are not permitted to touch upon that spot, but in Melville's day the island was frequented by whalers in search of dinner. The nearby Isla Marchena, known to Melville as Bindloe but not mentioned, might have been a better choice for his remark. It was not visited by whalers, and when two human beings eventually did touch it, they didn't live to tell the tale. But that's a story for another chapter.

```
If now you desire the population of Albe-
marle, I will give you, in round numbers, the
statistics, according to the most reliable esti-
mates made upon the spot :

   Men, . . . . . . . none.
   Ant-eaters, . . . . . unknown.
   Man-haters, . . . . . unknown.
   Lizards, . . . . . . 500,000.
   Snakes, . . . . . . 500,000.
   Spiders, . . . . . . 10,000,000.
   Salamanders, . . . . . unknown.
   Devils, . . . . . do.
   Making a clean total of . . . . 11,000,000,

exclusive of an incomputable host of fiends,
ant-eaters, man-haters, and salamanders.
```

Melville's population "statistics" as they appeared in the 1856 edition of *The Encantadas*. Any resemblance to a distinguished predecessor may not be coincidental.

Ere quitting Redondo in Sketch Fifth, Melville introduces us to someone we met here in a previous chapter—none other than Captain David Porter of the Salem frigate *Essex*. But the introduction is brief, for Melville has reserved the last two sketches to tell us more about the Captain. There, and indeed in all the remaining sketches, he recounts tales based, however loosely, on historical facts which, with one exception, can be tied to two islands. But perhaps for the sake of expanding the enchanted horizon, Melville distributes them around the archipelago, setting each tale upon its own island.

Sketch Sixth tells of "Barrington Isle and the Buccaneers." Melville finds the isle "well sheltered from all winds by the high land of Albemarle" and much favored by an earlier visitor:

"I once landed on its western side," says a
sentimental voyager long ago, "where it faces
the black buttress of Albemarle. I walked
beneath groves of trees—not very lofty, and not
palm trees, or orange trees, or peach trees, to
be sure—but for all that, after long sea-faring,
very beautiful to walk under, even though they
supplied no fruit."

The "sentimental voyager" was James Colnett, who actually wrote "At every place where we landed on the Western side, we might have walked for miles, through long grass and beneath groves of trees." This delightful place was "sheltered from all winds by Albemarle Isle." But this is not Barrington Isle. Colnett was referring to James Island, whose western side does indeed face Melville's "black buttress of Albemarle." Barrington is far away, quite removed from the shelter of Albemarle. In fact, none have landed on its western side, which is itself a buttress against all visitors. In speaking of it and of another island, Colnett remarks "We did not land on either of them." Neither did Melville.

Sketch Seventh takes us to Charles Island, now ruled by a certain Creole adventurer from Cuba. Melville forgets his name but dubs him the "Dog King" in recognition of the pack of hounds His Majesty keeps for protection. According to the tale, the Creole had fought valiantly for Peru and received title to the island in recognition of his services. This version of history must have raised a few eyebrows in Guayaquil and Quito, for then as now the islands were the property of Ecuador. And the Creole adventurer from Cuba was in fact a Southern gentleman from New Orleans—José María Villamil, now an Army General in the service of Ecuador.

According to Melville, His Majesty populated his kingdom by issuing a proclamation inviting subjects to "take ship for the promised land." In fact, Villamil did issue an invitation

Charles Island at about the time of Herman Melville's visit.

of sorts. After being appointed territorial Governor (nice, but not quite the same as King) by Ecuador, he proposed to a group of soldiers that they come live on one of his islands. Now this was surely an invitation they couldn't afford to refuse, for these were troops soon to be placed at the wrong end of a firing squad as penance for mutiny. Given this opportunity to stay alive just a bit longer, Charles Island was indeed a promising land.

It's puzzling that Melville played so fast and so loose with the facts behind this fiction. Surely he knew Galápagos was no territory of Peru, and in his day General Villamil was still very much alive. One wonders if he read *The Encantadas*.

In the next sketch we encounter another island which seems real enough at first. The title of Sketch Eighth, "Norfolk Isle and the Chola Widow" would seem to identify the place known today as Isla Santa Cruz. But it doesn't. The sketch begins "Far to the northeast of Charles' Isle, sequestered from the rest, lies Norfolk Isle." The island with this name actually lies due north of Charles, not far away at all, and certainly not sequestered from the rest. The sketch tells of the death of two whose hastily-built raft of logs sailed "just without a long reef with many jagged gaps, running parallel with the shore, about half a mile from it." There are such reefs near the Santa Cruz shore, but no such logs *on the*

From Abel du Petit-Thouars' 1841 voyage of the *Venus*.

shore, or anywhere for that matter. And a few pages later, the Chola widow walks across the island on a morning. People have died trying to cross far shorter distances on Norfolk Isle. It usually takes a week or two for death to find them.

Well then, where does one find Melville's Norfolk? Nowhere perhaps, but in the mind of its creator. And where does one find his inspiration for the Chola widow? Perhaps only on his own Norfolk.

Sketch Ninth begins with another lesson in Melvillian geography:

> Southeast of Crossman's Isle lies Hood's Isle,
> or McCain's Beclouded Isle: and upon its south
> side is a vitreous cove with a wide strand of
> dark pounded black lava, called Black Beach,
> or Oberlus's Landing. It might fitly have been
> styled Charon's.

The vitreous cove is now a popular tourist site on the island southeast of Crossman. But this island was known to Melville and others of his day as Charles, not Hood's. The wide strand of pounded black lava is still known as Black Beach, but it's on the island's northwest coast, not the south side.

And now David Porter returns to help finish up the tale. The Captain's *Journal* apparently found its way into Melville's library, where he read the report of events that had taken place a few years before Porter's own arrival. The Captain of the *Essex* had learned of the strange Patrick Watkins, ex-seaman and later gentleman tiller of the infernal landscape who had until recently scratched his existence out of Charles Island by offering fresh vegetables to passing ships in exchange for demon rum. But Melville had shown us Charles Island in a previous sketch, so he took the liberty of moving Watkins to a different island, and into a sketch named "Hood's Isle and the Hermit Oberlus." Other than that though, Melville pretty much lets Porter tell us the story.

Porter reports that Watkins, who had taken to calling himself "Fatherless Oberlus" (in Galápagos, everyone's a poet), quit the island a few years before he showed up. But the captain was intrigued by his story and jotted down this second-hand description:

> The appearance of this man, from the accounts I
> have received of him, was the most dreadful that
> can be imagined; ragged clothes, scarce sufficient
> to cover his nakedness, and covered with vermin;
> his red hair and beard matted, his skin much
> burnt, from constant exposure to the sun, and so
> wild and savage in his manner and appearance,
> that he struck every one with horror.

Melville the story teller offers his third-hand description of the horrid hero:

> His appearance, from all accounts, was that
> of the victim of some malignant sorceress; he
> seemed to have drunk of Circe's cup; beast-
> like; rags insufficient to hide his nakedness; his
> befreckled skin blistered by continual exposure to

the sun; nose flat; countenance contorted, heavy,
earthy; hair and beard unshorn, profuse, and of
a fiery red. He struck strangers much as if he
were a volcanic creature thrown up by the same
convulsion which exploded into sight the isle.

In comparing these two passages, we might say that while
Porter's description is good, Melville's is better. Porter gives
us prose; Melville, poetry. And never mind that neither of
them had met the man.

Captain Porter was also told of a note found in this wretched
creature's abandoned hut, in which an indignant Watkins/
Oberlus cries of injustices done him by recent visitors, and
then concludes:

On the 29th of May, 1809, I sail from the
enchanted island in the Black Prince, bound to
the Marquesas. Do not kill the old hen; she is
now sitting, and will soon have chickens.

(signed) FATHERLESS OBERLUS.

Not only does Melville edit Porter, he edits Oberlus as
reported by Porter, then adds a postscript followed by a
variation on a theme that has been circulating since Aesop.

Today I sail from the Enchanted group in the
good boat Charity bound to the Feejee Isles.

Fatherless Oberlus.

P. S.—Behind the clinkers, nigh the oven, you
will find the old fowl. Do not kill it; be patient;
I leave it setting; if it shall have any chicks, I
hereby bequeath them to you, whoever you
may be. But don't count your chicks before
they are hatched.

Melville reports that the bird was in fact "a starveling rooster, reduced to a sitting posture by sheer debility." And never mind that neither man had met the bird either. But then — a bit closer to truth, if not quite there yet — he follows Porter in reporting that Oberlus departed the island with a few others and arrived not at the Marquesas or the Feejees, but at Guayaquil, and alone. Both writers speculate that the others were sacrificed as the water supply grew scarce. Neither writer speculates on how one man with a gun could stay awake in a small boat long enough to do away with the entire crew.

The Oberlus sketch also opens with a borrowing from Spenser, this one selected to fit Watkins perfectly.

> That darksome glen then enter, where they find
> That cursed man low sitting on the ground,
> Musing full sadly in his sullein mind;
> His griesly locks long grouen and unbound,
> Disordered hong about his shoulders round,
> And hid his face, through which his hollow eyne
> Lookt deadly dull, and stared as astound;
> His raw-bone cheekes, through penurie and pine,
> Were shronke into the jawes, as he did never dine.
> His garments nought but many ragged clouts,
> With thornes together pind and patched reads,
> The which his naked sides he wrapt abouts.

Melville borrowed Spenser's description of a "… cursed man, low sitting on the ground" to introduce his "Hood's Isle and the Hermit Oberlus" sketch.

Finally, after drawing and embroidering so heavily on Captain Porter without making direct mention of him in the text, Melville reveals his source and brings the sketch to a close with an explanatory note:

> Note.—They who may be disposed to question the possibility of the character above depicted, are referred to the 2d vol. of Porter's Voyage into the Pacific, where they will recognize many sentences, for expedition's sake derived verbatim from thence, and incorporated here; the main difference—save a few passing reflections—between the two accounts being, that the present writer has added to Porter's facts accessory ones picked up in the Pacific from reliable sources; and where facts conflict, has naturally preferred his own authorities to Porter's.

As for Melville's "reliable sources," not a few humor-impaired scholars have spent not a few hours trying to track them down. But of course these "authorities" don't really exist; Melville was simply having a bit of poetic-license fun with the reader, a point not grasped by those who can't—or won't—read between his lines. And even if Melville had relied on some long-vanished authorities, he could have picked more reliable ones than he did. Besides that, Porter was a stickler for details; Melville wasn't. As a reliable though somewhat less than poetical source, Porter always wins.

The Captain also left us his report on a nameless seaman, whose departure from Charles Island was noted in verse on a white board perched atop a desolate tomb. Porter recorded the epitaph "more on account of the extreme simplicity of the verse, and its powerful and flattering appeal to the feelings, than for its elegance, or the correctness of the composition:"

> Gentle reader, as you pass by,
> As you are now, so wonce was I;
> As now my body is in the dust,
> I hope in heaven my soul to rest.

Melville concludes his tale of *The Encantadas* with something which he tells us was " … found in a bleak gorge of Chatham Isle." Not so. He "found" it—some of it, that is—on a bleak page of Porter. But it reads a bit better for having passed through Melville's pen.

> Oh Brother Jack, as you pass by,
> As you are now, so once was I,
> Just so game and just so gay,
> But now, alack, they've stopped my pay.
> No more I peep out of my blinkers,
> Here I be—tucked in with clinkers!

After bringing William Cowley, James Colnett and David Porter into *The Encantadas*, it's intriguing to speculate on why Melville did not turn to the work of William Dampier, whose *New Voyage Round the World* is often cited as one of the finest travel books ever. The book was surely well known to him, as it is to us from a previous chapter.

Perhaps there's a good reason why Dampier does not put in an appearance. In writing *The Encantadas*, Melville has generally improved on the work of his sources, who were sailors first, writers second. In the latter category they were often adequate, sometimes good, but never great. Dampier though was an indifferent buccaneer, a good navigator, and a superb author. Melville may not have wanted to try his hand at improving on another master.

It's not certain that Melville visited some of the real and the unreal islands of his *Encantadas*. But wherever his feet actually did fall, the experience must have been profound. Sketch First contains a description that has yet to be surpassed by any who would dare describe the islands.

It is to be doubted whether any spot of earth can,
in desolateness, furnish a parallel to this group. ...
Cut by the Equator, they know not autumn and they
know not spring; while already reduced to the lees of
fire, ruin itself can work little more upon them. The
showers refresh the deserts, but in these isles, rain
never falls. Like split Syrian gourds, left withering in
the sun, they are cracked by an everlasting drought
beneath a torrid sky. "Have mercy upon me," the
wailing spirit of the Encantadas seems to cry, "and
send Lazarus that he may dip the tip of his finger in
water and cool my tongue, for I am tormented in this
flame."

... the Encantadas refuse to harbour even the outcasts
of the beasts. Man and wolf alike disown them.
Little but reptile life is here found:—tortoises, lizards,
immense spiders, snakes, and the strangest anomaly of
outlandish Nature, the aguano. No voice, no low, no
howl is heard; the chief sound of life here is a hiss.

Again Melville is out on his own, bending his facts to suit his
fancy: that sound of a hiss is more often than not drowned
out by an assortment of whistles, shrieks, barks and
bleats, honks, chirps, grunts and groans as the Galápagos
menagerie goes about the business of the day, which mostly
has to do with mating and meals.

Perhaps Herman passed by after lunch.

Overleaf: "... concerning the peculiar reptile inhabitant of
these wilds—whose presence gives the group its second
Spanish name, Gallipagos—concerning the tortoises found
here, most mariners have long cherished a superstition, not
more frightful than grotesque. They earnestly believe that
all wicked sea-officers, more especially commodores and
captains, are at death (and, in some cases, before death)
transformed into tortoises; thenceforth dwelling upon
these hot aridities, sole solitary lords of Asphaltum."

From Sketch First: "The Isles at Large."

CHAPTER TEN

THE SMALL WORLD OF MANUEL J. COBOS

No sacar a este hombre.
Porque es veinte veces criminal.

Do not take this man away.
He is twenty times a criminal.

A sign posted on Isla Santa Cruz

At his hacienda in the little village of Progreso, 24-year-old Manuel Augusto Cobos chatted with two Norwegian journalists about his ancestry. Don Manuel assured the visitors that his deceased father's manners should be sufficient to prove the Cobos family had its origins in Spain. "The Spanish inquisition I am referring to," young Manuel added dryly. The year was 1922, and Manuel's father had passed on some eighteen years earlier. Although there was no official coroner's report, everyone knew that the death of the elder Cobos was brought on by the complications of lead poisoning and cranial bleeding — the work of a few bullets at close range, followed by well-directed machete blows to help finish the job.

Don Manuel the younger did not seem overly upset about all this, although he did take steps to make sure he didn't follow his father into a bloody grave, such as never sitting down to dinner without a pistol at his side. His precautions were not taken in vain. A few years after the Norwegian visit, some local workers seized his little armory and opened fire as he inspected his sawmill. He decided on the spot to take a few days off in the surrounding highlands, but eventually returned to restore order. Violence, it would seem, was a way of life on this island.

But to return to his father: "I was six years old ... and remember him only vaguely. I was sent to Paris and London to receive an education and learn languages." Meanwhile, his elder sister Josefina married a Rogerio Alvarado, and between them took over what was left after Cobos' death. Don Manuel took on the task of doing whatever he could do to keep the old sugar production plant going when he returned from overseas. Of course he missed student life in Paris. *"C'est ne pas gay ici,"* sighed Cobos, and then added, "but 15,000 kilos of sugar each month are also sweet!"

Don Manuel Augusto Cobos on the left, with Manuel Tomás Aguilera, Jefe Teritorial, in a 1933 photo.

He rose from his chair to bid his guests a pleasant *buenas noches.* Or perhaps a *bonne nuit.* As Cobos retired for the evening, it surely occurred to the journalists that they might inform their countrymen that here in Galápagos "survival of the fittest" was not necessarily a term reserved just for the animal kingdom. They decided against this though, as we shall discover later on.

Of course the murder of the elder Cobos was not the first such incident to occur here. The tranquility of the enchanted islands had been interrupted—and not for the first time either—some years earlier, perhaps because "Johnson from London" (we'll catch up with him later on) didn't arrive in time to prevent the murder of Don José Valdizán on Isla Floreana. Valdizán had started his orchilla lichen operation on that island after a similar attempt by Manuel Julian Cobos and his partner José Monroy had failed on Chatham Island, today better known to all as Isla San Cristóbal. But Cobos was no quitter: if there were no future in lichen, perhaps sugar would be his way to future wealth. Ecuadorian authorities were cooperative, and so Cobos put together a work force by emptying the jails on the mainland. Convicts were sent out to the island to supplement Valdizán's workers brought over from Floreana, and Don Manuel actually employed them in his operation.

But wages were not what they might have been. Cobos issued his own money—worthless on the mainland, but the only thing accepted in the local island store. Cobos owned the local island store. Employees who didn't like the arrangement might have taken the local island ship back to the mainland after completing their sentence, except for one little detail: Cobos owned the local island ship. It was called the *Manuel J. Cobos.*

Above: Manuel J. Cobos paid his workers with his own currency, where the name of the island is misspelled.

Below: An Ecuadorian coin countermarked with Rogerio Alvarado's initials ("R A" shown magnified next to the coin).

Some mainland currency was also introduced after 1883, when the Governor of Guayaquil appointed Cobos' son-in-law Rogerio Alvarado as "Director of Collections." Señor Alvarado had Ecuadorian coins countermarked with his own intertwined initials for restricted circulation, perhaps as a measure to prevent the use of money from outside sources. The countermark was applied to coins from 1884 to 1916, the year in which Alvarado's authorization was revoked.

How Cobos came to be a ship owner is unclear, but there may be a clue in an 1881 letter written by an angry American in Guayaquil to General S. A. Hurlbut, the U. S. Minister in Lima, Peru. With no resident American Minister in Quito, the writer hoped the General in Lima could find some way for him to retrieve his ship *Laura*, which he claimed had been seized by Cobos. He mentioned that Cobos had swiped two other ships from the port of Magdalena in Baja California.

> When these vessels were taken they were brought to the Galapagos Islands and thence to Guayaquil where they obtained the Ecuadorian flag by the influence of Mr. Cobos. One of these vessels is now here. Her name under the American flag was the Sue Greenwood, but now under the Ecuadorian flag she is named the "Angela Cobos." The other vessel robbed is now navigating between Guayaquil and the Galapagos Islands and belongs to this same Mr. Cobos. [He] is a particular friend of the Captain of the port of Esmeraldas and between the two, false affidavits have been procured.
>
> I intend to visit Esmeraldas but not to remain any time for fear of being assassinated, a common mode of getting clear of difficulties in this republic.
>
> Soliciting your attention and favorable consideration of this particular case, I have the honor to be,
>
> Your Obedient Servant,
> M. M. Staples

It is not known if the unfortunate Mr. Staples ever recovered his *Laura*, but perhaps one of the ships taken from Magdelena eventually became the *Manuel J. Cobos*. The other may have become not *Angela*, but *Josefina Cobos*, the name of another vessel known to be operated by Don Manuel.

Notwithstanding the man's ship acquisition techniques, there are tales that in the early days of the Cobos empire, he treated his workers with reasonable fairness. But over the years conditions deteriorated. Former resident Jacob Lundh speculates that Cobos was disturbed by what had happened to José Valdizán and feared the same fate might be his. And so it would be. As his workforce expanded with convicts who had nothing much to lose, he became progressively more paranoid, and no doubt for very good reason. Soon enough, Don Manuel Julian Cobos set himself up as the absolute monarch of all he surveyed, and with the nearest government office some 600 miles distant, there were none to dispute his right. The village of Progreso was little more than a slave labor camp.

Above: The *Manuel J. Cobos*, in a photo taken after it was renamed as the *San Cristóbal*.

Below: Camilo Casanova, banished to the uninhabited Isla Santa Cruz for publicly threatening Cobos.

A jail was constructed for those fortunate enough to survive Don Manuel's displeasure. Others were not so lucky—some were flogged to death, others shot without trial. A few were banished to other islands, where they could look forward to death by exposure. One of these men was Camilo Casanova, who had been sent out to San Cristóbal for reasons unknown. After attacking another man, Cobos had him flogged. The angry Casanova swore revenge, but made the mistake of doing so in public. The master of Progreso could tolerate

no such insubordination, and had him transported to the uninhabited island of Santa Cruz, there to await his fate.

Meanwhile, his own fate was being decided as more and more workers suffered under his rule. A group of five made plans to dispose of him, but Cobos got word of the plot. His firing squad put an end to the matter.

The next group would have to be more careful. The well-trusted Elias Puertas was one of their number, and the plan was to torch the sugar cane fields. This would bring out Cobos to see what was going on, and in the confusion of the fire he would make an easy target. But the group wasn't careful enough in selecting its members. Conspirator José Prieto apparently had a bit too much to drink one day and blurted out something about setting fields on fire. Cobos rightly suspected another plot, and Prieto was sentenced to a severe flogging the next morning to help further loosen his tongue.

Above: Elias Puertas, leader of the group that finally did away with Manuel J. Cobos.

It dawned on the plotters that when Prieto sobered up he would no doubt be happy to reveal their names in return for a lesser thrashing. And so it was decided that Puertas would intercede on Prieto's behalf, arguing that he was just a harmless old fool who didn't deserve such severity. If Cobos would not relent, then Puertas knew what he must do. As he almost expected, Cobos would have none of this:

> You know damn well that my orders must be
> obeyed to the letter. Prieto will be flogged
> today, at seven o'clock sharp, in my presence.
> Whomever is found guilty of planning to set
> fire to the cane fields will be shot at once.

Puertas realized that his own fate would be sealed shortly after seven. "No!" he cried, "You will punish no one. Today you die, or I do." Tradition has it that a few days before this encounter, as Cobos dismounted his horse his revolver slipped from its holster. The loss went unnoticed by Cobos, but not by Puertas, who quietly hid the weapon under his own poncho. Now he withdrew it and fired three shots into his master. But Cobos would not die easily—he was able to knock Puertas down, just as worker Pedro José Jiménez entered the room. Cobos fled into his bedroom and bolted the door, but not before Jiménez hacked at the back of his skull with a machete. As others joined in to batter down the door, Cobos leaped out a window and fell to the ground.

The mob approached the fallen tyrant and wasted a few more bullets on him, but by now he was beyond the reach of their fury. Nevertheless, their gun butts smashed his jaw before they were done with him. Then they turned and walked away.

Puertas saw to it that Cobos had an orderly funeral, and then in a last act of retribution, had him buried on the spot where the Cobos firing squad had carried out their executions.

The first resting place of Manuel J. Cobos, a tomb in the highlands of San Cristóbal, placed on the spot where he had several of his workers executed.

Some days later, the *Josefina Cobos* returned from a fishing trip. Puertas and his companions seized her, stocked her with food and water and invited anyone who wanted to leave to join them. The ship was re-christened *Libertad*, and more than 80 men, women and children departed the island forever in search of freedom.

But freedom also would not come easy. The ship reached the coast of Colombia, where it was seized by suspicious officials. The freedom seekers were sent to Guayaquil, there to be turned over to the local police. A photographer was sent to the dock, the story made the newspaper headlines, and of course the Government denied all knowledge of the abuses that had been going on for years. The gunboat *Cotapaxi* was dispatched to Galápagos to investigate, and it was soon enough discovered that the *Libertad* passengers had indeed told the truth about their suffering under the reign of Manuel J. Cobos.

"Guayaquil: Disembarkation of the Galápagos insurrectionists." A postcard issued on the occasion of the arrival of the escapees from Progreso.

The *Cotapaxi* continued on to Isla Santa Cruz to search for the remains of Camilo Casanova. The search didn't take long at all, for Casanova was there on the beach waiting to welcome his rescuers. He had survived for over three years on whatever he could catch, and eased his perpetual thirst by the blood of tortoises and the liquid he could squeeze from the cactus.

The Ecuadorian gunship *Cotapaxi*, sent out to Galapagos to investigate the situation. The painting shows the ship after it was renamed as *Calderón*.

On several occasions he had pleaded with visiting ship crews to take him from the island, but he was always refused. Popular folklore explains why: Cobos had mounted a sign on the island, with a warning in English and Spanish. Both versions are at the head of this chapter, where they may be read with horror by those who don't find it at all suspicious that a sign in plain view of visitors would not be noticed by a desperate lonely man on shore.

The ruins of the Cobos hacienda in Progreso. It has been said that Cobos departed this world via the window on the left.

A short stairway to nowhere. The interior of the Cobos hacienda has long since fallen victim to the years.

The remains of the jail where Manuel Cobos would lock up those workers who displeased him.

A few gears are now all that remain of the sugar cane processing plant at Progreso.

It is said that on some nights Manuel Julian Cobos may be seen riding his favorite white stallion through the streets of the village he founded, perhaps in search of his mortal remains. But some years ago his family exhumed the rough stone tomb in the San Cristóbal highlands and removed his body to a fine mausoleum in Guayaquil's cemetery, where he has been joined by his daughter Josefina and her husband Rogerio Alvarado. It is said that there is also a space for Manuel Augusto there, but he had other wishes. Shortly after his 86th birthday, he told Jacob Lundh that he wanted to rest where he belonged—on Isla San Cristóbal. He got his wish in February, 1994.

The Cobos family mausoleum in the cemetery at Guayaquil. The three plaques at the base are the tombs of Rogerio Alvarado, Manuel J. Cobos, and Josefina Cobos Alvarado.

SR. MANUEL J. COBOS

A photograph of Manuel J. Cobos from Bognoly & Espino-sa's *Las Islas Encantadas, ó Archipielago de Colon*. A search for a better photograph of Don Manuel has been unsuccessful.

CHAPTER ELEVEN

HOW ACADEMY BAY GOT ITS NAME

We are the Academy.

A crewman, on hearing news of
the San Francisco earthquake

IN THE EARLY YEARS OF THE TWENTIETH CENTURY, the California Academy of Sciences sought a vessel to send down to the Galápagos Islands to make a thorough study of the land tortoises. Academy Museum director Leverett Mills Loomis hoped the expedition could collect specimens of all the species while there were still specimens of all the species left to collect.

The Academy found what it was looking for in 1905. A year earlier, the U. S. Navy schooner *Earnest* had run aground while operating out of the Naval Station at Yerba Buena. The ship was stricken from the Navy lists, sold to the Academy, and re-christened as the *Academy* in honor of its sponsoring institution. A crew of collectors was assembled under the leadership of Rollo Beck. Joseph Richard Slevin—who would spend so much time in later years debating the whereabouts of Lieutenant Cowan with Waldo Lasalle Schmitt—was an important member of the ship's company. It was he who later published the *Log of the Schooner "Academy"* which combined the usual information found in other ship logs with day-to-day details of the crew's collecting activities. Slevin, whose specialty was herpetology, also kept a separate notebook on his own subject.

The schooner *Academy* at its Mission Street berth in 1905 ...

Charles Darwin would have been envious. H. M. S. *Beagle* returned to England with three tortoises. The schooner *Academy* returned to San Francisco with 266 of them. It might have been a better thing to return with 265. Expedition leader Rollo Beck had the dubious distinction of being the man to remove the last tortoise surviving (until Beck found it) on Isla Fernandina. But perhaps that was not such a bad thing after all—except from the point-of-view of the tortoise, of course. If Beck had not removed it, somebody else would have, and today we might not even have a tortoise shell in the archives. Not quite the same as a real live animal, but better than nothing.

With repairs made, extra water tanks installed, and food enough for 20 months, the *Academy* was ready at last.

... and its crew:

F. T. Nelson, mate   J. J. Parker (seated), navigator
A. Stewart, botanist   J. R. Slevin, herpetologist
E. S. King, assistant herpetologist   E. W. Gifford, ornithologist
Rollo Beck, expedition leader   W. H. Ochsner, geologist
J. S. Hunter, ornithologist, mammalogist   F. X. Williams, entomologist

> 1905. June 28, 10:00 am. The tug *Relief* made
> fast alongside and at 10:30 hauled out from
> Mission Street bulkhead, heading for the
> Golden Gate. ... Most of the party never
> having been to sea before succumbed rather
> early.

Slevin's *Log* begins with this entry as the *Academy* set sail on what would be the longest collecting voyage in Galápagos history. And in the entry for the second day, "Most of the party still seasick." On the third day a little something came up that might have brought into question the wisdom of venturing into the Pacific on a ship that had run aground not that long ago. But on the positive side, it would at least offer some distraction to those whose stomachs had not yet become accustomed to a horizon that wouldn't hold still.

> The main deck leaks considerably, making it rather uncomfortable below. Nelson and myself spending our watch below overhauling stores to prevent damage by water and plugging up leaks with empty sacks.

Not a propitious start for a long journey, but on the first day of July things started looking up: "Members of the party feeling better today, and Williams appeared at the table." So it would appear that food was once again a possibility.

The *Academy* proceeded on its slow track down the Pacific coast of North and Central America, making frequent stops for collecting along the way. At Mexico's Isla Socorro, Slevin may have spent a bit too much time collecting, as indicated by an entry in his own notebook, which he kept separately from the ship's log:

> July 28: Feet burned and blistered from yesterday's hunt for turtles. By putting on a plentiful application of cheese cloth, Vaseline and cocoa butter, I got on my shoes and went ashore with the boat early in the morning.

As too many gringo island visitors know, sunburned feet are not fun—others would surely take the day off to recuperate in the shade, but not Slevin.

After more collecting, the ship moved on to other islands, and then on September 23rd, Chatham Island at last came into view, complete with two albatrosses flying about the schooner. The next morning, "All hands enjoyed their first close up view of the Galápagos, a region that never ceased to be of interest during an entire year that followed." And the menu in the *Academy* dining room had a new offering:

"We now have goat meat every night for supper and cold goat for lunch" … which, not unlike Charles Darwin's observation on land iguanas, "… is liked by those whose stomachs soar above all prejudices." Some months later, the diners would repeat Darwin's experiment: "We tried some land iguana for supper this evening, but it was not considered a great success."

Within a few weeks the *Academy* found its way over to Charles Island, and a famous Galápagos landmark.

> Here we found the postoffice after which the
> bay is named. It consisted of a barrel erected
> on top of a post and painted red. An inscription
> on the post reads: erected by H. M. S.
> *Leander*. Crews of various vessels calling at this
> anchorage had painted or carved the names of
> their vessels on the post or barrel.

Among those noted by the men of the *Academy* was the U. S. S. *Oregon*, which stopped there in January, 1898 on a voyage that took it from Callao, Peru to Honolulu, Hawaii. Of course the *Oregon* was by no means the last oversized American warship to put into a Galápagos bay for a look around. But more on that in another chapter.

Above: An early visitor, the U. S. S. *Oregon* paid a call several years before the *Academy* arrived.

Slevin offered some background details about how the Post Office worked:

> The idea was that any ship homeward bound
> should pick up the letters, mark it ship's mail,
> and, on delivery in the United States, it would be
> forwarded to the main postoffice in Washington,
> without postage stamps being attached.

Mr. Gifford wrote to his father, and we found out on our return that it had been picked up by the British yacht *Deerhound* and forwarded to Washington. The rust from the barrel hoops had obliterated part of the address, so that all that could be deciphered was—Gifford, Alameda. The postoffice at Washington traced the addressee and delivered the letter.

1917: H. M. S. *Lancaster* crewmen gather at the Galápagos Post Office barrel a decade after the *Academy* visit. The ship had recently searched, without success, for German Captain Felix von Luckner's *SeeAdler*. The Count himself will make a brief visit to this island in a later chapter.

Alas, the U. S. Postal Service will no longer honor unstamped mail dropped off in a barrel.

The *Academy* made its way over to Black Beach, where the men found a party of natives cutting beef and hanging it up to dry, and heard about what had happened on Chatham Island a few years earlier.

Ochsner gave them some whiskey from our medicine chest and they seemed to relish this beyond everything. The word whiskey was the extent of their knowledge of the English language. They gave some nice, juicy oranges in return, saying that there were plenty and also plenty of fresh water up in the hills.

The chief of the hunting party informed us that Manuel Cobos, formerly owner of the plantation on Chatham, was killed two years ago and that one of the men who helped kill him is in his crew on shore. Just a month ago a member of his hunting party was killed in a fight, so we are not far wrong in judging from the looks of his party that they are a bunch of desperados. The camp cook, the only female in the party, looks like she could cut anybody's throat with pleasure.

A few days later the Governor's secretary arrived, accompanied by a military escort appropriate to his station.

We took the whole party on board the schooner: secretary, captain, interpreter and five soldiers. The latter made a fine looking army. One had an old French army hat about the vintage of 1880, some had no hats nor sandals, but were the proud possessors of undershirts and trousers, which seemed to be the uniform of the day. Their firearms were about the same period as the uniform hat and were old bolt-action rifles. One had a double-barrel shotgun, the firing pins of which were rusted fast. No ammunition at all was in evidence. No doubt it is too dangerous to let the soldiers get hold of any cartridges.

> However, what the army lacked, the
> commanding officer supplied. He was dressed in
> a light blue uniform of French design, with red
> epaulets, red stripe down his trousers, a huge
> red pompon on his hat, and a cavalry saber
> that, for size and polish, was the last word.

The next port was at last at Chatham Island, where the ship
was guided in by a beacon from shore:

> The wind died down towards evening and at
> 8:00 pm we picked up the Chatham light.
> The settlement at Wreck Bay consists of a
> warehouse, the plantation manager's house,
> several native huts and the light keeper's
> house. The Wreck Bay light consists of a
> lantern placed on the top of a pole. The sugar
> plantation can be seen from our anchorage and
> is about five miles inland.

The men went ashore and were escorted to the headquarters
of no less a personage than the governor himself, General
Julio Plaza. Here they were introduced to the local treat
known today as "puro"—although it was (and still is)
anything but.

> The General was found seated at his official
> desk, an old kitchen table with the drawer
> missing, attired in a white duck suit and a navy
> watch cap, probably donated by some sailor off a
> visiting warship. He gave us some very powerful
> home brew to drink, and, when he observed the
> tears streaming down our cheeks, informed us
> that it may be a little strong for us. Personally, I
> agreed with him, in that it was not only a little
> too strong but much too strong for any human
> being. Even now, 25 years afterwards, whenever
> I think of General Plaza I can almost feel my
> insides on fire.

The interpreter then said: "The General says
he can tell from your looks that you are
gentlemen." This remark rather flattered us, as
we had been out 110 days without a shave.

The next stop was Barrington Island, where in late October
the *Academy* collectors found a colony of the large land
iguanas that are unique to that island. Some months later
the men returned here and discovered that local residents
from Chatham Island had come over and exterminated
almost all of the animals. Not to be outdone by the locals,
the scientists made their own depredations on the tortoise
population over the next few weeks, and following
Darwinian precedent, Slevin made a note of the more
important testudinal details:

We had tortoise liver for supper this evening and
found it a little oily and of a peculiar taste, but
not at all bad when one becomes accustomed to
it. During future times we always lived on tortoise
liver when obtainable, with the exception of that
of the Duncan Island tortoises, which we found to
be dark and tasteless. The liver of the Indefatigable
tortoise is rich yellow, as is that of the tortoises of
all the other islands except Duncan.

Perhaps he should have added "… and James" where
Captain Porter noted tortoise liver "black as ebony."

On approaching Indefatigable Island, the *Academy* left its
mark—and almost, its bones—on the southern shore.

On nearing the spot where we were going to let
go the anchor, we struck on a submerged reef
just about the middle of the bay. No damage was
done, and we found that at low tide the top of the
reef was just exposed above water. We named this
bay *Academy Bay,* after the schooner, and it is now
shown as such on the Hydrographic Office charts.

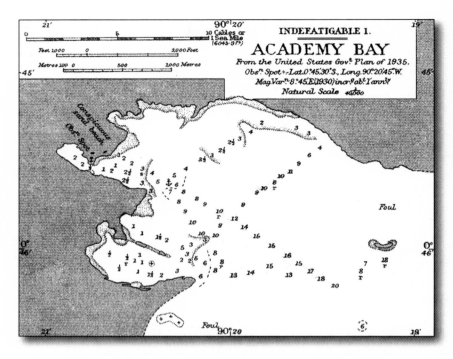

Academy Bay will be found on almost any chart issued since the voyage of the schooner that left its name there.

History repeated itself a few days later.

> During the day the vessel swung on her anchor chain and touched bottom at low tide. Shock not severe, but a little more so than when we struck bottom coming to anchor. The anchor was lifted off the bottom and the schooner hauled a little further out with the kedge.

While on the island, the men found recent traces of yet another unfortunate man who had run afoul of the law, Cobos style:

> Close by the water-hole, we found the remains of a grass hut, which we afterward found out was used by a negro who had been marooned

on the island by Manuel Cobos, the owner
of the plantation on Chatham. We saw this
man at Villamil and he told us of being on the
island for a whole year, living on raw tortoise
meat and what shellfish he could gather. He
was discovered by a passing vessel and taken to
Villamil.

Slevin does not give the man's name, nor any details about
why Cobos banished him to the island. But as we know
from a previous chapter, this was not the only example of
Slevin omitting information of interest.

Slevin reports a November 21st landing on the island now
known as Isla Baltra, where there was "... a fine lagoon,
separated from the ocean by a long sand beach on which
the surf broke furiously." In a footnote he mentions that on
a return visit many years later with Captain Allan Hancock,
"... this lagoon had entirely disappeared." Apparently
animals are not the only items on the Galápagos endangered
list.

The *Academy* scientists were of course collectors first, and
seamen second—and at times, a distant second. Slevin
describes a landing on the little island of Daphne Major.

Nelson landed the shore party and stood off
with the skiff, while the schooner beat to
windward of the island. While everybody was
busy working, Hunter saw the skiff drifting out
to sea with nobody in it. We hailed Nelson and
he answered back, saying that the skiff had got
away from him while he was up on the rocks
gathering some shells.

Circling around to the landing place, we fired
off our guns and waved our hats to attract the
attention of the schooner as she sailed by.

Ochsner and White put off in another skiff and picked us up. Hurrying back to the schooner, we ran down before the wind to pick up the lost skiff. As we approached it, a swell suddenly caught it just right, turning it turtle, the oars falling out and floating away. Nelson and others put off in the sailboat, which we had towing astern, to rescue the oars and the skiff.

Our navigator tried some fancy "seamanship" and as a consequence the main boom tackle fouled the mast of the boat and swamped it, throwing the occupants into the water. Nelson, coming up close behind in the skiff, rescued them. The sacks of sand used for ballast in the sailboat were dumped overboard and the boat bailed out.

Daphne Major Island, where the landing is never easy. In recent years, the island has been the site of Peter and Rosemary Grant's years-long study of "Darwin's Finches."

Once order was restored, the men made a second landing on Daphne Major to resume their work. Fortunately there had been no injuries, save possibly to pride in seamanship.

December 25: Christmas Day!! 181 days out from San Francisco. The cook made us a plumduff for dinner.

No doubt a turkey was unavailable, and by now they may have had quite enough of the goat.

The next few weeks, like all those since September, were spent depleting the islands of whatever creatures were unlucky enough to come within range. And then in February came the opportunity to reciprocate—or perhaps retaliate—with a gift to the governor. There had been yet another revolution in Ecuador, and a new governor had been sent out to the islands.

> February 24: Just as we were about to break out the anchor, the Governor, who came to say good-bye, and a boatload of sailors came alongside with a load of bananas. When Beck asked them if they wanted some whiskey there was a loud and immediate response of "Si si señor!!" Ochsner and I rose to the occasion, and, hurrying down below, got some clean alcohol out of a barrel, diluting it about 75 percent. A hurried trip to the galley, and some juice bailed out of a dish of stewed prunes gave our home brew the desired coloring. After shaking well, we poured the concoction into a whiskey bottle. In less time that it takes to tell it, we had a drink that seemed to hit just the right spot, as the sailors drank it down in great gulps.

> The Governor made some queer facial contortions and seemed to think all was not well, as he declined a second drink, a thing never heard of in these latitudes.

Slevin did not suggest to the governor that perhaps the brew was a little too strong for him.

In March, the *Academy* was over at Albemarle Island again, and there's a puzzling entry in the log, when the ship was well to the west of the village of Villamil:

> March 12: ... landed at low tide on a fine
> sandy beach, back of which we found the
> wreck of an old grass house, probably the last
> remains of what is known as the Old Cobos
> Settlement.

The tyrant of Chatham Island was not known to have property on this island, so the "Old Cobos Settlement" phrase may be a reference to a hut erected by yet another person banished by Don Manuel to a remote location.

At Iguana Cove on the same island a week later, some of the crew had a memorable experience as they tried without much success to load a trio of tortoises into the skiff.

> During this procedure our skiff turned
> broadside on to the swell and, an extra heavy
> roller coming in, the skiff capsized, throwing
> both tortoises, the oars, and the remaining
> contents of the skiff overboard. Fortunately,
> King, who could not swim, was left on the
> beach and saw the tortoises and some of the
> oars go floating out to sea. Beck could not
> swim either, but hung on to the stern of the
> skiff. Both Williams and myself felt perfectly
> at home in the water and finally got the skiff
> righted. Beck crawled in over the stern and,
> finding one oar, got it into action and sculled
> for the shore. We all landed on a rough ledge,
> getting somewhat cut up on the sharp edges of
> the lava.

But it may have been a good thing they were out of the skiff:

> An extra heavy swell coming in crashed it
> down on a sharp point of rock, smashing it to
> pieces. As it would soon be dark, we decided

to make down the coast for the schooner. As
we were making our way slowly along the
coast, we heard a whistle and saw a light. We
hailed the boat, told them we had lost our boat
and that nobody was hurt. Nelson told us he
would pick us up at the cove, and after what
seemed like a journey that would never end,
the skiff picked us up and brought us on board
for a much-belated supper.

Thus ended the 263rd and about the most
exciting day of the voyage.

And then on April 30th came some unexpected news when
the *Academy* returned to Villamil.

The Ecuadorian gunboat *Cotapaxi* was at
anchor, and from her we got a Guayaquil
paper announcing the fact that there had been
a terrific earthquake in San Francisco and
that the soldiers had been ordered out on the
streets. This was the first and all the news of
the great disaster that we had for some time.

The unwelcome news from San Francisco was most
upsetting, and of course the men knew nothing of the fate of
their families back home. In his notebook, Slevin wrote "We
made preparations to sail immediately for Chatham to try
and get news." But he contradicts himself in the ship's log,
which describes three more days of collecting at Villamil,
followed by a cruise to Hood Island for more collecting. And
then on May 29th—a month after getting the news about the
earthquake—"… weighed anchor and set sail for Chatham
Island, with the intention of going around the west end of
Charles." They spent most of the month of June there.

June 28: One year out from San Francisco
today!! One goat brought aboard for fresh meat.

Finally, on July 3rd they pulled into the Wreck Bay anchorage, where letters from home awaited them. Their families were safe. The next day, "Hoisted our colors at eight bells in honor of Independence Day." And then, a Captain Thomas Levick came aboard, with news that some meat that Beck had ordered shipped from San Francisco via Guayaquil had not arrived—not surprising considering what had happened there a few months earlier. Levick, who deserves (and gets) a chapter of his own, delivered some chickens a few days later, the first the crew had tasted since leaving San Francisco, and no doubt a welcome variation on the never-ending theme of warm goat for dinner, cold goat for lunch.

On July 5th one of the *Academy* crew learned of another revolution of sorts when he was called on to exercise some damage control.

> Ochsner went up to the hacienda to attend a wounded man who had accidentally been shot when one of the peons was trying to force a cartridge into a revolver. We learned later that some of the peons had stolen the revolver from a visiting ship and had planned to kill the Governor. They had a few odd cartridges and it was while trying to find one that would fit the gun that the accident happened. The Governor and the plantation owner never go about unarmed.

Ochsner patched up the patient's flesh wound, and whatever the Governor may have done about all this was not recorded by Slevin. But the incident may help further explain something said in the previous chapter—that Manuel Augusto Cobos never sat down to dinner without a pistol at his side.

A few weeks later, Slevin reports a potentially distressing bit of news, but fortunately there was a happy ending. The news: Expedition leader Rollo Beck—who should have known better—captured two goats on South Seymour Island, intending to turn them loose on James Island. The happy ending: "The two goats we had on board died from eating cotton and arsenic."

More months were spent collecting, and there's a puzzling entry in the log as the expedition was nearing its end:

> September 17: Cowley, Tagus Cove, Banks Bay Mountain and the top of James Island in sight from our anchorage.

Chances are, Slevin meant Cowley Mountain (the present Volcán Alcedo) and not Cowley Island, which would be invisible against the backdrop of Albemarle Island from the ship's anchorage to the north of Bindloe Island. Nor could he see Tagus Cove, which is on the far side of Albemarle. It's not clear what he meant, because there are no likely coves on the near side of Albemarle, and Slevin surely knew the actual location of Tagus Cove. The mystery will just have to remain unsolved.

On September 25th, 1906 the men of the *Academy* made their final landing on Culpepper Island. Later in the day

> With a fresh S. S. E. wind, we streamed the log, winged out the foresail and ran before the wind, bidding goodbye to the Galápagos on the first day of the passage back to San Francisco and the 455th day of the voyage.

It was not too long until the last dinner of goat was consumed, and on October 14th Slevin duly noted that "… our diet of canned salmon and beans is getting a little irksome to some of the party." One month later, "The cook parboiled and fried an albatross for supper this evening, some of the party wanting to get the taste of salmon out of their mouths, it being the 52nd day on a diet of salmon and beans." Like the iguana dinner of several months ago, the bird was not a great success as a main course. When a second attempt was made a week or so later, Slevin decided he'd stick with the salmon and beans.

November 9 — "500 days out from San Francisco today!!!" — The French barque L'Hermite was sighted, 125 days out from Dunkerque, France, bound for San Francisco with a load of cement. Despite its cargo, L'Hermite made port two weeks before the Academy, giving the first news that the vessel was on its way home.

> November 29: Everybody much elated over
> the prospects of getting in. Razors were broke
> out and we all took a shave, some for the first
> and some for the second time in 17 months.
> Old clothes are being thrown overboard so the
> Board of Health will not hold us up.

The Academy approached San Francisco and picked up their pilot. But they were not quite home yet.

> The wind dropped on us again and we lay
> becalmed. Being Thanksgiving Day, we could not
> get a tug, so, instead of the turkey we all longed
> for, we had our daily dish of Alaska salmon.

> We hailed a passing crab fisherman, in his
> fishing smack Louisa, and, for the sum of ten
> dollars, he agreed to tow us across to the
> quarantine station, where we arrived at 10:15
> pm, 65 days out from Culpepper Island and the
> 519th day of the voyage.

The voyagers were home from the sea at last, and now with a specimen collection far more valuable than even they could have anticipated. They had learned about the earthquake and fire months before they reached home port, and now they learned the extent of the damage. The institution that had sent them out no longer existed. It had been completely destroyed seven months earlier. The collections on exhibit when the *Academy* left port 17 months ago were gone. Almost nothing remained. Nothing, except the schooner *Academy* and the collection in its hold. The assortment of birds and beasts that were to have been an addition to the collection were now *the* collection—the foundation upon which a new California Academy of Sciences would rise.

Today's Academy Bay provides anchorage for tourist yachts while passengers visit the Charles Darwin Research Station.

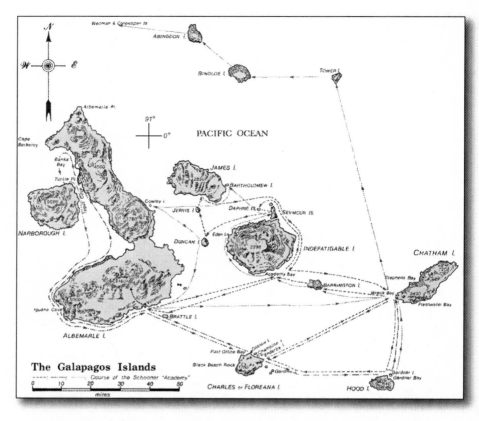

The meandering track of the schooner *Academy* during its 1 year + 1 day expedition in Galápagos.

CHAPTER TWELVE

THE LIGHTHOUSE KEEPER OF WRECK BAY

*...his real name was Thomas Levick. Why he did
not use this fine name instead of the ordinary
Johnson, he did not wish to relate.*

From a Norwegian settler's
description of "Johnson."

ATALE OF HIDDEN TREASURE, of carved initials, and of sudden death may be overheard now and then in the villages of Galápagos. As the story goes, an old man lived on Isla San Cristóbal long ago, and the old man knew of a buried chest. But he didn't know where it was. Maybe he knew when he was younger, but his memory wasn't so good any more, and there are many islands in Galápagos. All he remembered was that there was treasure on one of them—or maybe it was more than one of them. And so he would make his way from one island to another, carving the initials "T. L." here and there, perhaps to mark places from which he returned empty-handed. And then one day he found what he was looking for. He opened the chest, which of course was filled with coin. The old man rejoiced at his sudden wealth, but his pleasure didn't last. Within a few days he was dead.

Was the shock of final discovery more than an old man's heart could stand? Or was there no old man of San Cristóbal, and this just another of those "buried treasure" myths?

December, 1919. The writer Ralph Stock, his sister "Peter"
and Steve pulled into the harbor called (for good reason)
Wreck Bay at Isla San Cristóbal on the *Dream Ship*. We
know this because Stock's book *The Cruise of the Dream Ship*
gives us details, not including Peter's real name (Mabel),
nor Steve's identity. But never mind that; there are more
important matters to consider, such as a trio of approaching
visitors—and one of them an old man.

> Presently a boatload of three put off to us.
> They proved to be the owner of the island,
> a good-looking youth of about twenty-five;
> the chief of police, a swarthy Ecuadorian in a
> becoming poncho (presumably chief because
> there is only one representative of the law in
> the Galápagos); and a little, wrinkled old man
> with a finely chiseled face and delicate hands.
>
> The owner of Cristóbal informed us in
> excellent French (he had been four years in
> Paris previous to marooning himself on his
> equatorial possession) that the island was ours,
> and the fullness thereof; that he also was ours
> to command, and would we dine with him that
> evening at the *hacienda*, it being New Year's
> eve?
>
> The little old man, whom we soon learnt to
> call "Dad," sat mum, with a dazed expression
> on his face and his head at an angle after the
> fashion of the deaf. When he spoke, which he
> presently did with an unexpectedness which
> was startling, it was in a low, cultural voice,
> and in English! What about this Dutch war
> he had heard rumors of during the last year
> or two? "With Germany, was it? Well, now,
> and who was winning? Over, eh?—and with

the Allies on top? That was good, that was
good!" He rubbed his wrinkled hands together
and glared round on the assembled company
with an air of triumph, but without making
any appreciable impression on the owner of
Cristóbal or the chief of police.

Our author does not trouble the reader with the names
of his hosts, but we may recognize the "owner" as none
other that Manuel Augusto Cobos, son of the late Manuel
Julian C., murdered some years earlier. The name of *El jefe*
is unknown. As for the old man, ...

Dad was a type, if ever there was one, of the
educated ne'er-do-well hidden away in the
farthest corner of the earth to avoid those
things which most of us deem so desirable. He
had a split-bamboo house on the beach, a wife
who could cook, freedom, and God's sunlight.
What more did man desire? He had run away
to sea at the age of seventeen, run away from
sea two years later at the Galápagos Islands,
and remained there ever since. This was the
second time he had spoken English in fifty
years, so we must excuse his halting diction,
but the tales he could tell—the tales!

He was here when the pirates of the South
American coast murdered for money, even as
they have a knack of doing to this day, and hid
the loot at their headquarters in the Galápagos
Islands, silver and gold, boatloads of it. He
had built a cutter with his own hands, and
sailed it in search of this same loot, only to
encounter the sole owner, still guarding his ill-
gotten gains though reduced to nakedness and
hair. Dad had seen him first at a distance and,
mistaking him for a mountain goat, shot him

through the heart. It was the first man he had killed, and he could not stay on the island after that—especially at night.

Afterward, I asked the owner of Cristóbal if one could believe half the old man said, and he answered gravely that one could. "There is much, also, that he does not say," he added with a smile.

There is undoubtedly treasure still lying hidden in the Galápagos Islands. Two caches have been unearthed, silver ingots and pieces of eight. The finder of one built himself a handsome hotel in Ecuador, and the other drank himself to death in short order. But there is definite proof there is more.

As a field for the treasure hunter it is doubtful if any place in the world offers better chances of success today than the Galápagos Islands, but—there is always a "but"—the uncertainty of wind and current amongst the islands makes it impossible for a sailing ship to undertake the search, a motor auxiliary is too unreliable, and a small steamer is too large for the creeks and reef channels it would be necessary to negotiate. With a full-powered launch and diving apparatus, and a parent ship in attendance, and unlimited time and patience, and money—but these be dreams beyond the reach of the penniless world-wanderer: dreams, nevertheless, that will assuredly one day be realized.

Stock does not explain how he knew about the two caches already found, nor does he reveal the "definite proof" of more riches awaiting discovery. Perhaps "Dad" was his source.

"Peter" (seated on stairs) pays a call on Anita Johnson at
the lighthouse keeper's shack.

The ship's company spent the first morning of the New Year
exploring the beach.

> Mechanically gravitating toward Dad's split-
> bamboo abode, I came upon him seated on
> a log, staring meditatively at the crumbling
> skeleton of what had been, or was at one time
> going to be, a ship.

"Why didn't you finish her?" I shouted into his best ear. He stared at me in a daze, then burst forth in Spanish, until I succeeded in convincing him that he might as well talk double Dutch.

"Of course, of course," he muttered. "I forgot; Lord, how I forgot! It's queer to me that I can speak English at all after all these years; but I can; that's something, isn't it?"

"Sure thing," I yelled; "keep it up. Tell me why you didn't finish your ship."

He pondered the matter; then spoke slowly: "I told you of the other I built—and why. Well, I ran her on a reef—splinters in five minutes. Took the heart out of me for a bit, that did. Then I began to think of that loot again. I still do, for that matter: can't help it. You see, I think I know where it is. So I started on this one." He nodded toward the hulk, silhouetted against the crimsoning sky.

"I'd got to the planking when it occurred to me that I'd want a partner for the job, at my age; and who could I trust? They'd slit your throat for ten dollars in those days. They murdered the present owner's father in cold blood. I wouldn't put it beyond 'em to do the same to this one if it wasn't that he's a smart lad and carries the only firearms on the island.

"No one's come here since, no one that I'd trust ... Then, too, what if I found the stuff? What good would it do me—now?" He spread out his delicately shaped hands in a deprecating gesture. "I should die in a month

if I left here. Finest climate on earth, this is.
..." He laughed—a low cackle, reminiscent of
mirth.

"But that wasn't all that decided me. I'd got to
the planking, Guayaquil oak it was, and I was
steaming it on when a nail drew, and the plank
caught me in the chest, knocked me six yards,
and broke a rib. It's broken yet, I guess; there
was no one to mend it. Well, that finished it. I
wasn't meant to build that ship."

He stopped abruptly and stared down at his
battered rawhide shoes. The inference was
obvious.

"Well, what about it?" I suggested.

He looked up at that. "I've been thinking about
it ever since you came here," he confessed. "I'll
go with you; but mind this, you mustn't curse
me if nothing comes of it. I don't promise
anything. All I say is I think I know where the
stuff is, if someone hasn't got it."

"I'll let you know tomorrow," said I, and left
him sitting there.

Was the man senile? There was nothing to
make one think so. Was he a liar? There was
equally nothing to prove it. At least half his
story was a matter of island history.

. . .

I give this interview with Dad for what it is
worth, and simply because I see no prospect
of undertaking the search as it should be

undertaken. I am aware that it reads like the purest romance, but it is true in every particular, as anyone will soon discover on visiting Wreck Bay, Cristóbal Island, in the Galápagos group.

The old man still waits there on the beach for a ship and someone he can trust; but judging by his frail appearance (he is seventy-seven), he will not wait much longer.

The French flying ace Alain Gerbault left the service after the Great War, did rather well as a businessman, and found spare time enough to become a tennis champion. In England for some matches, he visited a shipyard to renew an acquaintance with a friend—Ralph Stock. A six-meter racing yacht, the *Firecrest,* stood nearby. Gerbault liked the vessel's looks. Stock introduced him to the owner.

On Saturday, July 18th, 1925, at 4:00 pm, Gerbault anchored his *Firecrest* in 6 fathoms over sandy bottom, just a few hundred yards north of the jetty in the Wreck Bay harbor at Puerto Chico—known today as Puerto Baquerizo Moreno. After securing the ship, he went ashore to present his papers. During the formalities, an old man came forward and, on learning that Gerbault was the only man on board, proclaimed in bad English, "You were two and you have drowned the other!" Then the old man settled down and revealed that he had come to Galápagos more than 50 years ago, married an Ecuadorian woman and forgot his native English. But he'd never properly learned Spanish. During his life he had done a bit of everything. He had been a sailor, a carpenter, trader—even skipper of a schooner—and at this very moment was in charge of the lighthouse. Gerbault had noticed a lighthouse on shore; actually it was just a lantern atop a great pole. A thatched hut sat at either side.

The old man declared that the *Firecrest* had the look of an English craft. Gerbault assured him he was correct, the man translated this to the others, but got not the slightest reaction from his audience. So he turned his attention back to the visitor, announced that he was born in London in 1848, and was delighted that Gerbault had been a frequent visitor there. Nothing more is known of this encounter, and the old man's name is never mentioned, perhaps because the old man never mentioned it. Gerbault hung around for a few days, then left.

The *Firecrest* had scarcely slipped below the horizon when, on August 2, 1925, a large sailing ship arrived at the same port. The three-masted Swedish vessel was renamed *Floreana* shortly after its purchase by a group of Norwegians who planned to colonize the island of that name. A small group of local dignitaries came aboard to welcome them, accompanied by a sprightly eighty-three-year-old man who introduced himself as "Johnson from London." The man from London informed the new arrivals that he was the official Lighthouse Keeper of Wreck Bay—a fitting job for one who looked a bit of a wreck himself. Apparently Johnson's on-again/off-again English was back on again, for he informed the ship's company that he was not only the archipelago's sole English-speaking lighthouse-keeper, but also the best English-speaking pilot in these waters.

Absent a Norwegian pilot, the new arrivals invited him to accompany them to Isla Floreana, where they would unload construction supplies and spend a few nights on shore before returning to San Cristóbal. But the old man warned them of the dangers of sleep. The island was a place where wild things roamed. The pigs were dangerous enough with their sharp curved tusks, but not nearly as fierce as the wild dogs!

> They have developed a malicious revenge-instinct against human beings, and during the night they come in large packs more blood-thirsty than wolves. Don't forget that Johnson from London has warned you!

The Norwegians loaded their rifles, and the wild dogs nearly did cost a man his life. During the night the old man's bladder needed attention, and as he crept out of the tent on all fours, one of the Norwegians heard something. He leaped from his bunk, grabbed a rifle and was about to fire off a few shots when he realized the prowling animal was no animal at all. It was Johnson from London on his way to find relief, and almost on his way to becoming a victim of his own stories. Johnson took care of business, slipped back into the tent and the night passed without further incident.

Above: "Johnson from London" in a photo taken by one of the Norwegian settlers.

As the Norwegians set about their work in the morning, Johnson declared his great admiration for their determination and skill. His only regret was that they had not arrived fifty years earlier. "Ah, then something might have become of Galápagos! But, better late than never."

Johnson told the Norwegians of a life-long obsession with treasure hunting. In fact, when he learned about a road construction project in Galápagos some fifty years ago, he offered his assistance, hoping the income would support him until the treasure-hunting paid off. The first part of the project was to be a road from Wreck Bay to Progreso up in the highlands. For his work, Johnson would receive an advance and then half the balance when the road was half done. But this half was not delivered and therefore neither was the last half of the road, which explained the miserable condition of the final kilometers on the way to Progreso.

The old lighthouse at Wreck Bay,
built by "Johnson from London."

Johnson from London knew the island lacked a lighthouse, and that he lacked an income. So he found a four-meter pole, propped it up and hung a kerosene lamp on top—from that day forward he was the Lighthouse Keeper of San Cristóbal. For this he received a small salary from the governor, but not enough to set aside a little something for treasure-hunting. He sought no support from the locals, whom he did not trust, and this despite Anita, his Ecuadorian wife. But honest Norwegians were quite another matter. In a moment of confidence Johnson revealed that his real name was Thomas Levick. Why he did not use this fine name he did not wish to relate. But if his new friends would help him with transportation and digging, they should receive their fair share of the find. In particular, there was a treasure on Isla Marchena which would be his—and theirs—for the taking.

The Norwegians put little faith in the old man's story, but nevertheless agreed to make a detour to the black volcanic island on their return to Wreck Bay. As they sailed around Marchena, Johnson stood with his telescope looking for the treasure site, which would be revealed by an old chain laid at right angles to the beach between the water's edge and a huge lava boulder. But there was no old chain. There was no huge lava boulder. There was no treasure. The *Floreana* proceeded to Wreck Bay.

Sketch of Isla Marchena by F. P. Drowne, 1897.

The twinkling spark of life in the eye of Johnson from London was gone. He was a broken man before the voyage was done. At San Cristóbal he had to be helped ashore and accompanied to his hut by the lighthouse. He died a few days later.

But the spirit of Johnson from London did not die, and his story lives on in the little villages of Galápagos. And if you look carefully, you may find the initials "T. L." carved here and there.

The initials "T. L." and above, the date "1911" mark a spot visited by Johnson from London as he searched the islands for treasure.

Little is known of Johnson from London beyond what the Norwegians have told us. But knowing of his alter ego, we can draw a sketchy profile of Thomas Levick, who first appears in the diaries of scientists from the Webster-Harris expedition of 1897. While the expedition ship *Lila and Mattie* cruised near Gordon Rocks off the east coast of Isla Santa Cruz, scientist F. P. Drowne met the man:

> We sighted a small boat with men in it
> near the shore, and it caused considerable
> excitement—they being the first we had seen
> in four months. ... We got alongside in a few
> minutes, and in response to our query, "Speak
> English?" one replied, "I used to," and we saw
> that he was an Englishman. He said that his
> name was Thomas Levick; that he had lived
> on the islands for 29 years, and now belonged
> to a small colony which had been started two
> months since on Charles, or, as he called it,
> Florianna Island.

Levick gave the visitors detailed information about tortoise populations, told them of fierce dogs, and said that until recently his island had been uninhabited, "on account of a certain old Spaniard having been killed there by convicts." If he offered more details, Drowne didn't jot them down.

Later on, scientist Rollo Beck recalled an interesting chat between the Master of the *Lila and Mattie* and one of the locals:

> Captain Lenbridge heard from an old sailor at
> Chatham Island an intriguing tale of treasure
> on Tower Island. The story, however, was not
> revealed until after we had finished work at Tower.

It doesn't take much imagination to guess who the old sailor was. "On returning to San Francisco," says Beck, "the Captain got confirmatory evidence of the treasure, and interested the owner of a thirty-ton schooner." Beck does not explain what "confirmatory evidence" is supposed to mean, but apparently it was persuasive enough to persuade him and a few others to join the Captain on a treasure-hunting expedition to Tower Island. They returned home empty-handed, and did so twice:

> We caught sight of Tower Island one evening just
> before dark, but drifted off during the night and
> did not succeed in getting near it again before it
> was time to turn homeward. The next winter we
> started out once more. ... When we arrived at the
> spot and commenced to search for the treasure,
> we found only a square hole in the ground,
> from which, no doubt, some earlier seeker had
> abstracted the contents, said to be valued at a
> third of a million dollars. The Captain and the
> cook were sorely distressed but the rest of us,
> being young, took it easily.

Sketch of Tower Island by F. P. Drowne, 1897.

Beck is again silent on details—how did he know the treasure was "said to be valued at a third of a million dollars?" Did he have inside information? Some have said that what Beck and company actually took so easily was not the distress, but the treasure itself. Yet there's no hard evidence to support this suspicion, and his lifestyle didn't show any notable sign of post-hunt improvement.

A few years later, the California Academy of Sciences sent the schooner *Academy* down to Galápagos on that collecting expedition described in a previous chapter, with Beck as expedition leader. He had nothing further to say of treasures or of old sailors, even though Levick again put in an appearance. The field notes of Academy scientist Joseph Hunter offer the following information about Hood and James Island, and how some of the animals got there, and how others left:

> Feb. 21, 1906—Wreck Bay, Chatham Island. In talking with Captain Levick of the island schooner, some interesting things were learned concerning the wild domesticated animals on the islands. He says that he turned goats loose on Hood in 1897. On James the hogs and burros were first let loose about 50 years ago when the colonists were taken away from the island. Levick says that he ate the last tortoise from Barrington Island 15 years ago and about the same time the last one from this island. He has been on the islands 38 years.

There never were colonists on James Island, and according to Levick's own chronology, the hogs and burros were let loose there more than 10 years before his arrival. So either he got his islands mixed up, or Hunter misunderstood the tale. As for the last of the Chatham tortoises, *Academy* scientists found a tortoise on the island a few days after Hunter's chat with Levick, and to this day a surviving population lives at the eastern end of the island. It's possible Levick knew nothing of this, but it's also possible that he was just "spinning a yarn" for his interviewer's benefit. He was good at stories—telling some that he forgot his English, and others that he was the best English-speaking pilot. That, and the Johnson from London alias.

Neither the Captain's first name, nor that of his vessel, appear in Hunter's notes. But a few years later a Spanish language source refers to a *capitán Tomás Levick, jefe de una embarcación menor de propriedad del señor Valdizán*—that is, to a Captain Thomas Levick, chief of a small boat belonging to Mr. Valdizán. That would have been Don José Valdizán, a businessman from Spain resident in Guayaquil, who moved out to Floreana in 1868 to see if he could make a go of harvesting orchilla lichen, using a workforce of convict labor. For a time, Don Jose's boat *Venecia* went back and forth to the islands, perhaps with Levick at the helm. We know the vessel's name thanks to German scientist Theodor Wolf, who made a passing reference to it in his *Visit to the Galápagos Islands* published in 1879. But this job didn't last, for Valdizán was the "certain old Spaniard" that Levick had told the Webster-Harris scientists about: a decade after he arrived on Floreana, the convicts murdered their master. Local folklore has it that Captain Levick hastened to the island to warn Valdizán of approaching danger, but arrived too late. He found Señora Valdizán and her daughter, escorted them to the safety of his ship, then returned to the scene of the killing, rallied the loyal workers and hunted down the murderers. Only one survived.

But is this just more of the stuff of legend? Perhaps so, because Levick said not a word of this to the Webster-Harris Expedition people. Surely he would have told them the tale of how he put down the rebellion, if there was such a tale to be told. But whatever his role, with Valdizán gone, so was his job as Captain of the *Venecia*. And that would put him on a different ship in 1906, the year Hunter referred to him as "Captain Levick of the island schooner." Perhaps this was the *Manuel J. Cobos*, or maybe the *San Cristóbal*— two names for the same ship. The former honored the ship owner who followed Valdizán, first to Galápagos to manage another convict labor force, and then to the graveyard when history repeated itself. But this time there was no rebellion. Cobos was hated by everyone, and Levick was probably as delighted as the others when the convicts did him in. And now, with one Cobos out of the way, the other was re-christened to honor its home port rather than the tyrant of the island.

The books of travel writer Rolf Blomberg were very popular in his native Sweden during the 1930s and 1940s. In *Underliga Människor och underliga djur* (Strange People and Strange Animals), Blomberg writes of his 1934 trip to Galápagos, and of a visit with Karin Guldberg, the Norwegian wife of Manuel Augusto Cobos. As often happened with the lady, the conversation turned to treasure hunting. Doña Karin suggested to Blomberg that he might find a visit with an old woman worth his time.

"A pirate's widow?"

"Yes. Down at Wreck Bay there lives an old woman in a hut built of driftwood and bamboo. She's called Anita Johnson. Her late husband lived here about fifty years and worked at a little bit of everything. Among other things, he took part in seizing a ship, and the captured treasure was buried somewhere in the islands. That he did not dig it up during his lifetime may surprise you, but the Galápagos Islands was a penal colony populated by murderers and other criminals. He could not do it by himself—the treasure is supposed to be hidden on one of the small northern islands—and there was no one he trusted to ask for help. At that time, murder was a daily event. And then over the years, Johnson became a little confused and would forget where he hid the gold. He told anyone who would listen about the treasure, and he fooled many yachtsmen and fishing-boat captains. He would take them into his confidence, then offer to help find the treasure and divide it on advantageous terms. The old man would go out on the boats, drink good whiskey—the passion of his life—smoke cigars and keep on talking. "Go ashore and look here," he could say when they arrived at some island, and the crew would dig in the soil a couple of days. They would sweat and curse the name of Johnson, and Johnson would excuse himself. "Look, I am getting old and have such a bad memory. But wait, I think I begin to remember! It was not on this island but on such and such a one…"

And so he would travel around the archipelago, drinking whiskey and smoking cigars, and this was treasure enough for him. And then, he died.

Doña Karin Guldberg at home on Isla San Cristóbal in 1991.

Doña Karin may have been thinking of a visit by William Beebe who, like everyone else it seems, met the old man, and described the event in his own book, *Galápagos: World's End*. After arriving at Wreck Bay and receiving the Governor aboard,

> Next came a sunken-cheeked ancient who announced as he stepped on deck, "I'm Johnson from London." In ten minutes we were in possession of the main facts of his long life. His opinion of those who had been his neighbours for a half-century was almost unprintable, and though we knew from experiment that the protean Governor understood no word of English, we felt excessively nervous as old Johnson made very personal remarks about him in a loud, cracked voice.
>
> Our visitors were invited to have a drink, of a liquid less precious to us than water, and we then discovered that the Governor had an English vocabulary after all. He was letter-perfect in the word "whiskey." As for Johnson from London, all speech forsook him for a while and then he murmured, "God, I ain't seen any whiskey for six years."
>
> When they saw that real ice was a part of the treat, they beamed with satisfaction, and after

being established on the forward deck with a
clinking glass and a cigar apiece, the Governor
overwhelmed us with a flood of rapid Spanish,
while the Englishman became confidential on
the subject of buried treasure.

He knows the very spot where the buccaneers
buried their plunder, but to us he located
it no more definitely than to say it was on
Albemarle, which is nearly a hundred miles
long. "Thirty years ago," he said, "I built me a
scow to go look for that treasure. But I couldn't
get nobody to go with me." He paused to
reflect and added, "That is, I could have got
somebody but—" and he drew a finger across
his throat, rolling a significant eye at us. A
penal colony is probably not the ideal place
to find companions for a treasure hunt. He
remembered Ralph Stock of the *Dream Ship*
which touched here a few years ago, and after
a few drinks recalled vividly Darwin's visit of
1835, and Admiral Porter's of 1813.

He may have whispered something of other riches lost and
found, for Beebe writes that "A chest with more than three
hundred thousand dollars' worth of gold was buried and
less than a score of years ago was salvaged from one of the
cliffs of Tower." But like Ralph Stock's 1919 report—written
less than a score of years ago—of "silver ingots and pieces
of eight," Beebe offers no further details, perhaps because
there weren't any. And in any case, at this point Beebe was
more interested in quite a different valuable—water. The old
man promised to deliver him to the source of this treasure.

Johnson would go with us to show the place
where, he said with a wide, free gesture, "I'll
show you tons of fresh water, right on the
coast." It is my opinion that the old man,

having been in the Galápagos for fifty years,
thought it time for a little change and a day
on a yacht with plenty of whiskey and cigars
appealed to him. However, he was as good as
his word. He showed us tons of fresh water.

After taking on a fresh supply of liquid treasure, Beebe
returned Johnson to the shack behind the lighthouse where
he lived with his mestizo wife. Then he and his water
supply left for Panama, and we return to return to Doña
Karin offering advice to Rolf Blomberg.

If anyone knows where the treasure is
hidden, it would be his old mestizo wife. Ask
Manuel to go with you, as he has a very good
relationship with her. You may get a clue, you
just never know."

I took a horse and galloped over to see Don
Manuel, who was supervising the work in his
coffee plantation. Yes, of course, he was willing
to go with me.

That very day—in a tropical shower—we rode
down to Wreck Bay. To us drenched horsemen
the sunburnt coastal plain was quite pleasant,
and we were in the best of moods when we
found the hut and knocked on the door. Mrs.
Johnson turned out to be a lovely old woman
with brown skin and good black eyes. Cobos
introduced us and she asked us in.

She made coffee for us in the kitchen, while I
looked around the cottage's only other room.
It was a homely and cozy mixture of new
and old, of valuable things and of cheap junk.
There were fine old ship models, seamen's
trunks, Chinese porcelain, and the cheap

junk. The walls were papered with illustrated periodicals and pages torn from colorful calendars. A large black tapestry covered something on the wall—I lifted the covering while the old lady busied herself in the kitchen. There were two beautiful portraits of the young Mr. and Mrs. Johnson: he a stately blond Englishman and she an enchanting woman from the South, a real beauty.

After a while, Mrs. Johnson arrived with coffee and a friendly smile. Cobos teased her and praised her fresh appearance, and she beamed like a sun at his every word. The conversation drifted toward treasure, with Cobos beating around the bush for awhile. Finally, he asked if she did not know on which island the treasure might be found.

Mrs. Johnson hesitated a moment, then went straight to the point: "I am old and poor, so if I knew where the treasure is, I would not doubt for a moment to tell you. I trust you, Cobos. I would ask my husband, 'Where is it?' And he would answer, 'It is on Isabela.' I would press for more details, and then: 'Did I say Isabela? I meant of course Floreana...' Finally, there was treasure to be found on five different islands.

"I have searched his papers and there is no map. And now I doubt there ever existed a treasure. I think that it was on account of good whiskey that he invented his story."

We don't really know if the old man found anything worth finding during his Galápagos lifetime. He may have acquired some small treasure after shooting the man he thought was a goat, but if so he said nothing about it to Señora Anita. He may still be searching for more: to this day his ghost roams the alleys of Puerto Baquerizo Moreno. If you doubt it, ask some of the old timers who have seen his shade.

There is some slight evidence that he may not have died empty-handed. Some years after Johnson/Levick embarked on his final voyage of no return, Nelson Campuzano of San Cristóbal spoke of Captain Pedro Campuzano, his father, who used to buy supplies for the old man. And why not?— Levick was a good customer who always paid his bills. In gold coin.

Where does one find gold coin in Galápagos? In the pocket of an old man? Surely not, unless that old man found the gold somewhere on an island. If he did, perhaps there's more still to be found. Perhaps you shall find it. Just look for an old chain and a huge lava boulder.

Captain Thomas "Johnson from London" Levick and his wife Anita at the time of William Beebe's visit in 1923.

Above: The pier at Wreck Bay, and in the background the lighthouse keeper's shack, home of Johnson from London and his wife Anita.

Below: Shacks on Isla San Cristóbal at the time of Johnson from London.

CHAPTER THIRTEEN

THE GALÁPAGOS DREAM

Den ecuadorianske regjering ønsker
enhver ærlig nordmand velkommen.

The Ecuadorian Government welcomes
every honest Norwegian.

February 1923
August F. Christensen

UGUST F. CHRISTENSEN — "AUG F." TO HIS FRIENDS — spent his youth aboard his father's whale-factory ship *Admiralen* working the southern coasts of South America. He also traveled extensively on the mainland, taught himself Spanish and English, and developed a great interest in the whale populations found between the Ecuadorian mainland and the Galápagos Islands. Always the entrepreneur, Aug F. eventually obtained permission for a Norwegian company, operating under the flag of Ecuador, to use the island of Floreana for its work. Back home in Oslo, he wrote several newspaper reports about the islands, and in 1918 became Ecuador's Consul in Norway.

Within five years, Aug F. had developed an ambitious colonization plan which included an agreement to give 20 hectares of land to any Norwegian who would come to Galápagos as a settler. But what would tempt an honest Norwegian to leave home for a new life on a remote island? As one enticement, Ecuador offered the incentive to live tax free for the first ten years and enjoy hunting, fishing and trapping rights on any colonized island.

Newspaper columnist Finn Støren's description of an island paradise and its current residents may also have exerted some influence:

> They were happy people. There were wives who prepared food. A cabin in which to live, food in unlimited quantities, together with total and infinite freedom to be enjoyed in the world's best climate. Is that not happiness? Could one wish for anything better? On San Cristóbal there are about 1,000 acres of cultivated land but there could be tenfold more. The soil is more-or-less free of rocks and easy to cultivate. About 10,000 cattle roam freely, but there is room for 50,000. It is a marvelous island, with water in abundance. Altogether there are five larger islands of similar fertility, some bigger, some smaller than Cristóbal. On these islands there should also be soil for new undertakings. Colonists could settle either on San Cristóbal, Isabela, Floreana, Santa Cruz or Santiago, all of which present great opportunities. The problem of water can be solved satisfactorily. All is arranged by nature so that an industrious and energetic colonist could be happy.

Støren assured his readers that they might enjoy excellent profits in fishing, whaling, seal hunting, agriculture and cattle ranching. Perhaps no one noticed that he mentioned both "water in abundance" and "the water problem" in the same paragraph, and that his authority came from less than one day spent on Isla Isabela, plus second-hand reports from his colleagues Per Bang and Jens Aschehoug. The two Norwegian journalists had lived for a time on Floreana after visiting Manuel Cobos, whom we met in an earlier chapter. But perhaps Støren thought the sources of his information weren't worth mentioning in public.

Next, Støren asked the obvious question: Why have the Ecuadorians themselves not taken advantage of all this? His answer was simple:

> They are not sailors, they have little or no understanding of the value of the ocean, and they already own good land on the continent. And so it is inconceivable for an Ecuadorian to look for an overseas challenge.

As for the Consul of Ecuador in Norway, it's doubtful that Christensen had even been to Galápagos at the time he proposed his colonization scheme and circulated the invitation to his honest Norwegian countrymen.

Right: August F. Christensen, in a photo taken aboard the *Floreana* on its way to the Galápagos Islands.

The local newspaper *Tidens Tegn* ("Signs of the Times") printed regular reports about the "Galápagos fever" that seemed to be spreading among its readers, and before too long the Swedish vessel *Start*—recently purchased by Aug F. and renamed *Floreana* in honor of its destination—sailed out of Sandefjord on the way to its island namesake. Aboard were some 20 pioneers; their number included a farmer, an accountant, a fisherman, blacksmith, teacher and a hotel manager. The *Floreana* arrived at the mouth of the Guayas River on July 9th, where the harbor pilot came aboard with the latest news: this very day marked the occasion of Ecuador's latest revolution! But there was no need to be concerned—the government remained in control, and all was peaceful in Guayaquil and Quito.

Galápagos development had been stalled since the murder of Manuel J. Cobos years earlier, and the Ecuadorians looked to the new arrivals to revive the archipelago's economy. Two weeks of welcoming parties followed, and then the

Floreana made its way to Wreck Bay, there to be greeted by "Johnson from London" and later on, by Manuel Augusto Cobos, who offered his Norwegian guests a tour of his sugar-refining enterprise. Later on, engineer Ludwig Ness recalled the dismal state of things:

> A factory such as this one I have never seen or heard of in all my life. The building itself was made of bamboo and rusty shells of corrugated iron. The machines were old, rusty, and highly unsanitary. The pipes through which the molasses flowed were not screwed together as we do it, and as a result much of the molasses was lost. The machines overheated and the poor foreman was scolded by the owner.

It would be best to move on, and so it was decided: the first Norwegian colony would be built at Post Office Bay on Isla Floreana. With their pilot—"Johnson from London" of course—the *Floreana* departed for its new home port. There it took them about two weeks to unload some 300 tons of equipment, and then construction began on their "Casa Matriz" (Motherhouse) headquarters.

The Motherhouse on Isla Floreana. Today, all that remain are the cement posts.

While exploring the Floreana terrain, a lava tube behind the building was discovered by one of the colonists. In the past it had been discovered the hard way by the tortoises that wandered the island. The Norwegians found their bones deep in the depths, for there was no way out for them. All the tortoises are gone now, and so is Casa Matriz.

Aug F. drew up a map of the island, showing the 50-acre plots of ground awarded to each settler, and the important landmarks—Wegger Hill, Øvreberg, Ranvig and Kamfjord Bays, and of course the Waardahl and Stub headlands. Like Casa Matriz and the tortoises, the names are gone now.

The Post Office Bay area on a Floreana map drawn in 1925 by Aug F. and Anton Stub.

Later on the *Floreana* began its first charter operation, transporting cattle and prisoners from Isla Isabela to Guayaquil. The cattle were winched aboard by ropes tied to their horns. Presumably, other means were used for the prisoners. When the ship reached the mainland, the Norwegians found that history had repeated itself; the recent attempt at revolution had been given a second chance, and this time met with success. The new administration regarded the settlers favorably, but the economy did not. For lack of work, the *Floreana* sat idle in Guayaquil, while out on the island the cattle ranching was not going well at all. Expected additional settlers from Norway did not arrive, and the colonists were running out of vital supplies. The teacher and the hotel manager had enough, and left for home. Put to the test, the pioneering spirit showed every sign of failing.

Eventually, a long-awaited second ship, the diminutive *Isabela*, arrived under the command of Paul Bruun, whom we shall meet again later on. But in the meantime, the *Floreana* had been sold off, all but a handful of the remaining settlers had decided to leave, and the management company back in Norway was close to bankruptcy. Yet despite all this, plans were in the works at home to form another company, this time with Isla Santa Cruz as its headquarters. Again an epidemic of "Galápagos fever" broke out in Norway, and soon enough the wooden schooner *Alatga* was purchased to bring out another 30 settlers. But demand exceeded all expectations and a second ship, the *Ulva*, was readied for the expedition. *La Compania de Santa Cruz* counted more than 80 members ready to make the long voyage to Galápagos.

The *Floreana, Isabela* and *Ulva* were the first three ships to make the long voyage from Norway to Galápagos.

After the obligatory stop at Isla San Cristóbal, the *Ulva* came close to meeting its end on the rocks that Captain Porter assured his readers weren't there—Arrecife MacGowen. But a quick-acting helmsman averted tragedy, much to the relief of the passengers, and the delight of the few remaining Floreana settlers who greeted the ship on its arrival at Post Office Bay. The *Ulva* spent a few days there, then proceeded to its destination at the uninhabited Isla Santa Cruz. But the island was not uninhabited after all—five Ecuadorians had been there for about a year, and one old Mexican was said to be up in the highlands, where he'd spent the last 15 years. But never mind them, the accompanying Ecuadorian officers invited the Norwegians to settle wherever they pleased.

The unfortunate *Alatga* in Norway. It would later be known to its passengers as *Aktafortvers* ("Back-forthsideways").

All things considered, the *Alatga* should never have left port. The diary of Sigvart Tuset contains an entry written when the ship finally reached Panama City.

> Of the 42 persons who traveled with *Alatga*
> from Tønsberg, four continued the journey to
> Galápagos.

What happened to make the others quit is not a pleasant story, which begins shortly after departure with engine failure. The voyage of a few days through the English Channel took two weeks, and the Norwegians faced a slow passage to the Canary Islands where they hoped the engines might be put back in operation. But the repairs were unsuccessful and the *Alatga* sailed on to the American Virgin Islands, where the passengers were not permitted to land without visas. Before reaching Panama the fresh food ran out and the voyagers had to make do with salt beef and canned goods. At the Canal, they discovered debts run up by the *Ulva* and were denied passage until the bill could be settled. Eventually, money was sent from home for transit fees and the repair of the engines. But the Captain gave the wrong instructions to the local machine shop and the repaired parts were useless. The first and second mates quit to work on farms in the Canal Zone.

To save money, the ship's water tanks were filled directly from Gatun Lake during the Canal transit. The water had an awful stink and a taste of decayed plants. On finally entering the Pacific, some passengers were laid low from vomiting and diarrhea. The potatoes had gone rotten, and the flour was a haven for maggots. The rigging was destroyed during a heavy gale and it was decided to return to Panama for more repairs. But sailing by dead reckoning, mistakes were made and the ship sailed off in the wrong direction. By the time they regained Panama City, five weeks had passed. Three futile months were spent there trying to obtain funds for repair work, and then the ship was sold. With the four exceptions mentioned by Sigvart Tuset, the entire ship's company dispersed—some to Central America, others to South America, and others home to Norway.

Tuset and his companions made their way to Guayaquil, where they arrived in time to arrange passage on Bruun's *Isabela*, scheduled to leave the next day on its return to Isla Santa Cruz.

Below: Harry Randall organized the largest expedition from Norway to Galápagos aboard his ship *Albemarle*.

Yet within the year, another expedition left Norway for Galápagos, this one under the direction of entrepreneur Harry Randall, who for a time was a theater director and artists' agent, later ran a cigar factory and then an import business in the United States. Back in Norway, he tried his hand at magazine publishing and was coauthor of a book titled *Galápagos—World's End: The Norwegian Paradise on South America's West Coast.*" The other authors were Aug F., Finn Støren and Per Bang, one of the journalists recently entertained by Manuel Augusto Cobos. The book played its part in spreading "Galápagos Fever" and Randall had no trouble booking 78 passengers on his ship *Albemarle*. Among them were the widower farmer Thorleiv Guldberg, his son Frithjof and daughters Snefrid and Karin. Lars Elholm later wrote about their arrival in paradise:

> About 3:30 in the morning the lookout announced there was something ahead that looked like a dark thundercloud, and he thought we must be very near land. But the helmsman insisted there were still several hours to go before the island would come into view and that it was indeed a cloud.
>
> There was a smell of rotten seaweed, and a few minutes later we heard breakers roar like a storm. Through the darkness we caught glimpses of white foam where waves broke against a shore directly in front of us. "Hard to starboard!" was called and at the last moment we managed to turn the ship and headed back out to await the dawn.
>
> With it came a proper view of San Cristóbal, so very different from the tropical island we had imagined. There were gray lava boulders along the entire shoreline, and higher up an intertwined jungle of thorny, ugly bushes. No tall trees, no green grass, and the disappointment was plain on all faces. We had staked all that we owned and gone through a lot of difficulties, but as we stood there looking at the island we understood that our difficulties were just beginning. We did not have long to wait.

A group went off to explore the highlands, and once again Manuel Augusto Cobos came on the scene, making a good first impression by revealing his admiration for the bard of Norway, Henrik Ibsen. Cobos and his brother-in-law Rogerio Alvarado persuaded the Norwegians to settle on their island, rather than continue to Floreana or Santa Cruz. Before long, the ship was unloaded and prepared to return to Panama to be sold. A map was drawn up to show the 50 acre plots assigned to each settler, and a village which did not yet exist was given a name: Campo Noruega.

But there was trouble brewing: the island highlands bear no resemblance to the "Norwegian paradise" promised in Harry Randall's book. On re-reading the newspaper accounts of Aug F., one settler laughed until he cried at what was now seen to be pure fiction. Randall was accused of cheating, and it was said that Cobos and Alvarado worked out a private deal to pay him for each Norwegian who would agree to settle here. In time, the colonists discovered that their land was close to useless, and Alvarado was pressured into giving them plots in a better location, even though this meant yet another move.

Many decide it is time to quit paradise and return to Norwegian earth. Randall prudently realizes that he'd better leave the island before it's too late, but the crew on the *Albemarle* toss him into the sea when he tried to come on board for the trip back to Panama. Later on, he would write in his diary about their departure:

> At 1 o'clock today, *Albemarle* left for Panamá with the following crew: Captain Deetjen who gets drunk whenever he is ashore; first mate Andersen, who drinks anything others pay for; second mate Lund, arrested by the police when we were in Las Palmas because of drunkenness and disorderly behavior; steward Lunde, former choir singer at the Opera Comique Oslo, an incurable and brutal drunkard who was arrested in Panamá; third mate Bjørnstad the same; he jumped overboard while drunk in Las Palmas; fully dressed and with his pipe in his mouth, he swam around the ship. As

a result of that he developed pneumonia. Jørgen Bjørnholdt, disowned by his family on account of drinking. Guttorm Pettersen, also whenever possible went ashore and returned drunk and unable to work; he was paid off recently when, in his usual state again, he refused to work.

Ship owner Stray gets dead drunk every time he has money; on our voyage he served as third engineer. Luckily, the two other engineers, Musikka and Stokkevaag, are decent people, as are the two assistants, but God forbid, what a crew!

If half of what Randall wrote were actually true, it were no bad thing that he was obliged to wait on the island for some other passage back to reality. In the meantime, Manuel Cobos insisted that Randall be his house guest for as long as he pleases, and the two friends spent hours together on horseback during the day, and more hours at night playing chess and talking. Yet despite their growing friendship, Randall was depressed by what he sees in the village:

In the two or three company stores found here, merchandise is never wrapped. The buyer always has a piece of cloth at hand and wraps sugar in one corner, flour in the other, salt in a third, and corn in a fourth. At the butcher's, where cattle are slaughtered just outside, the meat is sold while still warm. The blood is lapped up by the roaming dogs and pigs, and when the animal is tied to be slaughtered, all the dogs in the village gather to partake of the feast.

Wine and spirits are always at hand. But instead of washing wine glasses, the cook empties the remains on the floor, dries the glass with his fingers or with a dirty towel and afterwards places it upside down, back on the table, which remains set day and night.

> Lack of cleanliness is simply comical. Walls and
> floors are not tight, air passes through the cracks,
> and when one sweeps the upper story, dust falls
> down into the office and shop downstairs. All
> kinds of dirty people come and go upstairs on
> different errands. The communal water toilet
> is in a room without a door, so one risks being
> interrupted by a lady while in the middle of
> one's intimate business; I prefer the green woods.

After a month or so, Harry Randall arranged passage to Guayaquil, where the governor passed on some interesting news about the plots of land and the cattle that were distributed to the colonists: Neither Manuel Cobos nor Rogerio Alvarado owned the land that was sold, nor the animals that roamed upon it.

Despite all, a handful of settlers stayed on after the departure of the *Albemarle* and Harry Randall. A few others remained on Isla Santa Cruz. But within a few years, an informal census revealed the following statistics about the ships' passengers who could still be found in paradise:

From the *Floreana*, none,
From the *Isabela*, one,
From the *Ulva*, two,
From the *Alatga*, none,
From the *Albemarle*, seven.

Of these ten survivors, two would come to a bad end, and one would marry Manuel Augusto Cobos. That was Doña Karin, but the marriage didn't last.

CHAPTER FOURTEEN

THE VOYAGES OF THE VELERO III

Captain Hancock is a scientist and explorer.
No ordinary yacht will fill his needs.

—G. Bruce Newby, Naval Architect

APRIL 2, 1931. WITH CROWDS OF SPECTATORS LOOKING ON at the Craig Shipbuilding yard in Long Beach, California, the super cruiser *Velero III* was released from her tethers and slowly slid sidewise to water's edge. The ship keeled over, almost flat upon her side, and the judgment of those who knew about these things was confirmed: the radical design of the hull structure was unsound—the ship would founder before it would float.

But *Velero III* was having none of this; taking but a moment to compose herself, the lady gracefully assumed a position more appropriate for her station as the third generation in the *Velero* family. Her proud patriarch was the wealthy (obviously) California industrialist George Allan Hancock, who was about to prove the authorities wrong. Marine architects had informed him that *Velero III's* stern design was dangerous and would surely force the bow under, followed shortly by the rest of the ship. But Hancock was used to such pronouncements. Several shipbuilders had refused to work on his designs for the first *Velero*, and when one eventually agreed to do the job, the man refused to board the ship for its shakedown cruise unless a rowboat was in tow. Hancock obliged, but the precaution was unnecessary; the ship performed beautifully in a well-timed storm, and the builder, in spite of himself, was impressed.

243

Eventually the Captain required more than the little *Velero* could deliver, and a larger *Velero II* was built. Still later he acquired a British Mystery Ship recently decommissioned after the Great War. Outwardly resembling a slow-moving merchant vessel, the Mystery Ship was in fact a decoy set to attract German submarines, which preferred to destroy such ships by gunfire, thus saving torpedoes for more important prey. When a sub would move in for the kill the ship would  reveal itself as a fast-moving armored attack vessel with a steel ram extending forward just below the waterline. Such a ship was just what was needed to quickly transport produce to California from *Hacienda Barron*, Hancock's farm in Mexico. Rechristened *Oaxaca*, the vessel served its owner well until an unfortunate run-in with a poorly-marked channel left it on the rocks. The career of the *Oaxaca* was over, and the Captain moved on to *Velero III*.

Above: Captain Hancock at work in the chart room.
Facing page: The *Velero III*.

Hancock commissioned naval architect G. Bruce Newby to transform his ideas from paper to reality, to create a "super cruiser" (Newby's own description) with a profile resembling a Coast Guard cutter. Although the Captain wanted the interior appointments to be kept simple—Newby described them as "austere but pleasing"—no detail was to be overlooked in providing the owner and his guests with what he required; comfort but not luxury. Topside were two steel whaleboats, two wooden shore boats, and two smaller skiffs. Within, a grand stairway led from the Social Hall to the cabins below and aft, all equipped with special beds featuring the latest "Ace Coil" springs and "Beautyrest" mattresses from Simmons, all guaranteed to be the last word in creature comfort.

The public understandably saw *Velero III* as something it was not: the ultimate pleasure craft to transport a well-heeled captain of industry off to some exotic destination, accompanied by admiring friends who could afford to leave the cares of the city behind for weeks — perhaps months — at a time. But that was not what *Velero III* was all about. Hancock did not waste time in idle pursuits and when he traveled, he traveled for a purpose. His ship was a fully-equipped marine laboratory, his guests were distinguished scientists, his destinations were chosen for their research potential. And so it was only fitting that the first voyage of the *Velero III*, and the first of ten Allan Hancock Pacific Expeditions in the decade leading up to the Second World War, would be to the Galápagos Islands. The Captain knew of the islands from an earlier visit on the *Oaxaca*, and looked forward to this return visit, in company with several guests. Among their number were ship's "medicine man" Edwin Palmer, M. D., and scientists John Garth and C. B. ("Cy") Perkins.

While in Galápagos, the Hancock party meddled in the business of Mother Nature, and by so doing, probably saved a race of land iguanas from extinction.

On the morning of Thursday, January 14th, 1932, the *Velero III* made an anchorage off South Seymour Island. Once ashore, John Garth spotted his first land iguana, which Dr. Palmer asked him to capture for the benefit of his movie camera. The job was done with such ease that Palmer (perhaps the first Galápagos film director), had him repeat the scene for the benefit of the production. Whatever satisfaction Garth may have had with his bring-em-back-alive skills was short-lived: Cy Perkins pointed out that the catch of the day was half-starved, and thus not up to the task of eluding its captor. This proved the case with most of the animals in the surrounding area. Perkins noted that all but a few were quite thin, and some were little more than living skeletons.

On visiting North Seymour Island a few days later, the terrain appeared more favorable for land iguanas, with abundant cactus and no wild dogs or goats. There was only one thing missing to complete the picture: land iguanas. And this gave Captain Hancock an idea. Today the same idea would get him tossed off the island, but if it hadn't occurred to him then, there would be nothing to write about now. For better or worse, the Captain's idea was to capture the iguanas of South Seymour and release them on North Seymour. Then he'd come back in a year or so to see what happened to them. "A good idea I believe. No harm anyhow, as far as I can see" wrote Perkins in his diary. And so it was decided.

The next day a seventeen-man landing party was dispatched to the north end of South Seymour to stage an iguana roundup. The afternoon release of the animals on North Seymour was as well recorded as any Hollywood opening, with both motion-picture and still-camera coverage. Nevertheless, the stars of the day did not much care for their spotlight, and many needed a gentle prodding to induce some action for the cameras. Once coaxed out of the transport cage, the saurian celebrities ignored their admiring public and beat a hasty retreat to shelter under the nearby cactus plants.

On North Seymour Island, Captain Hancock supervises the delivery of iguanas rounded up on South Seymour Island.

The ship departed South Seymour the following morning, and after several more weeks of exploration, the first voyage of the *Velero III* was done. But before the end of the same year, Hancock was ready to revisit Galápagos and look in on the newly-tenanted North Seymour. The Captain invited writer George Hugh Banning to join the group, and this second voyage reached Galápagos in January. On arriving at North Seymour Island, Banning jotted down some reservations on what had taken place here the previous year:

> The practice, and, especially, the irresponsible practice, of rearranging the island fauna, might lead the investigations of others somewhat afield. Hear ye, therefore, and be it known nevertheless, that some seventy iguanas, including a second transport, have been carried across the channel from the southern to the northern Seymour, investigations having shown to our utmost satisfaction that the emigrants of last year were still there and doing splendidly.

A third voyage brought the Hancock party back to North Seymour one year later, where Garth recorded seeing numerous iguana burrows, though the animals themselves kept out-of-sight (fearing perhaps yet another ride in a cage?). On this trip, Dr. Palmer recalled that "We had removed to North Seymour 72 land iguanas in 1932 for lack of food, but today the vegetation [on South Seymour] was very fair and there seemed to be no dearth of iguanas of which we took many pictures, and several were taken for mounting." It's tempting to speculate that if this had been Captain Hancock's first encounter with the iguanas of South Seymour, it might not have occurred to him to intercede in their affairs, and this story might have ended on a much sadder note.

Again in 1934, December 13th brought the fourth voyage of the *Velero III* to North Seymour for another site inspection. Hancock went off scouting for his charges, finding two in excellent condition, an old egg, and an island generally honeycombed with fresh burrows. From all evidence, it was judged that the colonists were doing quite well.

Hancock made his final visit to Galápagos on the seventh voyage of the *Velero III* in 1938. The eighth voyage ventured no farther south than Panama, and the remaining two were confined to Baja California. And then it was 1941. The *Velero III* was acquired by the U. S. Navy, where it became the U. S. S. *Chalcedony*, assigned to weather station duty out of Pearl Harbor. At war's end, Hancock acquired the *Velero IV*, and his former vessel passed to the American Independent Oil Company. Business must have been good, for $1,000,000 was spent to convert it from the comfortable austerity of the Hancock era into the luxury cruiser *M'y Ahmady* for Ahmad Al-Jaber Al-Subah, Sheik of Kuwait.

And the rest, as they say, is history.

The captain of the *Velero III* is remembered in Galápagos today by Banco Hancock, found almost submerged about midway between Islas Floreana and Santa Fe.

A JUNE 19TH, 1991 POSTSCRIPT. Representatives of the Ecuadorian Navy and Air Force, the Charles Darwin Research Station and the Galápagos National Park Service gathered on Isla Baltra, known in the days of Allan Hancock as South Seymour Island and now the site of the airport. The occasion was to welcome the arrival of some three dozen young settlers—all five-year olds, all land iguanas raised at the Charles Darwin Research Station on nearby Isla Santa Cruz.

Their parents were none other than the tenants of North Seymour Island. In previous years, scientists had dropped in on the little island to the north to see how the colony was getting on. The Hancock elders were still there—iguanas live to a ripe old age—but youngsters were rarely spotted. And so it was decided to intercede once again with Mother Nature. Adults were brought over to the Research Station so that their offspring might be raised under the most favorable conditions.

The project worked, and it worked well. And now it was time to bring the youngsters to their ancestral home. In subsequent years, the North Seymour adults have been left at home, but their nesting sites have been monitored. Freshly-laid eggs are now transported to the Research Station for incubation and hatching.

National Park Warden Cirilo Barrera escorts the descendants of the Hancock transfer to their ancestral home on Isla Baltra.

All things considered, the repatriated iguana population is doing rather well, although there have been casualties. Evolution will not be hurried, and the creatures still don't understand that a parked vehicle is something beyond a convenient source of shade from the equatorial sun. The Galápagos land iguana is never in a hurry to move, so by the time an engine starts and a wheel turns, it is probably too late. Nevertheless, the iguana population of Isla Baltra is slowly increasing, which is something that might not have been said were it not for the voyages of the *Velero III*.

Of course George Allan Hancock had interests in creatures other than iguanas, but that's another story. Or rather, another chapter.

CHAPTER FIFTEEN

MARGRET AND THE BARONESS

I can hardly resist the feeling that in
my time I have indeed slept upon evilly
enchanted ground.

—Herman Melville: *The Encantadas*

D ID MELVILLE HAVE A SPECIFIC ISLAND IN MIND as the
place of evil enchantment? Perhaps he was thinking
of Charles Island, now better known as Floreana, and
then known as the late abode of Irish Patrick Watkins,
described by Captain David Porter in a previous chapter.
To anyone careless enough to tarry here, Watkins would
offer a generous cup, and then another, and again another.
In time—of which Watkins had plenty—the unwary visitor
would reach that rum-sotted stage in which navigation
was out of the question. At this point the indisposed guest
would be stowed out of sight until his shipmates gave up
the search. And then there would be one more somber
seaman to join the ranks of Irish Pat's brigade at the dawn
of a new and sober day. Or so the legend of the great South
Sea would have it, and Melville offered this bit of advice
to those who might see a welcoming light penetrating the
blackness of a Galápagos night:

That is Charles Island; brace up, Mr. Mate,
and keep the light astern.

Yet the island was not without its charms, one of which was water, a liquid luxury never to be underestimated in Galápagos. Floreana had it, its neighboring isles didn't. Seventeenth-century mariners knew of this oasis, which out of respect the Spaniards called Santa María de la Aquada. And when British buccaneers discovered what the Spaniards knew, the island became for a time their exclusive retreat. The merry boys would come here to relax in highland caves near a welcome spring and for their greater comfort they fashioned benches in the walls. Here they would recline to dream of calm seas and prosperous vessels awaiting their piratical pleasure. But that was a long time ago; three centuries and more have passed since the cave dwellers dallied on Floreana. In Darwinian terms their residence was brief, and except for their caves and their benches, there is nothing here to recall them.

Not too long after the last buccaneer sailed away, the enchanted—and at last, reasonably safe—waters began to attract the rival whaling fleets of England and her former colonies. One day, somebody established a post office on a Floreana beach, the one that Captain David Porter used to his great advantage. But even that was a long time ago; soon two centuries will have passed since Hathaway and Porter followed the pirates and Patrick into history.

The post office lives on however, now as a tourist attraction, and no doubt the only such establishment in the world where stamps are neither available nor required. If you would drop off mail here, you must first inspect the barrel's contents for messages addressed to your little corner of the world. If you find one, you are to take it with you and see to its proper delivery. This is the custom, if not the law, and you do well to remember that Floreana is not pleased with those who lack the proper respect for her ways.

These days there is a fairly regular traffic of tourists who walk the few feet from shore to barrel, drop off their mail, take the obligatory souvenir photograph, stand around for a moment, then depart with a post card for some perfect stranger back home.

The Post Office barrel continually changes its look as visitors drop off souvenirs around it. The barrel itself is not always easy to spot.

There is more to see here, though not many do. Walk on a few paces, then stop and look about. Here and there one sees concrete slabs, the earthly remains of the Norwegian colonists' Casa Matriz headquarters from the 1920s. A few of their roads—if you would call them that—are marked off with stones. Walk past an intersection—it's the only one— and then on just a bit farther to a few concrete steps now leading nowhere. But don't stop. At the head of the steps is a path, also marked off with stones, and the path soon passes a small tree, and next to the tree is a deep hole. This is the entrance to the lava tube discovered by Rolf Sønderskov in 1925.

Ask your guide to bring along a sturdy coil of rope. Tie one end about the tree, toss the other into the hole and drop in for a closer look. At the bottom you'll find a crawl space leading to blackness. A few feet on hands and knees and the space opens up. But don't stand. There's one more drop-off ahead, after which you find yourself in a very large subterranean cave. Bring a flashlight (in case you should want to get out again) and begin walking down a gentle incline until your feet find water. The incline continues and the water is soon waist deep. At some unknown point there is an opening to the sea, but no one has had sufficient curiosity to find it. That is, no one who has come back to talk about it.

But now it's time to return to sunlight, past the ghosts of Norwegian fishermen, past Hathaway's Post Office, and onward to a little more Floreana history.

At about the time of the Norwegian venture, William Beebe's *Galápagos: World's End* caught the public fancy. Although the author offered a reasonably accurate picture of the equatorial landscape, not a few European readers read into his description a bit more than he actually wrote. Readers in pre-Hitler Germany perceived Galápagos to be a rustic garden of Eden, something their troubled homeland certainly was not. Yet for most of them, the islands remained a distant and unattainable dreamland.

Below: Dr. Ritter as a young man in Germany.

For most, but not for all. Friedrich Ritter served the Kaiser in the trenches of the first World War, survived, then went on to practice medicine and preach philosophy. His vocation brought him to the Hydrotherapeutic Clinic in Berlin, where his avocation brought him to Dore Strauch Koerwin, a young woman whose maladies included early multiple sclerosis and a terminally-dull husband. The good doctor diligently worked on the lady's body and mind, and soon enough the pair were spending a bit of time in Ritter's office, and a bit more of it on the roof of the office building. Here, Dore absorbed Ritter's view of the world, a wacky wonderland where another Friedrich (Nietzsche) stood at one pole, Laotse was at the other, and the doctor himself was poised at epicenter. It was a world well-suited to Dore, who would later write that a woman's lack of emotional control kept her nearer the earth than a man. Dore made perfect sense at all times, if only to herself. As for Herr Koerwin, he allowed Frau Dore to get away with murder, much to her disgust. She wanted a *real* man such as Friedrich to be her master. She got her wish.

The doctor prescribed a life of contemplation for himself and his disciple. And as a likely venue in which to put his philosophic theories to practice, he selected Galápagos, and the island called Floreana. Here he—and now, Dore too— would learn to stifle their animal instincts and intellectualize the emotional side of their curious relationship. Dore was strictly cautioned that Herr Doktor would tolerate none of that cheap physical stuff. Or as he himself put it with Teutonic tact, "I cannot have a love-sick woman full of romantic notions trailing after me into the wilderness." But if Dore thought she could limp along at his surly side, well then she might as well give it a try for all he cared.

Given the Ritter philosophy and Dore's willing acquiescence, it may come as no big surprise that their respective spouses offered little objection to the joint venture. In fact, Dore even persuaded Frau Ritter to take a position as housekeeper to her husband. Herr Koerwin agreed to the arrangement on one condition: that Dore must promise never to come back to him again.

In preparation for departure Ritter had all his teeth pulled. As a vegetarian he saw little need for them; as a pragmatist he knew there would be no dentists in paradise. Dore's teeth, such as they were, remained in place, and at last the deadly duo departed Germany in July of 1929. For Dr. Ritter, it would be a one-way trip.

Their first few years on Floreana were passed in a solitude punctuated every now and then by the arrival of other would-be settlers on the *Manuel J. Cobos*. This derelict vessel made regular passages between Guayaquil and Galápagos, with "regular" defined as whenever the owners could round up enough business to make it worth the bother. This worked out to about once every six months or so. The captain, Paul Edvard Bruun, was a Norwegian of dubious credentials who had somehow or other established himself in Ecuador. According to Dore, the story around Guayaquil was that Bruun had been obliged to leave Norway in some haste after the Great War when the wrong side won and it was discovered he had been retailing British naval secrets to the Germans. So Bruun sailed off to sea in his tiny boat *Isabela*, and on the way to Ecuador he "lost" his identity papers in a typhoon. This remarkable tempest conveniently washed away his past while sparing his present—the ship itself and its crew of three. The Ecuadorian authorities, who do love a good story, promptly issued Bruun whatever he needed to stick around and become a local captain.

Some years after transporting Friedrich and Dore to their Floreana hideaway, Bruun announced that he would join them as a settler. He had now had quite enough of the *Manuel J. Cobos* and saw greater opportunities on Floreana, where he and his Norwegian compatriot Knud Arends would revive the fishing industry, if not the fame of Norway. Within a few weeks he was dead.

Another *Isabela* now entered his life, and this one terminated it. After establishing himself on Floreana, Captain Bruun went off in his motor launch to nearby Isla Isabela to pick up supplies at Villamil for his enterprise. But he overlooked his fuel supply and on the way back to Floreana, just what you would expect to happen happened. So the Norwegian anchored his little *Norge* in a sheltered cove and tried his luck in a rowboat recently swiped from Dr. Ritter. But as Bruun had recently had enough of the *Manuel J. Cobos,* so the gods of Galápagos had now had enough of Bruun.

The wind quickly demolished his improvised sail. The end was near, but Bruun didn't know it yet. He managed to row back to Villamil and there the gods had their next little joke: the now-punctual *Manuel J. Cobos* sailed into view, and its new captain offered to transport Bruun, Ritter's rowboat, and the necessary fuel back to the *Norge,* there to stand by until Bruun was ready to follow his wake back to Floreana.

But Bruun was no one's follower. He challenged the captain to a race and, the wager accepted, rowed off with a few Indians to fuel the *Norge* while his recent rescuer got underway with all due haste for Floreana. But he needn't have hurried, for the Norwegian and the *Norge* were not to be reunited. As salvation steamed smartly out of view, one of Bruun's Indians dropped an oar, reached overboard for it, and that was the beginning of the end. The boat was swamped by one wave and then by another. The crew lost whatever racing interest they had previously enjoyed and prudently abandoned boat. All except Bruun. He stuck it out until only his stubborn skull could be seen above the surf. Then a great wave lifted him clear of his craft, and the next after that delivered him from a watery grave by smashing the life out of him against the rocks. The shore-bound Indians dragged their former Captain up on the beach, dug a hasty grave, then made their way back once again to Villamil, this time by foot.

Captain Paul Edvard Bruun, late of Norway, Guayaquil and Floreana would not be the only twentieth-century entrepreneur to come to a bad end in this evilly enchanted ground. In fact, even Dore herself would one day write that "these islands are, in truth, one of those places of the earth where humans are not tolerated." But she would need to spend a few more years here before coming around to that way of thinking. For the moment, she and her doctor were suffered to survive. And with Bruun gone to whatever heavenly haven awaited him, the couple had their earthly, earthy paradise all to themselves. Their estate, by the way, had come to be called "Friedo" after the first names of the landlord and his limping lady. And now it seemed they might live on here more or less undisturbed, except by each other of course.

And soon it was 1932. In Germany Heinz Wittmer made a living of sorts on the staff of the Lord Mayor of Cologne, Konrad Adenauer. But given the way his country was about to go, this was a position without much future. Perhaps Heinz sensed he might go nowhere, or worse. Among his modest assets were counted Margret, a new wife who thought she might be slightly pregnant, Harry, a young and sickly son from before Margret's time, ... and a copy of William Beebe.

The German physicians wanted Harry placed in a sanitarium for a few years, but Dr. Beebe's book offered another prospect. Heinz and Margret would take the lad to Galápagos, where a more hospitable climate might do better for him than the winters of home. Margret's impending confinement was of course a consideration, but Heinz had heard of a Dr. Ritter who had settled there and who would surely help if there should come a need. And so one more set of pioneers embarked on a search for enchantment, and on landing at Floreana, more than doubled the census. Friedrich and Dore, who were now "The Ritters," were not pleased.

Yet Heinz and Margret were an unassuming enough couple. They might even have been judged likable, if only the Ritters had been capable of liking anyone but their respective and individual selves. Heinz lost no time in accurately assessing Ritter's personality—or lack thereof. As for Dore, small talk did not slip lightly from her lips. Many years later, Margret recalled their first meeting. "What," asked Dore, "do you think of Nietzsche?" The new arrivals quickly agreed between themselves: it would be best to give these people lots of space.

The Wittmers in 1938. Margret with her second-born, Ingeborg Floreanita, and Heinz with his ever-present pipe.

The Wittmers took up their first residence in the pirate caves, sufficiently removed from Friedo as not to burden the Ritters with neighbors. Their homestead may still be visited by anyone with time for a two-hour stroll into the highlands–just follow the one and only "highway" leading away from the dock area. While there, have a look at an "ancient" stone face carved into the rocks. Stories of its existence drifted back to civilization and brought Thor Heyerdahl of *Kon-Tiki* fame to the islands. He asked Herr Wittmer for help in finding the mysterious monument. With a sheepish grin, Heinz said that would be no trouble at all, for he knew exactly where to find it, having carved it himself some years earlier. The Heyerdahl group had a good laugh, followed by a toast to "homo Wittmerensis" and then went off elsewhere in search of the great Inca.

Above: the author and the Inca. The author is the one on the left.

Heinz and Margret would refer to their earliest household as "Asilo de la Paz" or haven of peace, a name not new to Floreana. It was the name General José Villamil used here a century earlier, when he attempted to colonize the island with that gang of Ecuadorian soldiers who were otherwise scheduled for execution. But by the time of the Wittmers, this venture had also been abandoned and all the principals were now long dead.

The Wittmers were hardly unpacked when the weirdest entourage of them all arrived, against which the Ritter household would appear to be normalcy itself. The new group comprised one Baroness Eloise Wehrborn de Wagner-Bousquet, a descendant—according to no less an authority than herself—of both Franz Lizst and Richard Wagner. Waiting in respectful attendance upon her ladyship were her companions Alfred Rudolf Lorenz and Robert Philippson, with supplementary services rendered by Manuel Valdivieso Borja, a local citizen who had with favorable notices come to the attention of Baroness and Company. Don Manuel, tall, dark and Latin, was expected to be quite useful to the Baroness in realizing her plan to transform Floreana into an international resort. As the lady graciously informed the local press before quitting the mainland, "My hotel and residence station will be arranged to provide comforts for tourists and immigrants of the better races." Indeed, it was to be known as Hacienda Paradiso. Again, the Ritters were not pleased. This time, neither were the Wittmers.

For a time Lorenz enjoyed top billing in the lady's pecking order, but he was soon replaced by Philippson, whom the Baroness took to identifying as "baby" or, when dignity demanded, "my husband" although her real husband had been mislaid somewhere back in Europe. While Valdivieso continued to render supplementary services, mostly to the Baroness, Lorenz' social standing deteriorated quickly, along with his mental and physical health. Within a few months, he was little more than a slave to Eloise and her husband du jour. For a while Valdivieso obligingly helped Philippson thrash Lorenz, but given the realities of Floreana's demographics, he soon enough realized he was a stranger in his own land. Eventually he packed it in and left to seek saner ground.

To wile away her idle hours, the Baroness (Margret took to calling her "Madam") found some amusement by shooting animals and nursing them back to health. One fine day she tried out her little hobby on something a bit higher up the food chain. The Norwegian Knud Arends, former partner of the late Captain Bruun, had come over for a hunting expedition, and Madam apparently mistook him for a cow and "accidentally" placed a bullet in his belly. Madam herself insisted it was all a big mistake, and deputized Philippson to accompany the target back to Guayaquil for treatment. Meanwhile, Madam continued the business of establishing herself as the terror of Floreana, much to the delight of the international press, if not of her fellow residents. Thanks to her well-publicized antics, the little kingdom by the sea was soon marked by the international yachting set as a spot definitely not to be missed on the watery grand tour.

The Danish journalist Hakon Mielche dropped in one day on semi-official business: while at nearby Isla San Cristóbal, the governor prevailed on him to deliver the mail to the Floreana residents. First stop, Paradise, where with critical eye Mielche preserved Madam and her consorts for posterity.

The Baroness was small, but one could not say that she was beautiful. In front of her swollen lids she wore strong spectacles and her mouth, though too large, was yet unable to cover her long, yellow, rabbit teeth. She moved in that hopping manner which jockeys call a "canter." Baby looked as though he had been a gigolo in a very cheap restaurant somewhere in Berlin.

His eyes were a watery blue, his hair was curly and his smile much too sweet. A German cook (Lorenz), tubercular and with one foot in the grave, smiled sicklily from the background and brought tea.

After a few hours in Paradise, Mielche moved on to the Eden of the Ritters.

Ritter was fairly small, his legs had been screwed on wrong, so that his toes pointed inwards. His nose was long and pointed, he had watery, protruding eyes and the hair of a prophet. His disciple, Miss Dora, smiled a toothless welcome. The couple had at their disposal only one pair of false teeth and this was Ritter's day.

Mielche was not one to overlook a watery eye, a bad hair day or a smile—sweet, sicklily or toothless. Perhaps he'd heard about Dr. Frankenstein's monster, he whose "teeth of a pearly whiteness formed a more horrid contrast with his watery eyes."

After exchanging pleasantries with the Baroness and the Ritters, his final stop would be the Haven of Peace, there to deliver an old newspaper and a few letters to Heinz Wittmer. Given his recent experiences at Paradise and Eden, Mielche wondered what weirdness would be served up at the Haven, but Wittmer was a pleasant surprise:

His quietness had a beneficial effect on the young postman who had spent the entire day among pirate queens and naked philosophical dentists with rat-like movements and dirty toes. Wittmer was the island's one and only stable point.

Back in simpler days when the prophet of Floreana and the not-yet toothless Miss Dora were the island's solitary residents, the American industrialist/philanthropist and amateur cellist Captain G. Allan Hancock would stop by on the several voyages of the *Velero III*. The Captain was intrigued by the Doctor and—when not engaged in transplanting land iguanas—would enjoy a visit to Friedo. Ritter liked the visits too, for Captain could always be counted on to leave gifts. On subsequent visits Hancock added the names of the Wittmers and the Baroness to his gift list, much to Ritter's disgust. The doctor believed he should have exclusive rights to the Hancock largess, by virtue of being first in line. Now and then his quaint notion would be given a little jolt by geography: Madam lived nearest the beach and could get her hands on the booty first. She would, however, share when occasion demanded, as it did in January 1933, when Margret presented Floreana with its first native-borne citizen. To celebrate the event, Madam sent up a can of milk. The gift came from a case that Hancock had left for Margret and baby Rolf. But he made the mistake of leaving it in care of the Baroness.

"The Ritters" with Captain Hancock during his January 1934 visit.

For Dore Strauch, Hancock's third visit was no doubt a memorable, if not entirely pleasant, occasion. The lady's teeth had not been faring well in this island Eden and Ritter—if not Dore herself—decided they must go. So he brought her, a pair of forceps and a few bone chisels down to the *Velero III*, turning the whole works over to Doc Palmer, ship's physician and now, dentist too. The Captain marked the event with another little gift—a set of dental tools for Ritter to fashion plates for Dore.

Left: Rudolph Lorenz in January, 1934, just two months before the disappearance of the Baroness and Philippson.

Below: The Baroness and Philippson during Captain Hancock's January, 1934 visit to Hacienda Paradiso, and their signatures in John Garth's notebook.

Over the years, the social climate on Floreana did not improve. And then one fine day in March, 1934, as Margret would write later on, the Baroness came up to announce that she and Philippson were off to Tahiti with friends who had just arrived on their yacht. According to Margret, Madam desired Lorenz to "let bygones be bygones," to remain in charge of the hacienda and await further instructions. On March 28th, the Baroness took her leave of Mrs. Wittmer, of Floreana, and quite possibly, of this world. Neither she nor Philippson were ever seen again.

Obviously, the story about the yacht and Tahiti was a lie. But whose lie? Did the Baroness lie about the yacht, or did Margret lie about the Baroness? If there were in fact a yacht, then it's conceivable Madam would have gone off to Tahiti to see what mischief she could get into there—in which case she might have stopped by Margret's to leave instructions for Lorenz. But in that case, the world would surely have heard more news later—about the yacht, the friends, and to be sure, the further adventures of the Baroness Eloise Wehrborn de Wagner-Bousquet. Or if the yacht went down in the Pacific, then that news would have eventually reached the papers, and we should at least know its name. But there is no record of a yacht calling at Floreana. There is no record of a yachting party from Galápagos reaching Tahiti. There is no record of a Tahiti-bound yacht lost at sea. There is no record—none but Margret's.

Given the evidence—or in this case, lack of it—it's a bit of a stretch to accept Margret's report at face value. No doubt Madam was entirely capable of lying about whatever suited her purposes, but it's unlikely she would have concocted a nonsensical Tahitian tale on the eve of her demise. On the other hand, if Margret was in on the lethal little surprise that awaited her neighbor, a concocted story about friends on a yacht might serve as a convenient "explanation" for a disappearance—not a very convincing explanation, but better than no explanation at all. It may have been more than enough to satisfy authorities who were as pleased as Margret and family to be rid of this foreign pest.

And now with the Baroness conveniently disposed of (one way or another), Lorenz sold off everything Madam had left behind with amazing efficiency, then set about getting himself off the island. Some months later he succeeded in hitching a ride over to Isla Santa Cruz with Trygve Nuggerud, a Norwegian fisherman whose boat *Dinamita* was locally celebrated for its fickle motive power. Not content with deliverance from Floreana, he persuaded Nuggerud to take him over to nearby Isla San Cristóbal, where he might have better luck booking quick passage to Guayaquil. His plan was to spend a few months there recovering his health before continuing on to Germany and home. Nuggerud made the fatal mistake of obliging him, and the pair sailed off. And that was the last time anyone saw them alive.

In November 1934, Alfred Rudolf Lorenz and Trygve Thorvaldsen Nuggerud achieved some passing fame when news of their whereabouts reached the international press. Their desiccated corpses were discovered on the unforgiving shore of yet another enchanted place, the waterless Isla Marchena. Far to the north of San Cristóbal, far from the wake of friendly ships, far even from the slimmest hope of salvation, the pair waited until it was too late and then they waited some more. Finally, chance brought the American tuna clipper *Santo Amaro* close enough to see a sign of their distress. Atop a lonely pole, a few rags waved in the sightless breeze to mark an unhappy beach and two sun-baked bodies face down and asleep forever on the sand. It was not at first certain which was which, or even if it was them at all. In fact, the *Santo Amaro* crew thought they had found a man and a woman, and that news was relayed by wireless to Los Angeles. By chance, Captain Hancock had planned his next Galápagos departure for later that same week, and he thought the bodies would be Heinz and Margret. But before leaving the harbor he learned that the Wittmers were still quite alive on Floreana, and surmised correctly that it was Lorenz and Nuggerud who lay silently waiting for him on the beach.

But what strange business would have brought them to Marchena in the first place? The best guess is that *Dinamita's* engine had once again failed, and this time for the last time. As the current swiftly carried them away from their intended destination, captain and passenger probably abandoned ship in the lifeboat, which was also found on the beach. The *Dinamita* itself and another crew member were never found.

December, 1934. On Isla Marchena, the lifeless bodies of Trygve Nuggerud (left) and Rudolph Lorenz were photographed by the Hancock Expedition a week after they were discovered by the *Santo Amaro* crew.

Hancock was anxious to reach Galápagos, for he had received an ominous note from Ritter. "We hope you will come once more to the island. Then I will tell you what I cannot write, because I have no proof of it." Did Ritter have news of what had really happened to the Baroness? If so, Hancock wanted to know about it. But the doctor would now have to wait upon events. The course of *Velero III* was shaped for Isla Marchena, where the Captain found and photographed his late acquaintances. He regretted that he had arrived too late to do any good, then sailed off to Floreana and the Ritters. And again he regretted a late arrival. The doctor was dead.

Friedrich Ritter, philosopher and physician, prophet and vegetarian, had been done in by a chicken.

A strange end for a strange person, but Ritter was known for frequent dietary lapses. On one such occasion he went to the cupboard for a jar of his own potted pork, but discovered the meat had gone quite bad.

This was on November 13th, 1934. Radio personality Philips Lord had just arrived on his four-masted schooner *Seth*  *Parker*, named after the country preacher character he played on his radio show. He looked on as Dore tossed the pork to the chickens, who enjoyed it immensely and expired later in the day.

Right: Philips Lord's *Seth Parker*.

While Lord was visiting with the Wittmers the following morning, his ship's crew came up to report that the chickens had died of meat poisoning

Never one to quit in the face of adversity, Ritter next set about potting the birds, against such time when he might again feel a lapse coming on. But alas for his skills at preservation, the birds followed the beast's example and turned bad. Ritter, a slow learner when it came to such matters, insisted that with a little boiling they would be as good as new. But he was wrong. Dead wrong. That night he and Dore enjoyed their last supper. The date was November 19th, 1934; earlier this day news of the Marchena bodies reached the American newspapers.

The next morning Ritter was one very sick philosopher. And to make matters worse, there was only one physician in town—him. Dore watched his condition deteriorate for a day or so, then wandered off to find the Wittmers. Margret was at home and at once accompanied her back to Friedo, where together they presided over the deathbed festivities. Years later, both witnesses described the scene in their respective books. The accounts offer the reader a superb example of Galápagoan comparative literature:

Dore:	Margret:
Suddenly he opened his great blue eyes and stretched his arms toward me.	Whenever she came near him, he would make feeble movements as if to hit or kick her.
His glance was joyously tranquil.	He looked up at Dore, his eyes gleaming with hate.
He seemed actually to say to me: "I go; but promise you will not forget what we have lived for."	[He] wrote his last sentence: "I curse you with my dying breath.
It seemed to be as if he would draw me with him.	His eyes filled with a wild feverish flame.
Then he sank back, and I began to caress his forehead tenderly.	Dore shrieked, and drew back in horror. Then he collapsed soundlessly, falling back on the pillows.
He became quite still, and that was death.	He had gone.

Friedrich was dead, and on that one point the girls agreed. But that's about all they agreed on, and one of them was lying, but nobody knew then—or now—which one. And Hancock never did find out what was on Ritter's mind. Did Herr Doktor know something about the fate of the Baroness? Did Lorenz? Did the two of them share some terrible secret? Neither were in a position to say. For that matter, what did Margret know?

If Hancock had arrived a bit earlier, he might have left Galápagos with a few answers, and perhaps with one or more islanders to return to Guayaquil in custody. Instead, he got to take Dore back to the mainland, whence she would return to Germany. She had better luck than Lorenz: Hancock's engines did not fail (they wouldn't dare), and Dore Strauch Koerwin Ritter made it all the way home.

1934. The Ritters, the Baroness and the others are gone now, and Margret can at last relax at home, seen here in a Hancock expedition photo. Her stepson Harry looks down from the second story.

At last, Heinz and Margret Wittmer became sole proprietors of the little German colony, and the prophecy of Hakon Mielche was fulfilled.

> When Ritter and the Baroness have turned to dust and "Paradise" and "Eden" have sunk into a smoking hell, Wittmer will still be sitting in his cosy little house smoking his pipe. The sun will rise and set, and he will forget to count the days.

Wittmer kept at his pipe until 1961, when he became somewhat of a *cause célèbre* as the first Floreana resident in recorded history to die of natural causes. Although Dore beat him to the grave, she got to hers from Berlin in 1942. Heinz rests in the family plot near the Wittmer home.

Others who have departed this life on Isla Floreana are buried in a small cemetery along the road to the highlands, and here one finds the grave of Saydee Reiser, an American tourist who strayed from the trail in 1964. After an intensive search was called off, local hunters discovered her under a tree. In 1980. She had at least one thing in common with the Baroness: Margret was the last Floreana resident to see her alive.

As for the Wittmer children, Harry died in a boating accident, Rolf runs a charter boat operation, and his younger sister Ingeborg Floreanita has a farm up in the highlands. Her late (one assumes) husband, Señor Garcia, disappeared without a trace while hunting on the island in 1968. Dr. Ritter remains alone in death under a few rocks near the place where he lived, which probably suits him just fine.

Right: Dr. Ritter at rest on Isla Floreana.

And that leaves Margret to account for.

For many years she ran a Black Beach guest house just down the dusty path beyond the *Escuela Fiscal*. She was that strange old lady whom too many visitors never did get to meet. But tourists were always welcome at Casa Wittmer—lunch, dinner, stay an hour or two, longer if you like. Some came, sat down, had a beer or maybe some of Casa Wittmer's special fruit wine. A popular island pastime was trying to play "Who killed the Baroness?" and at least a few people were sure that Frau Wittmer knew more than she cared to admit. But the feisty Frau had been grilled by the best of them, and eventually only the slowest learners continued to ask the same tired questions that she had already not answered so many times before. Others preferred to leave the inquest to someone else and just enjoy the visit. They'd have a little something to eat and let Margret do the talking. There were tales to be told to those who would listen. Some might buy a bottle of her homemade wine, then go back to the ship and move on to the next landing, which would not be anything like this one.

Margret is gone now. She died in March, 2000, in her 96th year.

Margret Wittmer in 1988.

CHAPTER SIXTEEN

A MONUMENTAL TALE

*Raising a monument to Charles Darwin was
more than an act of biological piety. It was
the beginning of a campaign to save a living
laboratory from extinction.*

Victor Wolfgang von Hagen

ANTHROPOLOGIST VICTOR WOLFGANG VON HAGEN recalled his
first reading of Darwin's *Journal of the H. M. S. Beagle* back
in the spring of 1933. One sentence in particular caught
his attention:

> The *Beagle* sailed for the Galápagos on the
> 15 September and landed on Chatham (San
> Cristóbal) Island.

Dr. von Hagen set down his recollections in an unpublished
memoir written some 50 years after the fact, and may not
have had the chance to edit it before his death a few years
later, for the quotation is actually a composite of a few
entries Darwin wrote in his Diary. His September 7*th* entry
begins "The Beagle sailed [from Peru] for the Galápagos,"
and later, "on the 15th she was employed in surveying the
outer coast of Chatham Island." And then on September
17th, he landed (the ship of course, did not) on the island.
And the *Journal* that von Hagen mentioned was actually
The "Beagle" Diary, in a new edition just edited by Darwin's
granddaughter Nora Barlow.

As von Hagen read the *Diary*, it dawned on him that the 100th anniversary of Darwin's arrival in Galápagos was fast approaching. He thought it would be a splendid project to launch a new expedition to awaken interest in preserving the island habitat and at the same time honor the man behind the *Diary*. But surely this was not a very original idea, and no doubt others were already at work on something appropriate for the anniversary celebration. He was mistaken: With the exception of the ornithologist Robert Cushman Murphy, the scientific community had all but forgotten the date, and there was not the slightest interest in doing anything to celebrate it. But Murphy had known Darwin, and would do whatever he could to make the project a reality.

Dr. von Hagen went to Ecuador to make preliminary arrangements, and as an example of what may best be described as being in the right place at the wrong time, he described his arrival at a hotel in Quito.

> The owner of the Metropolitan Hotel said I would have the honour of having the room that had been reserved for the Vice President himself. As the bellboy opened the door, a bulky figure burst out of nowhere, tackled me and we fell just below the window. At that moment a burst of gunfire shattered the glass. The gentleman urged me to keep my head down (as if I needed urging!). "Please excuse me," he said in most-polished Spanish, "I am the Vice President."
>
> I extended my hand as more bullets whizzed over our heads. He wished me health and happiness and crawled out of the room.

It seems that Dr. von Hagen had arrived just as the latest revolution was getting started. This one was an attempt to remove President José María Velasco Ibarra, arranged and orchestrated by the Vice President. If von Hagen's story is to be believed, it would appear that the President's men knew his adversary was scheduled to be at the hotel, and had arranged this little greeting for him.

But if the Vice President were indeed at the hotel, why was his room given to von Hagen? And why did the official need a room in the first place? Presumably, the country's Number 2 man would have a home of his own, and would hardly need to take up lodging in a downtown hotel—unless of course it might be a more convenient podium from which to conduct a revolution.

But is von Hagen's story to be believed at all? Perhaps not, or at least not entirely. The office of Vice President did not come into existence in Ecuador until 1946, more than 10 years after this incident took place. Now there's always a possibility that the story teller's memory was faulty: someone else tackled him, and after the passage of a half century he got his officials mixed up. And then there's the possibility that the story teller was just "telling a story" for the sake of adding a bit of human interest to his narrative. But more on that sort of thing in another chapter. The remainder of this one will stick a bit closer to the truth.

Taking the rest of his account at face value, von Hagen changed into something presentable, arranged for a different room not ventilated by bullet holes, and then went off to keep an appointment with the other side of the faction—the President himself.

Right: Five-time President José María Velasco Ibarra.

At the Presidential Palace, the former history teacher turned history maker looked a bit pale— but if revolutions didn't agree with his system, he would learn to adjust in due course, for in later years Velasco Ibarra would be brought in and pushed out of office four more times. But now to the business at hand: Dr. von Hagen explained he was here for two reasons: to observe the problems of Galápagos conservation, and to put up a monument to Charles Darwin to mark the occasion of the naturalist's first visit to Isla San Cristóbal on September 17th, 1835. The monument would be dedicated by the "Darwin Memorial Expedition" on the centenary of that event. To mark the occasion of his own visit, von Hagen presented the President with a small medallion showing Darwin as a young man on one face and H. M. S. *Beagle* on the other. Sr. Presidente was suitably impressed, von Hagen received official permission to proceed and then took his leave, to proceed to a meeting with the Minister of Post and Transportation.

Above: Dr. von Hagen's Darwin Medallion, with a quotation on the reverse: "The voyage of the Beagle has been by far the most important event in my life and has determined my whole career. Darwin. 1835 - 1935."

To further celebrate the anniversary, von Hagen had designed a series of six postage stamps showing Darwin, an iguana, a tortoise and other images of Galápagos. He hoped the stamps would be issued to coincide with the dedication of the monument, and that an Honorary Postmaster would be appointed to place a special cancellation seal on envelopes posted in Galápagos on the day of the dedication. To fill the office of Honorary Postmaster, he proposed himself, and further proposed that profits from sales of the issue to collectors worldwide would be used to support the establishment of a research station in the islands. Through the good offices of his friend Juan Trippe, president of Pan American Airways, he would arrange for the first Pan American clipper flight to Galápagos, where it would pick up the stamped envelopes for worldwide delivery. The Minister thought all this was a grand idea, and von Hagen was understandably delighted.

> This was, unbelievably, the easiest of all my projects; the designs were given to the Quito representative of Thomas de la Rue Ltd., specialists in such stamp issues, final designs were made later in the year, approved, and the memorial stamps were actually issued.

Dr. von Hagen departed Quito for an eight-month expedition into the upper Amazon, assured that things would go just as he would expect them to go. But alas, he forgot this was Ecuador, where things never go as one would expect them to go.

Emerging from the jungle in May, 1935, he proceeded out to Galápagos with a bust of Darwin stowed in the hold of the *San Cristóbal*. A mason came along and was dropped off on the island of the same name to supervise construction of the pedestal for the bust. von Hagen continued on to Isla Santa Cruz to do some botanical research, then returned to Isla San Cristóbal in time for the inauguration. The pedestal was waiting, and so was a little surprise:

> The masons had done a good job, but, as they had not been working under supervision, they had found a heart-shaped stone which they put in the centre of the monument and wrote thereon, in large conspicuous letters:
>
> AURELIO BORRERO
> — MASON —

> This legend completely dwarfed the name of Charles Darwin.

There was yet another surprise: no plane, no stamps, no envelopes.

Back at the Presidential Palace, there had been yet another revolution, and this one was successful. Velasco Ibarra was out, and so were the stamps and all the rest. But since the monument was done, there was no reason not to proceed with the dedication.

There was a simple ceremony. A few idle Galápagueños, half teethed and half clothed, stood by, mainly for the wine that was to follow. I made a short speech in Spanish; the commandant, who did not know any more about Darwin then he did about Wedgewood, responded. He accepted the monument in the name of the Republic of Ecuador and that was that. It would certainly have delighted Charles Darwin to know that a small group of sea iguanas, which he called "the little imps of darkness" were then scampering about the base of the monument.

Above: The Darwin monument, shortly after its 1935 inauguration on Isla San Cristóbal.

Meanwhile, back at the Presidential Palace, the smoke eventually cleared and the stamps were issued. They were issued late, but they were issued. But Pan Am never did get to fly out to the enchanted islands.

Three of the commemorative stamps issued to celebrate the 1935 Darwin Centenary.

The Darwin monument still stands, but few tourists who fly out to Isla San Cristóbal know it's there. They depart the airport and proceed more-or-less directly to a waiting ship which immediately leaves for somewhere else. The monument, now behind a fence surrounding Ecuador's Second Zone Naval Base, remains out of sight. Of the handful of visitors who linger in the village of Puerto Baquerizo Moreno, only the persistent few get to see it, for it takes a bit of sweet talk to convince the guard at the Navy Base gate that one is not intent on foul play. For those who do make it past all these obstacles, fewer still might think it had been worth the bother. As monuments go, this one doesn't go very far, and there may be more interest in the story of the Darwin bust, than in the bust itself.

That story begins almost a century ago during another centenary. This one marked the 100th anniversary of Darwin's birth, and the 50th anniversary of his *On the Origin of Species*. On February 12th, 1909, the American Museum of Natural History inaugurated the new Darwin Hall of Invertebrate Zoology. Earlier, the New York Academy of Sciences had awarded the prominent American sculptor William Couper a $1,000 commission to create a bronze bust of Darwin. The bust—a gift to the Museum from the Academy—was unveiled on that day and placed in the Hall. The March, 1909 issue of *The American Museum Journal* informed its readers that "The bust is pronounced by those who knew Darwin personally, and by his sons in England, who have seen photographs of the clay model, the best portrait in the round of the great naturalist ever made."

Above: William Couper's bronze bust, commissioned by the New York Academy of Sciences for presentation to the American Museum of Natural History.

Shortly after the inauguration of Darwin Hall, the Museum thought to present a replica of the bust to Cambridge University in England. Accordingly, Couper made a second bust, and an American delegation presented it to Christ's College during their own Darwin Centenary festival held later in the year. Later on, the Museum's Dr. Henry Fairfield Osborn wrote to Couper to tell him about the event:

> I have been intending to write you regarding the Darwin bronze, which was very gratefully accepted by the authorities of Christ's College. Unfortunately, it was exhibited in a very small room with other memorabilia of life size, and its heroic size threw it somewhat out of proportion. Sir George Darwin said that he regarded it as a very good likeness. Professor Francis Darwin was rather reserved in his opinion. The general opinion seemed to be that it ranked with the best of the portrait busts of Darwin. The occasion, however, was such a hurried one, and there were so many events crowding in upon each other, that I await more mature judgment, which I am quite sure will be very favorable.

Couper took the professor's reservations in good humor, replying to Osborn that "I am in hopes that as soon as Prof. Francis Darwin becomes used to seeing his father's head so large, he will feel differently about it."

And then, as the Darwin-in-Galápagos centenary drew near, Victor Wolfgang von Hagen approached Dr. Robert Cushman Murphy at the Museum, to see if it would be possible to get a plaster cast of Couper's bronze bust. von Hagen had already arranged for a bronze plaque with an inscription written by Darwin's son, Major Leonard Darwin.

The Museum made the necessary arrangements a few months later, and in fact had two casts made. The casts were delivered to the Museum, and one of them was sent to von Hagen in Ecuador, for which he was billed the princely sum of $60 (plus shipping and handling). The bust was shipped to Guayaquil and from there von Hagen had it sent up to Quito, where a local artist used it to create a mold for a new bust of poured concrete. Bronze filings were mixed into the concrete in the hope that this would give the bust a bronze-like patina. The purpose and location of the second plaster cast are unknown.

The original bust presented to the American Museum of Natural History went into storage when Darwin Hall was dismantled in 1940. And then in 1960 the gift was finally returned to the Academy of Sciences, where it now resides in a small outdoor courtyard at the Academy's headquarters in New York City.

Above: Couper's original Darwin bust in the courtyard at the New York Academy of Sciences.

Right: The Darwin bust at the University of Guayaquil.

Still another version of the Darwin bust may be found just beyond the iron fence surrounding the University of Guayaquil. It may come as no small surprise that this one was also arranged by Dr. von Hagen as part of his plan to engage local University professors in a Galápagos Committee to stimulate public interest in the formation of a research station out in the islands.

Eventually the Charles Darwin Research Station did come into existence, but it would take another two decades for that to come about. Writing in 1979, the Darwin Foundation's G. T. Corley-Smith looked back on how it all began:

> Dr. Victor Wolfgang von Hagen and other early Galápagos enthusiasts vigorously advocated both protective legislation and the establishment of a scientific station. The Government of Ecuador decreed some of the islands as nature reserves and in 1935, von Hagen led the "Galápagos Memorial Expedition" to San Cristóbal to erect a monument to the great naturalist, with an inscription written by his only surviving son, Major Leonard Darwin.

> It was a gallant effort, but produced no positive action. The Government appointed no wardens in the islands to enforce its decree and international scientists failed to set up even a modest research station. Dr. von Hagen pleaded his cause in Europe, where in 1937 Sir Julian Huxley headed an imposing "Galápagos Islands Committee."

Then World War II intervened. Matters of conservation were put on hold and the Galápagos Islands became the stage for a drama never dreamed of by Charles Darwin. But Dr. von Hagen would find himself playing an interesting role in it, as we shall discover later on.

Eventually the war would be over, and Corley-Smith could conclude his reminiscences on a positive note:

> ... the Charles Darwin Foundation for the Galápagos Isles was created in Brussels on 23 July, 1959, the centenary of the publication of *On the Origin of Species*.

A few years earlier, he had written directly to von Hagen to acknowledge his contribution:

> The members of the Executive Council of the
> Charles Darwin Foundation, meeting at the
> Headquarters of the World Wildlife Fund at Morges
> on 8 May 1978, unanimously wish to put on
> record their appreciation of the pioneering services
> rendered by Mr. Victor W. von Hagen to the cause
> of conservation in the Galápagos.

The tourists who fly out to Isla San Cristóbal and set sail without seeing Charles Darwin will eventually wind up on Isla Santa Cruz at the Research Station which bears his name. Here they will see the tortoise rearing pens, and perhaps pay a call on Lonesome George. But they will have missed seeing something just as important back at the Second Zone Naval Base on San Cristóbal.

Another load of tourists arrive at Isla San Cristóbal. And most probably don't know that Charles Darwin slept here.

Perhaps there will be time for a quick look before the return flight to the mainland. If not, there's always the monument at the University of Guayaquil.

Still standing after all these years. The Darwin monument on Isla San Cristóbal in 2005. Talk nicely to the guard at Second Zone Naval Base and you may be able to have a look.

CHARLES DARWIN

landed on the Galápagos Islands in 1835 and his studies of the distribution of animals and plants thereon led him for the first time to consider the problem of organic evolution. Thus was started that revolution in thought on this subject which has since taken pla ce. _ Erected September 17th 1935 by the members of the Darwin Memorial Ex pedition. _ Victor Wolfgang von Hagen Alexander R. Brown III, Christine Inez Brooks, Christine Inez von Hagen Dard Hunter.

Above: The plaque at the base of the pedestal. The two Christines were von Hagen's mother-in-law and wife, Brown his brother-in-law, Hunter the famous authority on paper manufacturing. In recent years the plaque has been painted white, making the lettering (such as it is) almost unreadable.

To return to Victor and Christine von Hagen in Galápagos, with the Darwin bust secure on its pedestal, the dedication ceremony over and done with, they could now devote full attention to finishing their research work, then make their way back to the mainland on the *San Cristóbal*. And that's just what happened—almost.

Although the von Hagens did of course leave the islands, their departure was not in the manner expected. But more on that in the next chapter.

Yet another replica, probably based on the bust presented to Christ's College in 1909, and placed on the rear porch at Down House, Darwin's home in the village of Downe. Although the village added an "e" to its name in 1842, Darwin retained the old spelling for his home.

Dr. Victor Wolfgang von Hagen aboard the ship *Golden State*, which he had hoped to bring to Galápagos as part of the Darwin Memorial Expedition. But with little or no interest from potential supporters, plans for the ship had to be abandoned, and the von Hagens proceeded to the islands on their own.

South Seymour
Island—now, Isla
Baltra—was even-
tually chosen as the
best location for a
military base, code-
named Base Beta.
The photo is from a
1959 U. S. Air Force
mapping mission.

The landing strip
on the right in both
illustrations re-
mains in use today
for tourist flights to
and from mainland
Ecuador.

CHAPTER SEVENTEEN

THE GALÁPAGOS FILES

There was something in a Panama paper, ...
something about Hitler having escaped in a submarine
to Floreana and being sheltered by the Wittmers.

Teniente Santos, *Armada del Ecuador,*
to Margret Wittmer

EVER SINCE THE PANAMA CANAL OPENED ITS GATES for business, both friend and foe recognized it for what it was—a splendid target, if it should come to that. If so, it would need to be defended, and long before "Defended from what?" had an answer, the United States had started to quietly look around the neighborhood for potential defense positions. One prime location for such a defense was a group of islands straddling the equator, conveniently near the shipping lanes to and from the Canal.

In his 1914 book *Ecuador,* author Reginald Enock opened and closed his Galápagos chapter with speculations about what the future might hold:

> The archipelago of the Galápagos is a territory
> of considerable interest, although relatively
> little known and unfrequented. It is possible
> that these islands may play a more important
> part in the future, due to the circumstance that
> they lie almost in the direct path of vessels on
> the route across the Pacific from Australia and
> New Zealand to the Panama Canal.

Of recent years the prospective strategic value, due to the building of the Panama Canal, of the islands has motivated various negotiations by foreign powers for their acquisition. In 1909 some sensation was caused in Ecuador by the publication of ex-President Garcia's private papers, showing that there had been proposals for sale of the Archipelago, first to France and then to the United States. In 1911 there were dealings between President Estrada and the United States for a proposed lease of the islands for a term of ninety-nine years, under a payment of £3,000,000 to Ecuador; but the American offer was refused, as its acceptance would have affronted Ecuadorian patriotism.

1286 – U. S. ARMORED CRUISER "WEST VIRGINIA."   800 OFFICERS AND MEN.
LENGTH 502 FEET.   MAIN BATTERY 18 GUNS.

An early visitor: The U. S. S. *West Virginia* stopped in Galápagos in 1909, reason unknown.

In the same year as the Garcia sensation, the armored cruiser U. S. S. *West Virginia* was seen in Galápagos, dropping in at Islas Floreana and Isabela. The purpose of the visit is unknown. Perhaps the territory was under study while that lease was being negotiated. Or perhaps the ship was just passing by on its way somewhere else.

In Ecuador, a 1913 editorial cartoon portrayed an Uncle Sam with a bad skin condition making an offer for a galápago symbolizing the islands.

A decade later, and just back from returning troops to America after the Great War, the U. S. S. *South Dakota* departed Panama on its way to Manila to take up position as flagship of the Asiatic fleet. But first, a visit to Galápagos. Extracts from the crew's journal "Ess Dee" described a main street of mud in the little settlement of Progreso, a sugar mill running on antiquated machinery, and some 200 men working under the direction of Rogerio Alvarado, son-in-law of the late Don Manuel J. Cobos. These are not the sort of details one would expect visiting sailors to jot down, and it's tempting to speculate that the visit was something more than a social call. However, there's nothing to indicate that the ship's company was gathering intelligence for future reference. There's also nothing to indicate that they were not.

Even if these early visits were truly nothing more than social calls, subsequent visits were something more than that; the U. S. Office of Naval Intelligence began serious compilation of strategic information on Galápagos in the early 1930s, with surveys of potential sites for submarine bases, and each island studied as a possible site for an airbase.

In 1936 the U. S. Navy returned with specific instructions to gather more intelligence, and this time to do it with the aid of a 28-year-old who knew nothing—or, who said he knew nothing—about his upcoming role. After celebrating the

Darwin centenary in September of 1935, Victor Wolfgang von Hagen and his wife Christine had stayed on for a few months of research and collection work. In November, millionaire Frederick Lewis dropped in with some 20 or so Sea Scouts aboard his yacht *Stranger*, and von Hagen joined them for a study cruise around the islands. February of the following year found the couple back on Isla Santa Cruz, their equipment packed and ready for shipment as soon as the schooner *San Cristóbal* arrived to return them to the mainland. But on the morning of February 24th they found not the expected *San Cristóbal*, but the unexpected U. S. Navy.

For the moment, people in the United States knew more about what was going on than von Hagen did. The February 3rd *New York Times* informed readers that "First Tests will be Made of Use of Galápagos Islands as Base for Defense Forces." The operation would be under the direction of Rear Admiral F. J. Horne on the aviation tender *Wright*, accompanied by the tender *Gannet*. Dr. von Hagen picks up the story, which differs in a few details from the newspaper report:

> A motor dinghy was lowered and in minutes several officers came up to the small wharf. Not one of them spoke Spanish. They knew of our presence there, for Frederick Lewis of the MS *Stranger* had informed the U. S. Navy Headquarters in San Diego. I went forward to present my wife and myself to Lt. Clyde Smith of the U. S. Navy Air Force and commander of the *Lapwing*.
>
> He gave me a letter—"sealed orders" is the proper name. Invited by the Admiral to take ship, we went back to our own camp and as fast as possible, loaded all our collections, personal materials, said our farewells and were transported, bag and baggage to the *Lapwing*.

We had hardly boarded, when a large hydroplane circled the ship, made a landing and slowly drifted toward us. It held its position until the principal officer got out of the plane and was brought aboard. We were face-to-face with a Hemingwayesque figure with an immense smile. His name: Commander Spencer.

He brought a message from Admiral Horne, commanding the small fleet from the aircraft carrier *Ranger*. It was the first time the U. S. Navy had visited the islands in 123 years.

Here, von Hagen has counted back to David Porter's 1813 visit—perhaps he didn't know, or didn't want to know, about all those other ships that had visited since then. As for the current visitors, von Hagen states that Admiral Horne was directing things from the U. S. S. *Ranger*—the first U. S. Navy ship built from the keel up as an aircraft carrier.

31 CANAL ZONE PLANES WILL DRILL IN PACIFIC
First Tests Will Be Made of Use of Galapagos Islands as Base for Defense Forces.

Special Cable to THE NEW YORK TIMES.

BALBOA, C. Z., Feb. 2.—Thirty-one planes from the United States Fleet airplane base at Coco Solo will engage in manoeuvres in the Pacific off Colombia and Ecuador and around the Galapagos Islands under the direction of Rear Admiral F. J. Horne, commander of the air base forces.

Rear Admiral Horne sailed on the aviation tender Wright, accompanied by the tender Gannet, with the first port of call Buenaventura, Colombia, on a cruise of three weeks. The tender will be joined by the planes from the Coco Solo base, which will engage in bombing practice and similar tests.

This excerpt from the February 3rd, 1936 edition of the *New York Times* places Rear Admiral Horne on the U. S. S. *Wright*, accompanied by the U. S. S. *Gannet*. The presence of the U. S. S. *Ranger* and *Lapwing* is not even mentioned in the report.

Naval intelligence documents indicate that when the American ships arrived, the von Hagens were already aboard the schooner *San Cristóbal*, ready to depart for

Guayaquil. But due to his wife's poor health, the couple were granted permission to transfer to the *Lapwing* for the voyage back to the mainland.

Not unlike other chapters in the enchanted history of these islands, something is not quite right here. If von Hagen was given those "sealed orders" that he mentioned, then it would seem that the Navy had come looking for him. And in that case, he would hardly have boarded the San Cristóbal, as stated in the intelligence report. In his own account, von Hagen doesn't help much to clarify the matter:

> The Admiral had cabled Washington and in turn was given permission to take Christine and myself aboard the *Lapwing*. At that time, or at any time at this point in history, a woman on a warship at sea was strictly forbidden: we were not shipwrecked, nor isolated, nor in danger: in point of fact, the *San Cristóbal* was expected to arrive any day.
>
> We were being picked up for another purpose. I was to write a short history of the Galápagos, then give more details. I had a portfolio of maps of landing places made by a topographer aboard the *Stranger*. There were charts where hydroplanes might land, especially on Barrington Island. I entered the movement of vessels in and about the Galápagos, mostly tuna-fishing boats. Wild life, especially feral pigs and goats, were listed. On our four days aboard the U. S. S. *Lapwing*, Christine typed my 40-page report, the first detailed intelligence on the Galápagos Islands the Navy ever had.

How odd that von Hagen would have come aboard with all this strategic information conveniently in hand—just the sort of thing that would fit nicely into an intelligence report—yet he not knowing anything of this in advance. Just a coincidence, or is someone throwing up a bit of an informational smokescreen? Perhaps there's an answer somewhere, waiting to be discovered.

But of course von Hagen wasn't the only pre-war visitor whose activities invite questioning; A rather well-known amateur angler came calling just a few years later. The Third Presidential Voyage of the U. S. S. *Houston* brought Franklin Delano Roosevelt to the islands in July, 1938 to have a look around. Although billed to the public as simply a presidential "fishing expedition," Chilean reporter Galvarino Gallardo speculated that the visit was "… something more than a mere incident in the course of a pleasure trip, and therefore cannot be overlooked by the public in this hemisphere."

We already know that the President had hoped to find the grave of Lieutenant Cowan. But beyond that, was he also angling for more than can be caught on a hook? Perhaps not directly, but while he attended to rod and reel, others made note of places visited, and their observations were added to a growing intelligence report about the islands.

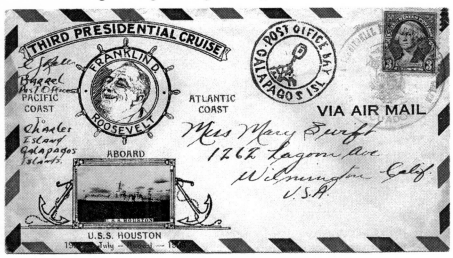

F. D. R. drops in. The U. S. S. *Houston* brought the President to the islands on a "fishing expedition" in 1938. The ship's company took advantage of the event to drop off letters in the Galápagos Post Office barrel.

Apparently 1938 was a busy year for other Galápagos "fishing" expeditions. Several months before the presidential visit, the *New York Times* reported that the American yacht *Haida* had been discovered taking soundings there. When local authorities approached, the *Haida* hastily departed. The actual purpose of the ship's visit remains unknown, for there is no mention of it in naval intelligence files.

Naval traffic kept up over the next few years as the islands were carefully studied for their strategic military value in case it should become necessary to protect the Panama Canal from enemy attack. No cove that might shelter seaplanes, no bay that might accommodate submarines, escaped notice.

And this brings us back to an earlier chapter, in which Waldo Schmitt and Joseph Slevin wrote about Captain Sherwood Picking. As Commander of Submarine Squadron Three, his assignment was not to look for a grave, but to gather more important information for the Navy. Nevertheless, he did find the time for a detour over to Isla San Salvador where he searched, without success, for Lieutenant Cowan.

All this advance homework paid off: two months to the day after Pearl Harbor, the U. S. Office of Naval Intelligence published its *Field Monograph of Galápagos Islands,* with more than 500 pages of detailed information collected over the years. At about the same time, construction began on the air base and naval station on Isla Baltra. There was every good reason to expect that both would be needed soon: More than a year before the Jap attack on Pearl Harbor, Imperial Army General Kiyokatsu Sato described his country's plans for the destruction of the Canal.

> The struggle for Hawaii constitutes the first stage of a Japanese-American war. On the assumption that Hawaii was captured by our navy, the Japanese forces would undertake, as the next step, the task of destroying the Panama Canal and the main squadron of America.

If the Japanese Navy succeeded in crushing the
American fleet in the Pacific, landing on the Pacific
coast of America would become easy. At the same
time the Panama Canal must be destroyed, as the
maintenance of traffic through it would facilitate
supplies to the American Navy.

Attacks should be made on the canal by an effective
air fleet. The destruction of the canal and the
American fleet would literally be half the battle.
This would end the second period of the war.

The second period of the war did not end quite the way
the General had anticipated, but it did end. And several
thousand American troops did their part to bring about
that end from a tiny island in the shipping route between
the Big Ditch and the Rising Sun. But much of that story
will be told in the next chapter.

Intelligence gathering continued even after Pearl Harbor,
and in 1942 the U. S. S. *Erie* visited Wreck Bay at Isla San
Cristóbal, Academy Bay at Isla Santa Cruz, Post Office
Bay at Isla Floreana, and Port Villamil at Isla Isabela. An
impressive array of panoramic photo views were added to
the files, along with a report on the German residents of
Galápagos.

Mr. H. Wittmer is a reserve officer in the
German Army. His present rank is unknown. ...
He has claimed great friendship for, and personal
acquaintance with both Hitler and Goering. A
picture of Hitler was prominently displayed in
his home in the GALAPAGOS ISLANDS until
recently. It is said that Mr. Wittmer left Germany
at about the time that Hitler went to jail. This
could not be confirmed.

The complete report was a curious mix of good and bad
intelligence (some things never change). Hitler was jailed
and released almost ten years before the Wittmers left

Germany in July of 1932, a fact apparently known to everyone except those who are paid to know about such things. Wittmer's reported friendship with unpleasant people in the Fatherland seems unlikely, for he was in fact on the staff of a Hitler enemy—the Lord Mayor of Cologne, Conrad Adenauer. As for Der Fuhrer's picture, it was a gift from Count Felix von Luckner, a German naval commander during the First World War, and visitor to the Wittmer's Floreana home in 1937.

Count Felix von Luckner. In 1945, he successfully negotiated the preservation of the city of Halle, and was later made an honorary colonel of the 104th U. S. Infantry "Timberwolf" Division.

Although the picture may indeed have been displayed at Casa Wittmer for a time, it should come as no surprise that it was nowhere to be seen when the U. S. S. *Erie* paid its call. How then did its presence come to the attention of Naval Intelligence?

The question remained unanswered until 1948, when Ainslie and Frances Conway's *The Enchanted Islands* was published. In the years before the war, the American couple had lived on Floreana and were quite friendly with the Wittmers. Frances described her first visit to Casa Wittmer in 1937:

> Frau Wittmer called our attention to a large,
> flag-draped portrait on the wall behind us.
> It was Adolph Hitler, very much idealized,
> uniformed, and bemedalled, "Nice, no?" Frau
> Margret asked. "The Count von Luckner give it
> to us."

In late 1941, Frances returned to the United States, Ainslie went over to Isla Baltra to work at the U. S. military base, and a few months later someone on the U. S. S. *Erie* compiled that report about Germans in Galápagos. It's not hard to guess who supplied the information about Wittmer's portrait of—if not friendship with—Adolph Hitler. Although there is no direct evidence that Ainslie had a hand in drafting the report (which is unsigned), there is a bit of circumstantial evidence: The Naval Intelligence document also notes the recent departure of the four Angermeyer brothers, but misspells their name:

> The Englemeyer brothers have recently left
> Academy Bay for Guayaquil. ... The military
> Commander does not expect them to ever return.

The Angermeyers went to the mainland in search of a larger boat for their fishing operation. By coincidence they went aboard the *Pinta*—on the same voyage that transported Frances Conway there. She remarked about it in her book:

> When the *Pinta* was ready to pull up anchor, a
> sail-boat belonging to the brothers Englemeyer of
> Santa Cruz had been lashed to one side of her, ...

It was the same misspelling that appeared in the intelligence report. Now even if neither Ainslie nor Frances knew how to spell Angermeyer, and neither thought the Wittmers were spies, apparently there were others who thought that perhaps they were. But what they might be spying upon, and how they might be doing the spying, was never made clear. The Wittmer navy consisted of one row-boat. Eventually it was concluded that the couple posed no serious threat to the American way of life, and they were left in peace on their island.

Right: The Conways at their farm on
Isla Floreana.

For a time, the military considered building a landing strip there, and the Wittmers got busy raising tomatoes to sell to those who would come soon to build it. But then the Yanks decided against the project, and the Wittmers were left to their solitude, with nothing to report on to anyone, save possibly the state of their tomato crop. There is some doubt this intelligence would provide much fuel for the Nazi war machine, even if the Wittmers had been so inclined.

Throughout the war years, Heinz and Margret occasionally entertained visiting American servicemen and—except on one notable occasion—the meetings were quite cordial. But at war's end, and just before the American tenants finally handed the keys to the base over to their Ecuadorian landlord, a detachment of armed troops pulled a surprise invasion of Floreana. They were looking for Adolph Hitler— rumor had it that he was hiding out at Casa Wittmer. They didn't find him.

Below: U. S. Naval Intelligence Map showing distances from Galápagos to Panama and other key locations.

CHAPTER EIGHTEEN

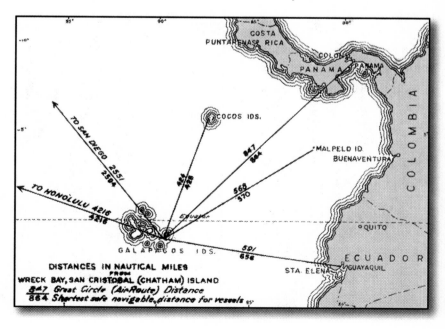

WHO KILLED THE IGUANAS?

... boredom ... we really cannot blame
them for what they did.

Dr. Irenäus Eibl-Eibesfeldt

JULY 1, 1946. THE WAR WAS OVER, the Canal was safe, the Ecuadorians wanted their islands back. And so, with Galápagos goats looking on as observers, the Stars and Stripes came down for the last time over the "Beachhead on the Moon" — as Contributing Editor Carl Solberg from *Time* put it in his cabled report. With the brief ceremony over and the lunar landscape again in the hands of its owners, the Americans were happy to return to earth — perhaps even happier than their hosts were to have them gone. The last of the bombers disappeared into the clouds, bound for Panama and points north.

But the Americans would return. Not right away of course, and at first it would be just the occasional yachtsman looking for a brief stopover on the way to somewhere else. Later, a few tourists would catch the weekly flight from the mainland out to the same island and the same airstrip that served during the war. The visitors would return home and spread the word. Now there are two flights a day and tourists enough to fill them both.

On disembarking, one's first impression may be that one has been had. The land is flat, featureless, and the cactus (if that is what that sorry-looking stuff really is) could only be called "vegetation" by one with superior imagination — perhaps the very one who sold you this trip in the first place. The second impression is not much better. There is a line. In fact, there is a very *long* line, and you're at the wrong end of it. At the right end stands an inspector, who is there for a reason of course: passports will need to be stamped, papers will need to be issued, and of course there will need to be a "little something" to take care of all this. At the moment, the little something works out to US $100, cash only if you please. Eventually, the first few people are stamped, papered and taxed. The line moves. It moves slowly, but it moves. Each and every tourist personally validates Darwinian theory by evolving to the head of the line to complete the formalities of entrance to the Galápagos National Park. Now all that remains is one small step — out into the sun to partake of an old Ecuadorian tradition; the wait. Sooner or later a bus will show up to take the tourists to the dock and the awaiting ships. With little else on this rock but you, your fellow travellers, and the bus, it may not be immediately clear what delayed it. It's probably best not to ask.

While waiting, spend a few moments imagining what it might be like to live here. Not here, as in the Enchanted Isles, but here as on this dismal rock that doesn't seem capable of supporting much of anything beyond itself and an occasional slithering lizard. Yet this was home for several thousand Americans during the Second World War, and that is why we're on this rock today, waiting for that bus. America believed — and so did Ecuador — that the Galápagos Islands would be of use in the defense of the Panama Canal. In the unhappy days following December 7th, 1941, there was damned good reason to believe the Japs would follow up their visit to Pearl Harbor with a similar call on the Canal. They had in fact already announced their plan to destroy it before invading the American west coast. These nearby islands seemed a likely spot to place a reception committee, and the Americans were given permission to build a landing strip and send out an aircraft squadron to sit around and wait upon events.

A wartime flyover of Aeolian Cove. The seaplanes are gone now, replaced by yachts awaiting tourists from the mainland.

At that time, the island—code-named Base Beta—offered its temporary tenants the very worst aspects of war and peace. There was absolutely nothing here to get the adrenalin flowing: the Japanese were preoccupied elsewhere in the Pacific and had little time to even think about the Canal and its Galápagos defenses. The Germans were simply too busy destroying their own continent to be very effective elsewhere. They did make a few attempts in the Caribbean, sinking whatever their U-boats could find, before the 6th Air Force found their U-boats. But they didn't have much luck striking Panama or reaching its protectors in the Pacific, whch meant the enemy here was neither bombs nor bullets. Here, the enemy was good old-fashioned boredom.

The Rock-Si Theater, Galápagos Beer Garden and a bowling alley provided some diversion for the servicemen
marooned on "The Rock" during WWII.

With no inviting town just down the road for a bit of R &
R, the military did what it could to provide the troops with
onsite activities to fill their off-duty hours. There were sport
fields, a boxing ring—later on, even a bowling alley—plus
the base movie theater and the Galápagos Beer Garden.
Later on, the men built a service club out of rocks, *La Casa
de Piedra* (the Stone House), featuring what was claimed to
be the longest bar in the world.

And then there were the
accidents. The wreckage
of a fighter plane crashed
on "Little Seymour." No
records have been found
in the miltary archives,
and the fate of the pilot
is unknown.

And there was fishing. A few small boats were pressed into
service for expeditions around the nearby islands, and the
catch was always a welcome break from the usual menu
at the mess hall, which was not celebrated for its haute
cuisine.

A 1944 fishing expedtion off Isla Seymour Norte, with Daphne Major barely visible in the right background (just beyond the fishing rod).

One such expedition provided a bit more diversion than had been anticipated, and it left its mark on the nearby island of "Little Seymour," known today as Isla Seymour Norte. Years after war's end, the U. S. Air Force was engaged in a Galápagos Islands mapping mission. With photo reconnaissance planes flying overhead at 6,000 to 25,000 feet, many smaller islands were captured on a single exposure. The one of Base Beta itself introduced this chapter, and there was another one of "Little Seymour." This photo showed the terrain and a little something else—a series of white concentric circles in the southeast section of the island. On close examination, an "S. O. S" could be seen within the circles on an aerial photograph taken in 1959.

There was no record of any plane or ship going down in the area, and so no reason to suspect that some survivors had made it to the island to fashion a distress signal that might be seen from the air. How then, did the message appear?

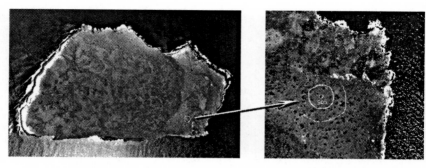

"Little Seymour" Island and an enlargement (rotated 90°)
showing an "S. O. S." signal. How did it get there?

The answer did not come until years after the war. Dr.
William G. Kennon, Jr. was stationed at the Base Hospital
on Isla Baltra. He recorded his recollections in 1981.

> On Christmas day, 1943, we were out fishing in a
> little inboard-motor Chriscraft, about 16 feet long.
> We shipped a little water, swamped our engine and
> couldn't get it started again. We started drifting up
> towards North Seymour Island. We had no oars,
> only a small paddle and we couldn't direct the boat
> very well. It drifted to the island and got battered
> up pretty badly, but we climbed up onto the rocks
> and made our way to the top of the island. The
> squadron commanding officer was part of our
> fishing party. He said "One of my flights is due here
> in about 30 minutes. I think they're going to drop
> some bombs right here."
>
> Well, there weren't a lot of places to hide, but we
> found two or three old sandbags that had been left
> up there. We cut holes in the bags and wrote out
> a big "S. O. S." right across the area where they
> usually drop their bombs. Next, we set fire to the
> sacks and added some dead wood to the blaze. We
> made quite a bit of smoke with our little fire, and
> pretty soon one of the infantry outposts on Baltra

saw it. Somebody flew over in a small liason plane;
he was a friend of ours and recognized us. He
flew very low, cut his engine and leaned out and
laughed. Needless to say, we weren't in a laughing
mood, and we made it known to him that we
wanted off. They finally sent somebody out and
got us off in time to get back to Baltra for a big
Christmas dinner at the officer's mess.

It is not known if any fish survived the day's activities, but
chances are the men had to make due with turkey.

Captain Bill Knight and his "Knight Mare" on patrol over
Base Beta on Isla Baltra.

Given the facts of life on "The Rock," there was no
opportunity for the type of non-serious action that might
appeal to a young and healthy American male. The nearest
available females were about 600 miles due East, and there
was no ferry service. Some troops stationed at a radar outpost
on Isla Isabela amused themselves by carving socially-
unacceptable statues of reclining figures in the rock—not
quite the same as the real thing though. Others would get
to fly to the mainland while looking for enemy vessels that
never cut a wake through the water below. Then after a few
hours sleep they would fly back, again searching in vain
for trouble which never showed up, and with little or no

chance to get themselves into more-interesting trouble on the continent.

How then to fight the only enemy in sight: boredom? Popular wisdom has it that the American troops turned on the local land iguanas for target practice. It's a believable legend: imagine being barely 20 years old, newly drafted and sent to a place that could very well be the next Pearl Harbor—a place the Japs would need to wipe out before they could take on the Canal. You have nothing to do but stand around and wait for something terrible to happen. But of course, nothing terrible does happen. In fact, nothing happens, period. The birth of the Charles Darwin Research Station is still some 20 years in the future, and it will take almost as many more years until the world of tourism wakes up to the possibility that this God-forsaken place might actually be a "destination." But in the meantime, this home so very far away from home is just "The Rock," a term of endearment formerly reserved for Alcatraz, another prison watched over by gun-toting guards. But on this little rock in the Pacific, the guards are also the prisoners. At the end of a boring day they take their amusement firing shots at some stupid lizards. So the story goes.

Eventually the war ends and everyone goes home. Some years later the scientists arrive and note the absence of land iguanas. They recall the island was occupied by Americans during the big one and set down the following observations:

1. Iguanas were here before the war,

2. Americans were here during the war,

3. Iguanas are missing after the war. Therefore, ...

4. Americans killed the iguanas.

In due time hypothesis becomes theorem, and today there's hardly a wildlife study that does not include the obligatory "senseless slaughter" reference. Despite the absence of a single reliable first-hand account, the hypothesis is so believable that few challenge it. It's almost as though we *expect* young men to do such things. The troops are judged guilty, in absentia and without trial.

Perhaps this harsh judgment should be appealed, if not on the basis of newly-found evidence, then at least on re-examination of the old. By studying World War II documents it's possible to reconstruct—at least partially—an account of what did, and what did not, happen here during the war.

Construction of an airstrip began just after Pearl Harbor, and it was ready for the first landing in April, 1942. A month or so later, the American Smithsonian Institution sent Dr. Waldo Schmitt out to Galápagos to investigate the possibility of establishing a small laboratory adjacent to the military facilities. Schmitt was of course no stranger to the islands; he had been a part of the Hancock expeditions of the early 1930s and later on accompanied President Franklin Delano Roosevelt here in 1938, aboard the U. S. S. *Houston*. Then he was back a few years later with Captain Picking and the submarines. But you already know about that from previous chapters.

This time there was no yacht for Waldo, and no cruiser either—not even a submarine. This time his vessel was the Tuna Clipper *Liberty*, which after a five-day voyage from Panama dropped him off at Base Beta. He made notes about the iguana situation in his diary:

> Some sections much favored by [the iguanas]
> have been completely denuded of all vegetation
> in the course of land leveling operations. The
> goats and remaining iguanas have been driven
> into, or concentrated in, perhaps half the

range that they formerly occupied. Thus, the
animals come into closer competition for food.
Due to the indiscriminate use of pistols during
the early phases of the military occupation,
so many iguanas were killed that a severe
epidemic of carrion flies resulted. [But] this, of
itself, brought about some degree of protection,
in order to eliminate the pest of flies.

Unfortunately, Schmitt did not elaborate on this, but we do know the remark about the pistols was not based on personal observation. For in his diary he wrote "Army killed iguanas with pistols, & let carcasses die … I guess [this] made a bad flie (*sic*) pest." However, this entry was made ten days *before* he arrived in Galápagos. He apparently heard about it from someone else, but he doesn't say from whom. By the time he actually got there he was able to jot down a cheerier note: "Killing of animals [is] out," perhaps by order of the base commander who had distributed a memorandum on the status of the islands as a game preserve. It stated that "The killing of all animals and birds is prohibited."

Left: Dr. Schmitt at work, perhaps in Galápagos.

But assuming Schmitt's earlier second-hand account to be reliable, it would appear that these regrettable actions were of brief duration and had ceased prior to his arrival. In any case, the Smithsonian didn't want to take any chances on the future, and a memorandum was sent off to the State Department to warn of the potential for diplomatic embarrassment.

It is recognized that disturbances through
construction and actual occupancy are
unavoidable, but it is important and necessary
that all hunting for game or sport, and all

other unnecessary molestation of the wild
life be controlled and prohibited by the
military authorities. ... Should any [animals]
be destroyed needlessly, much resentment
inevitably will arise.

Accordingly, the Secretary of War instructed the
Commanding General, Caribbean Defense Command that

... you take appropriate action to prevent any
unnecessary molestation of the wild life in the
Galápagos Archipelago and to prohibit the
introduction of domestic animals that may prey
on the native fauna.

"Franklin" and
"Eleanor" (last
name unknown)
with a young
friend of un-
known origin.

The orders were issued to all military units, for both the
State Department and the Smithsonian were aware that
interested foreign agencies were monitoring the situation
and could be expected to take action if the United States
permitted the Galápagos habitat to deteriorate needlessly.
In short, the protection of flora and fauna was taken very
seriously.

But could the servicemen themselves be expected to take
their orders as seriously as did their government and the
Smithsonian? In retrospect, perhaps they took them a bit

too seriously. The orders made no distinction between endemic and feral animals—an unfortunate loophole that the resident goats used to their advantage, much to the annoyance of some other (human) residents at Base Beta. The June 19, 1945 edition of the base newspaper *Goat's Whisker* published a report on the situation.

VOL NO.2 NO 23   JUNE 19, 1945

"THE GOAT'S WHISKER HAS THE LARGEST CIRCULATION AND BEST
READER AUDIENCE OF ANY PAPER IN THE GALAPAGOS ISLANDS"

GOATS MAY BE BANNED FROM PX BEER GARDEN

It turns out that some recent arrivals had complained to the PX officer about the presence of the beasts, much to the disgust of the old-timers, who regarded the goats as fixtures. No action was taken, pending further study of the matter. And so, along with their PX privileges, the animals prospered under a well-intentioned but misguided Uncle Sam.

When not raiding the trash cans or drinking with their army buddies down at the PX, the goats had the unsettling habit of wandering (staggering?) across the runway at the most inconvenient moments, and at least a few landings had to be aborted on their account. But such close calls notwithstanding, it would seem that troops and herds lived in more-or-less peaceful coexistence.

Military mascot "Billy Bender" in residence at Base Beta.

But what of the iguanas? Is it likely that the troops would cheerfully spare the goats yet systematically risk official displeasure by taking on the iguanas? The evidence, such as it is, suggests not. For whatever else the airmen did to pass their leisure time, they took pictures. They photographed the planes they flew in, the buddies they flew with, their baseball games, the goats, and of course, the ubiquitous iguanas. The pictures have one thing in common; the iguanas are reasonably plentiful, and all are quite large. Although there's no shortage of baby goat pictures, there's not one juvenile iguana to be seen in all the photos in all the albums. Not one. Over the war years, several thousand military personnel called Galápagos home. Not one of them saw a baby iguana. One medic attached to the base hospital recalled that

> Someone who acted as though he spoke with authority said, "You know, you only see large iguanas here on The Rock. You never see any small ones." After that I specifically noticed the size of the iguanas that we had, and all of them were fairly large.

Now, who (or what) was killing off all the young iguanas while sparing their elders? It could hardly be the work of bored humans, who if so inclined would surely find the faster-moving (when sober, of course) goats were far more attractive targets. And whatever the cause of the missing young, the effect had been observed long before World War II. William Beebe noted it in 1923. Some ten years later the members of the Hancock Expedition observed that the iguanas were not thriving on this island and they transported some of them to nearby North Seymour Island. Still later, Dr. Loren P. Woods from Chicago's Natural History Museum recalled that "when he visited Seymour

in 1940, prior to the establishment of the military base, he found only a very few Land Iguanas—*all of them large adults.*" Seymour—actually, *South* Seymour— was the former name for this island, and the italics are in a report of his trip.

Dr. Edwin Rowe and a young patient.

With all of this offered for consideration, it would seem grossly unfair to continue blaming the American troops for a phenomenon that had begun long before their arrival. To be sure, the heavy construction work, with subsequent air and road traffic, took its toll on the surviving adults. But even this did not totally finish them off. For in January 1954, Dr. Irenäus Eibl-Eibesfeldt reported finding an iguana carcass here. He writes "The sun had shriveled up the creature's body but still I could make out from the bullet holes that the lizard had been shot." After noting that the island had made life miserable for so many bored troops, he adds that " ... we really cannot blame them for what they did." And in so writing, he blames them.

But how long had this unfortunate creature baked in the sun before it was discovered? A few months? A year at best? Presumably, Dr. Eibl-Eibesfeldt's skills lie elsewhere than in forensic science, for at risk of stating the obvious, the very existence of an iguana carcass in 1954 should have convinced the German scientist that the American serviceman could not possibly be blamed for, as he put it, "senseless devastation" in Galápagos.

The legend lingers on. In the year 2002, author Michael D'Orso told his readers how the Americans spent their time on The Rock. They " ... wound up with little to do but drink beer and shoot iguanas."

By now the bus should have arrived.

Lieutenant Lewis
Nelson and friend.

Above: Life on "The Rock" depicted in the November 1944 issue of *The Caribbean Breeze*.

Below: A wartime ad featured the emblem of the 51st Fighter Squadron stationed at Base Beta.

OLDSMOBILE DIVISION OF GENERAL MOTORS

CHAPTER NINETEEN

A VISIT TO CASA WITTMER

I wondered who were better off, they or we.

Ernest Reimer, writing about the Wittmers.

At WAR'S END, CAPTAIN VERNON C. LANGE, 29th Bombardment Squadron, 6th Air Force had no regrets about his two tours of Galápagos duty, and even thought of bringing his wife here one day for the honeymoon they missed when war called him away. With the right supplies they might camp out for as long as they pleased, and perhaps even pay a call on the Wittmers of Floreana. He had already met the family when he made an impromptu visit to their island. Although a bomber pilot most of the time, every now and then Lange would take off in a single-engine observation plane to drop (literally) mail at the remote radar outposts on Isla Isabela, where no plane could land. But these aircraft could come down in a reasonably-flat field. Now it just so happened that a reasonably-flat field was near the Wittmer house. So one day Pilot Lange and Navigator Ernest Reimer "borrowed" a Stinson L-1 for a few hours—just long enough for a visit to the Wittmers, which Reimer would later remember as a "Social Visit Extraordinary." After the short hop over the water from the airbase, the pair landed on Floreana and set out to find Casa Wittmer.

Instead, Casa Wittmer found them, or rather young Rolf Wittmer did. The gun-toting 10-year-old appeared out of the bushes, commanded the Americans to "halt" and waved his rifle in their general direction as an inducement. Reimer startled the boy with his "Put away your gun, sonny. We're here to visit your parents" delivered in fluent German. Rolf allowed them to pass, then followed them up the path towards home. Lange and Reimer spent a pleasant few hours with the family, swapping the latest news on the war for a home-cooked meal washed down with some of Margret Wittmer's own fruit wine. And soon it was time to go. The Americans signed the guest book, snapped photos of Rolf and his sister Floreanita, accepted Heinz's cordial invitation to drop in again soon, and flew back to Baltra.

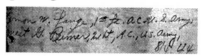

August 4, 1944. The Guest Book at Casa Wittmer, signed by Vernon Lange and Ernest Reimer during their brief visit.

They never returned. Soon afterwards the 29th Bombardment Squadron was called back to Panama, and when they came back to Galápagos a year later, no light planes were available for another visit. And then the war was over and it was time to go home.

Time passes. Lange gave up the military life, never did get to Galápagos again and eventually settled on the west coast. After retirement, with a bit of free time on his hands, he enrolled in a writing class which led to an assignment: to write his life story. Of course, he recounted life on Baltra, and the diversion of a visit to the Wittmers. Written almost a half century after the fact, the author wondered how the years had treated his Floreana hosts.

Margret was of course still going strong, serving up meals and drinks to the regular stream of visitors who dropped in at Casa Wittmer. I had met Frau Wittmer some years earlier, and made a point of dropping in on her whenever I visited her island. So Lange sent me the photos he'd taken years ago and asked that I give them to Margret. On my next visit, I asked if she still had her 1944 guest book, and with a "What a stupid question" look in her eyes she disappeared for a moment, then reappeared with book in hand. I showed her the page Lange and Reimer had signed, then handed her an envelope. "So, vot's diss?" she demanded. "Open it, and you'll see." And there were the photos of her young ones taken so many years ago. Margret stared at the photos, and then at me. The wheels spun as she calculated my age—about as old as her son she reckoned, and therefore certainly not a photographer from 1944. I explained the Vernon Lange connection, accepted a glass of home-brew fruit wine, and we toasted the memory of wartime visitors.

Above: Rolf and Floreanita Wittmer in 1944.

I sat with a newly-arrived group of tourists a few days later at Hotel Galápagos in the village of Puerto Ayora on Isla Santa Cruz and we spoke of places we'd been. "What brings you to these islands?" I asked Jean Skamser. "Well," said Jean, "there's this man in my writing class. He was here during the war, ..." Said I, "Oh yes of course, you mean Vernon Lange." The lady needed a few seconds to recover, then needed a complete explanation of how it came to pass that I knew of her classmate. I assured her that the legend of Vernon Lange's wartime exploits had long been a part of Galápagos folklore. But she wasn't buying that, so I tried the truth instead; that we had corresponded, he sent me the photos, and I had presented them to Margret Wittmer just a few days ago. And that's the end of this little story.

Well, almost. Ms. Skamser wrote to me a few weeks after she returned home. She had visited Casa Wittmer, seen the same guest book, asked about the photos (by now, Margret was wondering just how many people knew about 1944), then returned to her ship to finish John Treherne's *The Galápagos Affair,* which tells of the unsolved "Who killed the baroness?" mystery, and in passing mentions a manuscript Margret had written shortly after the affair. She sent it to G. Allan Hancock, who didn't read German and so commissioned a translation into English. A footnote identified the man who did the job. Sidney Skamser. *Sidney Skamser?* Jean put 2 & 2 together — "That's my uncle!" — and made a quick phone call.

"Oh yes," recalled Uncle Sidney, "now that you mention it, I did do some translation work for Hancock years ago. I think I got 50 bucks for the job. How did you hear about it?" "Well," said Jean, "there's this man in my writing class ..."

A SOCIAL VISIT EXTRAORDINARY

Navigator Ernest Reimer shared his recollections
of the visit to the Wittmers with the other
members of the 29th Bombardment Squadron.

Captain Vernon W. "Fox" Lange, a tall, rangy Minnesotan, and I decided to take a small plane to Floreana. We'd try our luck landing in a pasture near the Wittmers and pay a social call. Soon the outline of Floreana broke through the haze and Lange expertly guided the plane between the hills and over the trees towards the Wittmer farm. As we flew over their place we saw a woman and two children below, waving at us. We continued past their place and descended onto the pasture; as we flew over it at about five feet we both could see rocks covering the field. They ranged in size from small pebbles to some that were six inches in diameter. Fox made several passes at the field locating the best landing strip; as we had no interphone communication it was my difficult task to just sit and watch. Finally on the fifth pass the wheels hit and the plane rolled to a stop within two hundred feet. As we crawled out of the plane we exchanged smiles of relief. Positioning the plane for take-off and securing it well we started off in the general direction of the Wittmers. We had to climb and go around a hill covered with high underbrush. The hot morning sun beat down and the difficult going through the brush soon left us wet with perspiration. The branches and vines caught at us and, in the extreme quiet of the morning, it seemed as though they had taken it upon themselves to bar the way. There seemed to be no life here at all, and the eerie atmosphere kept us close together as we forced our way onwards. The going was hard and we stopped frequently to catch our breath.

After a hike of approximately thirty minutes the ground began to level off; we had reached the top of the hill and were only a short distance from the Wittmers. The underbrush was thinning out now and soon we came to a stone fence. On the other side of the fence was the dry bed of a small stream. Across this, nestled against the side of the hill was the home of the Wittmers. Save for a bird or two and the sound of the gentle wind through the trees there was no movement, no noise at all. Lange and I looked at each other and wondered about the correct etiquette of a call such as this. We decided the best thing to do would be to holler from this side of the fence. We yelled our greeting and immediately some dogs began barking and from around the corner of the house came bounding two huge police dogs. They were followed by a boy holding a rifle, with what at that moment did not look like a friendly expression on his face. The boy stood there, rifle in his hands, a dog on each side, their barks and growls resounding throughout the stillness; this, however only lasted a moment for Mrs. Wittmer then appeared and with welcoming smile and outstretched arms bade us enter. We climbed the fence, crossed the dry bed and came up to the house.

Welcome, welcome" she greeted us, "We were just wondering if you had really landed. You only flew over us once and we thought that maybe you would land. Rolf here wanted to go down and see but I told him to wait a bit. Come in, come in, it's so good to see someone again."

We introduced ourselves and, in turn, met her two children, Rolf of the rifle, age 11 and Floreanita, a pretty little girl of seven. Both children were extremely well mannered, polite and intelligent. They were dressed in home-made but well-made clothes. As Mrs. Wittmer led the way into the house she sent the boy to fetch his father from the farm.

Their home was in the shape of a small rectangle; the kitchen and dining room each comprised one quarter of it and the other half consisted of bedrooms. On the hill side of the house the hill itself formed half of the wall and the other three walls were constructed of large stones. The floor was packed earth and the whole place, while small, gave the appearance of very comfortable living.

Mrs. Wittmer, and when he appeared, Mr. Wittmer, were both enthusiastic in their welcome. We were the first visitors in six months and our news of the outside world was received gratefully. They had no radio or newspaper and this seemed to be the only thing they missed. We spent some time in bringing them up-to-date on world events.

We met all the family except the eldest son, whose bad eyes prevented him accompanying his father from the fields. The first thing that struck us about these people was the excellent health they seemed to enjoy. Their life of isolation no doubt had its disadvantages, but good health certainly made up for a lot of them. We asked what they did in case of sickness and they replied that they had thus far been able to handle anything that came along. The conversation turned to the children and Mrs. Wittmer explained that she had no trouble at their birth and that both children had enjoyed good health all their lives.

That the children's education had not been neglected was very evident as we observed them. Their parent's plans called for the children to be formally educated in England at the war's conclusion and I believe that these two will have a head start on any other children of their own age. Their self-reliance and assurance were remarkable for their age. The island had many wild bulls that were a nuisance and sometimes destructive on the farm; it was Rolf's job to kill these bulls and he considered it a poor one unless he placed the first bullet between the bull's eyes. Mr. Wittmer in one of the photos wears an apron made from the hide of one of these bulls.

Mr. Wittmer produced a bottle of lemon-colored, home-made punch; the taste was indefinite but along the wild plum line. It was delicious and we questioned him as to its contents. His only reply was that it was a combination of fruit juices. As we were conversing with Mr. Wittmer, his wife was busy preparing some coffee and cake and it was hard to realize that we were hundreds of miles from civilization; in their solitude through the years the Wittmers had maintained a perfect mode of living. They could return and at once fit into any small community. When we learned that their only contact with the outside world was an Ecuadorian boat that stopped at inconsistent intervals, sometimes not for months, it increased our amazement.

Their source of fresh water was a small stream in a cave behind the house and they had rigged up a half-inch pipe that caught the free-falling water and carried it directly to the kitchen sink. One of Herr Wittmer's hobbies was carving smoking pipes; he showed us about eight of them in a beautiful hand-carved pipe stand.

They subsisted almost entirely upon their own products; the boat bringing them whatever the land could not furnish and as we marveled at the completeness of their life they told us of the long time it took to accumulate their belongings and of the difficulties they encountered the first few years. The method of communication was still the mail barrel in Post Office Bay, where a letter would wait until a passing boat picked it up; it was in this manner too that they received their mail.

We questioned them about the past and they were very pleasant in their answers but were reticent to speak about the Baroness, so we did not press the matter. Mr. Wittmer pointed out where the Baroness had her home, just across a small valley.

We wanted to take some pictures of the family and their home, so we went out to their front yard. Here, growing in abundance were many beautiful wild flowers of every description and color. There were many baby chicks and ducklings running about the yard and along with the dogs, chickens and geese it paralleled many a scene on an American farm.

Right: A Wittmer family photograph taken in 1944 by the American visitors from Basa Beta.

On the path leading down to the fields there was a little knoll and from here Mr. Wittmer pointed out his farm lands that were visible from this point. We did not have time to go down and see the manner and style of his farming, but judging from what we had already seen I'm sure it lacked nothing.

The knoll was perhaps three hundred feet from the house and yet as we looked back we had difficulty picking it out for it blended in perfectly with the background. Other than a red roof section or a yellow window curtain, there was nothing to indicate a modern Eden.

We asked them if they were happy; if being free from all the limitations that society imposes and therefore doing without the benefits of society brought about a philosophy resulting in a life of contentment. The smiles that came to their faces showed that they had been asked this many times before and I imagine we got the same answer as the rest. A shrug of the shoulders and a smile that said, "look for yourself." They had been there for fifteen years and although the war worked its hardships on them in a more severe way than the rest of us they never once left their isle. They might not have the complete answer but I think they have come a lot closer to it than the rest of us.

The time slipped away much faster than we realized and we had to say goodbye to this extraordinary couple. We promised to send them copies of the pictures we took of their children and Rolf and Floreanita were sent along to guide us down the path to the field where we had left our plane. I can still see Rolf, rifle in hand, striding manfully down the trail ahead of us. I don't believe his rifle was ever more than a few inches from his grasp.

The airplane was something completely new to these two children, for we were the first ones ever to land on Floreana; they had seen planes in the air but had never been close to one on the ground. We let them inspect the plane as much as they wanted and even placed Rolf in the cockpit, but the usual childish enthusiasm for airplanes was lacking. Both of them were very quiet as they looked at this man-made contraption; it did not register with them. Its many gadgets, dials, switches and levers were too much and bewilderment showed on both faces. We told them to stand about two hundred feet away and watch us take off. They silently obeyed, but as soon as the engine caught and started with a roar both kids turned and ran as fast as they could to the shelter of the trees. There they watched us taxi and take-off with perhaps more confidence.

As we flew back towards the electric lights, movie shows, radios and all the other things we would feel lost without, I wondered who were better off, they or we. — *Ernest Reimer*.

Vernon Lange with the Wittmer Children.

CHAPTER TWENTY

ISLANDS FOR SALE OR LEASE

The Galápagos Islands belong to Ecuador. ...
But we ought to own those islands by all means.

Senator Kenneth McKellar (Democrat, Tennessee)
Congressional Record, August 18, 1944

WHEN THE BISHOP OF PANAMA ACCIDENTALLY PAID A VISIT to Galápagos some years ago, it apparently never occurred to him to claim the islands for his King. And in fact for the next 300 or so years, it didn't occur to anyone else to claim them either. So there they sat, appreciated by assorted buccaneers and whalers for their resources, but not appreciated enough by anyone else to plant a flag.

Eventually Ecuador got around to it in 1832, claiming the islands as her own and raising no objections from her nearby—and considerably stronger—neighbors. Even arch enemy Peru didn't care enough to launch a counter claim.

But it didn't take very long for other parts of the world to sit up and take notice—after all, if Ecuador thought enough of the place to annex it, then surely there must be something there worth annexing. Yet Galápagos was a long way away from Europe, a long way even from the United States, and in the age of sail it would be difficult to maintain control over such a remote outpost. And besides, with no native tribes to subdue, why bother?

Still, England, France and assorted other nations would now and then make half-hearted attempts to buy or lease the property, and from time to time Ecuador would make half-hearted hints that something might be arranged if the price were right. Then the locals would raise a ruckus and either the landlord or the prospective tenant would drop the matter. The United States made a three-million dollar offer in 1854, on learning that the islands were a rich source of what is politely referred to as "guano" thanks to millions of birds that lacked toilet training. The offer was ratified by Ecuador, then dropped by Uncle Sam when it was learned that the birds were not quite as sloppy as had been thought.

Then came the Panama Canal, and at about the time the first ship made its way through the locks, the Galápagos Islands sailed out of the equatorial backwaters and into modern history. The islands may have had little value as a source of guano, but now they had immense value in defense of the Canal, and the last two chapters told of that role before and during World War II.

As the war progressed and the rising sun began setting in the Imperial East, America's Galápagos interests showed no immediate sign of waning, at least not in the halls of Congress. Under an August 28th 1944 "Brotherly Greed" heading, *Time* Magazine described the antics of "Three Southern Senators not noted for their broad view of the world." The *Time* report referred to the following bit of nonsense introduced into the Congressional Record by the Senator from Tennessee, Kenneth McKellar:

> *Resolved further*, That the President be, and he is hereby, requested to enter into negotiations with the Republic of Ecuador with a view to obtaining the Galápagos Islands as permanent possessions of the United States.

The Galápagos Islands belong to Ecuador. I believe
we have some air bases or maritime rights there,
but we ought to own those islands by all means.

Ecuador owns the islands and I have no doubt
we can make a peaceful arrangement with her by
which we can acquire them. We have Ecuador's
interests in mind. The Monroe Doctrine is still in
force. We have duties under it.

The only way [the Panama Canal] can be preserved
from attack from the west is by owning those
islands and it would seem that fair-minded people
anywhere in the world would understand this.

The Senator from Tennessee did not say how one might
simultaneously take over the Galápagos Islands and still
"have Ecuador's interests in mind." Nor did he reveal the
connection between the Monroe Doctrine—in which the
United States views foreign intervention in the western
hemisphere as dangerous to its peace and safety—and his
harebrained scheme.

One might suspect that McKellar's little oration was a lone
voice of legislative lunacy within an otherwise-sensible
Senate. One might be wrong. From Buncombe County
in North Carolina, Senator Robert Rice "Buncombe Bob"
Reynolds chimed in. The chairman of the Military Affairs
Committee—described by *Harper's* Magazine as "... a cross
between a carnival broker, a shell-game operator, and a
traveling salesman"—liked McKellar's resolution so much
that he re-read it, then suggested that we should also take
over Bimini and Nassau from the Brits, and while we're at
it, grab St. Pierre and Miquelon from the French. That, and
a small chunk of Greenland and Iceland. And then from
Kentucky, Senator Albert Benjamin "Happy" Chandler let
the two congressional crazies know they were not alone:
"I just want to assure the Senator from Tennessee and the
Senator from North Carolina that I will be with them when
the showdown comes."

The "Brotherly Greed" trio. Senators Kenneth McKellar (Tennessee), "Buncombe Bob" Reynolds (North Carolina), and "Happy" Chandler (Kentucky) effectively destroyed any potential deal between Ecuador and Uncle Sam.

It's a wonder these deranged Democrats even knew where the various islands were, or who their present proprietors were. As for McKellar's designs on Galápagos, *Time* added a footnote:

> Promptly, the anguished Ecuadorian Congress set swiftly about amending its Constitution to forbid the sale or transfer of any of its territory.

They needn't have bothered. Although both governments had been dancing around the subject for years, and both would come back to it one more time in the future, the publicity surrounding the "Brotherly Greed" affair was enough to kill off any immediate prospects of a deal.

But a year later, the press reported that the United States was about to lease one of the islands, and Ecuador was about to get a $20,000,000 loan. Like every other such scheme in the past, this one had no future. And as time passed, the strategic importance of Galápagos diminished. Today the islands sleep on under the equatorial sun, with the flag of Ecuador in no danger of being lowered.

CHAPTER TWENTY-ONE

THE SHORT UNHAPPY LIFE OF FILIATE SCIENCE ANTRORSE

*The great dream ended, not with a bang
but with a whimper.*

An observation by one of the dreamers

I̤N 1959, A TUG BOAT SKIPPER AT THE PORT OF SEATTLE came
across a magazine article about some islands out in the
Pacific, and it gave him an idea. He would start a colony
there to take advantage of resources that could be exploited
by anyone willing to turn away from civilization and put in
some hard work in the wilderness. So Don Harrsch quit his
job, came up with the lofty slogan *"Filiate Science Antrorse"*
("Together with Science we move Forward") and founded
the Island Development Company to pursue his idea.

Now Harrsch was not only smart enough to get his tug
in and out of the docks at home, but also smart enough
to know he'd need expert help navigating this project
through the murky waters separating dream from reality.
And so one of his first steps was to call on the University of
Washington's Psychology Department, looking for advice
on how to choose the right expedition participants from
those who applied to him. The faculty did not blow him
off, but instead referred him to the school's Department of
Sociology, where a sympathetic professor heard him out
and proposed that the whole project become the object of
a study.

329

Don Harrsch points out the Galápagos Islands in a 1959 photo in the *Seattle Times*.

Harrsch readily agreed, and a university research group was organized to track the progress of the expedition. The group's role would be limited to one of observation—they would play no active part in influencing the outcome, other than to advise some prospective participants to exercise caution before committing their life savings to the scheme. Notwithstanding their interest in Harrsch's project, the group members were unanimous in their early prognosis that the scheme would fail. And they were correct.

The study group learned that Harrsch had dropped out of school after the eighth grade, drifted through various jobs and eventually joined the Army. But that didn't work out; after four AWOL incidents he received a dishonorable discharge, followed later on by getting his name in the police records on a weapons charge. That, according to a paper published several years later by members of the group, and disputed by Harrsch. He admits to the weapons charge, but states he left the Army with a Bad Conduct—*not* Dishonorable—Discharge. Or as he put it, "Me and Uncle Sam were incompatible."

But whatever the actual details of his military record, the group noted Harrsch's relaxed bearing and saw here a man of potential vigor, which he would certainly need to call on for the work ahead. He was perceived as intelligent, energetic, and highly self-confident. The opinion was that "naively hopeful persons would have little difficulty in regarding him as a leader," although to that assessment the group appended a qualifier: "at least on first acquaintance."

At the time happily married with two small children, Harrsch proclaimed himself an atheist with a strong interest—and faith—in science. In fact, he thought atheism should be the official doctrine of the Galápagos community. A faculty member not part of the study group later advised that atheism was not a suitable doctrine, and should be replaced by "scientific humanism." Harrsch agreed, and began calling himself a Humanist in an apparent attempt to enjoy some advantages of a religious association. In a 10-page typewritten description sent out to prospective applicants, he referred to participants as "a colony of scientific philosophists"—a phrase that sounds like something coined in a university Sociology Department.

Harrsch frankly pointed out to his readers that "They must not fool themselves into thinking they are escaping into a Garden of Eden. They shall all toil as most of us have never toiled before." But he assured his prospective followers that they could count on "... the help of the Ecuadorian Government, which will be considerable." American veterans who had been stationed in Galápagos during the war were skeptical: "It's not an attractive spot," was one opinion. "It's a harsh, arid area" was another.

Nevertheless, plans were announced to send the first boatload of colonists to the islands. But first,

> A PBY airplane will be purchased to send a
> group of scientists to the islands. They will give
> us such information as where to land, where to

> live, soil samples, nearest water, etc. These men
> will be down there for about two weeks. Some
> of our members will go with them and remain
> behind at the point chosen for our landing.

Later on, the plane would be used for air freight operations: "It is expected to do very well." But there would be no plane, and no air freight business later on.

If any of Harrsch's followers were actually familiar with the territory, they might have pointed out to him that he could use a quick geography lesson.

> We are engaged in negotiations for land on
> Isabela Island, and upwards of 20,000 acres
> is forthcoming very soon. Cartago Bay seems
> to be the place to establish residence. About
> 30 miles away is a small island known as
> Seymour. The United States had an airbase and
> we expect to acquire lumber from the buildings
> there, which is available to all islanders.

Cartago Bay is on one side of the narrow Perry Isthmus, and a more hostile environment for humans would be hard to find. Also—but not that it mattered—the island known as Seymour (actually known as Baltra by then) was about 50 miles away, and the wooden buildings had long since been dismantled and carried off by the locals.

Perhaps Harrsch was subsequently advised that his first choice of venue was not a good one, for by the time the first ship was ready to depart Washington, nothing further was heard of Isabela Island. Harrsch mentioned that the University had given him invaluable research help in island selection, and that island would now be San Cristóbal. He added that "This research shows that San Cristóbal has a lake large enough to insure an adequate water supply, and a sizable underground river." There is indeed a lake there, but no underground river.

Meanwhile, back at the University the study group offered an interesting overview of both the man and the plan:

> The leader perceived the Galápagos Islands as rich in marketable resources, and at various times referred to the possibilities of profit from coffee-growing, cattle-raising, lobster-fishing, seaweed gathering, tourist entertaining, and scientific research, especially biological studies.
>
> He drew plans for a specific complement of occupational types, including cattlemen, teachers, physicians, construction men, ship's crew, and, of course, administrators and bookkeepers. The organizational plan had the general form of a cooperative in which all but minor forms of property were to be owned communally.

Profits were to be split into three parts, distributed to individuals, to the community, and to a fund for scientific research. Workers would be paid on a differential scale of from two to five "wage units," according to the nature of each job. The president (Harrsch, of course) was to receive a considerably higher wage than any worker, as well as a bigger and better house, and one supplied with household servants. Harrsch would later explain that this leadership lifestyle was on the recommendation of local authorities, who advised that the community must thus fit into the Ecuadorian class system if it is to gain the proper respect of the natives.

The final document of organization, unworkable and inconsistent in the opinion of the study group, nevertheless persuaded some three dozen families to commit $2,500 each for one share of stock in the new company. Some were drawn in by a newspaper ad:

> Wanted: Swiss Family Robinson. Is your family one of the 50 adventurous families with the spirit of America's early pioneers needed to establish a model community on a beautiful Pacific island?

Others came by word-of-mouth, or from reading news of the venture in the local papers. An August issue of the *Seattle Times* ran a three-column report about the project.

100 FAMILIES SOUGHT:
Galapagos Islands Colony Planned by Seattle Firm

The paper noted that two local men, Clarence Elliott and Henry Lutterman, were already on the way to Galápagos to make a preliminary survey, and that prospective members would need to take "psychological tests to be sure they can get along with each other." But as time passed Harrsch was still short of families and had to lower his selection criteria, eventually settling for anyone with the money and the desire to join. He was not happy about this, telling the study group that the participants were "...too narrow and not good thinkers, but [he] believed he would be able to impose his own attitudes on them." He was wrong.

The troubles began. In late 1959, Harrsch purchased the 30-year-old tuna clipper *Alert* for $13,500 and departed with thirty persons. Or, he tried to depart. U. S. Coast Guard officials came up with a list of "recommended" repairs that should be made before sailing. Harrsch told the paper that the Coast Guard list was "... something of a quibble. Twenty-four recommendations sound like an awful lot wrong," he said. "But then, when you note they listed different fire extinguishers as separate points, you see how it adds up."

Ship's engineer Roland Dorsey added that many of the recommendations would be followed, "since there will be women and children aboard." He also noted that the main diesel engine "ticks like a clock." But apparently this clock had a casing in need of repair. The *Alert* successfully cleared the Port of Seattle's Libby wharf, made a brief stop at Lopez Island, traversed the Strait of Juan de Fuca separating Canada and the U. S., but got no farther than about 100 miles down Washington's Pacific coast. Then the Coast Guard brought the vessel into Westport after water leaking into the engine room reached a dangerous level.

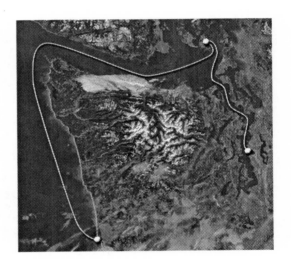

The *Alert* made it from Seattle north to Lopez Island, then out into the Pacific and south as far as Westport. Here, the ship was ordered into port for repair work.

White pattern in center is Olympia National Park.

The ship's pumps were out of action, and the *Alert* was ordered to stay in port until a full inspection was completed and "... all the nautical ills it reveals are cured. ... Don Harrsch, the expedition leader, is threatened with arrest if he does not comply with all Coast Guard regulations." The January 16th *Seattle Times* reported Harrsch's response: "The *Alert*, he said, could be made seaworthy in three days." After all, there wasn't that much that needed to be done, other than attend to a few little details: "The only things we haven't repaired are the bilge pumps and the life-saving equipment."

Ten days later, the paper reported *"Alert* free to Sail Again for Equator." The authorities still did not approve. According to Commander Lynn Parker, sufficient repairs had been made to allow the ship to depart, but "It does not, in the opinion of the Coast Guard, indicate in any way that this vessel is seaworthy."

Another week passed. Then on the last day of the month, the paper at last reported *"Alert* Leaves Westport for Galápagos." And on the next day, "Coast Guard Fears for Colony Ship." A severe gale was blowing off the Oregon coast, storm warnings were issued, and the cutter *Medoc* was sent out to escort the *Alert* back to port if conditions got much worse. Somehow the ship managed to weather the storm, yet all was still not well with the clock, and more bad weather plus more mechanical problems made for a slow voyage. But eventually the ship reached Wreck Bay, Isla San Cristóbal, on March 16, 1960.

Their arrival was not an entire success: under a "Reception Cool for Galápagos Colonists" headline, the *Seattle Times* reported that the island governor told the *Alert* passengers they were not permitted to land because "... they lacked adequate immigration documents." Fortunately, Ecuador's Minister of the Interior intervened—the governor was ordered to admit the colonists, all of whom had valid Ecuadorian visas.

Once on shore, the plans were that the colonists would immediately ship 20 tons of lobster back up north on the return trip for a $40,000 profit. Galen Kaufman, who had signed on as a cook "because I'm sure no sailor" was enthusiastic. "Our first money-maker will be lobsters. We've already got a contract with a California firm to take all the lobster we can supply." And local fishermen would catch those lobsters for them, "... under an agreement with the Government of Ecuador."

There were indeed local fishermen on the island, but no local lobsters in the surrounding waters. A few perhaps, but not enough to bring in much profit. And tuna fishing was no better, but that didn't matter either—the *Alert's* refrigeration system wasn't working properly. Until repairs could be made, the catch would need to be stored in the local refrigeration plant. Harrsch had put $30,000 down on it, but it was in worse shape than the facilities on the ship.

Two columns of pillars and a broken wall—all that remains today of the old refrigeration plant.

And then there was the coffee plantation up in the highlands, with an "owner" who was not quite what he seemed to be— just a squatter with no clear title to the land, but with clear vision of an opportunity for a fast buck. Trying to make the best of a bad situation, some of the colonists planted vegetables, and one of the gardeners described how that went:

> Pigs, burros and chickens ate everything we
> planted. So we built a fence. ... No sooner
> than the second crops began to shape up
> nicely, the rains came. For weeks on end the
> sun did not appear on the hill. Our garden
> died.

Meanwhile, back on the mainland it was election time and
the local Communist Party recognized an opportunity
when they saw it.

> Ecuadorians awaken! The small band of
> Americans in the Galápagos is but a prelude to
> a major-scale invasion. Yankee imperialists are
> about to take our islands.

A local newspaper editorial chimed in:

> Don't let the same thing happen to the
> Galápagos that happened in Texas.

Next, an Ecuadorian attorney got into the act:

> I helped establish the colony in the Galápagos,
> then discovered the leaders of the American
> group to be a bunch of adventurers with
> cockeyed ideas. They proposed to cure
> everyone in the islands of whatever diseases
> ailed them ... to re-educate the islanders to
> their way of thinking ... with belief in God
> relegated to a minor role. They claimed to
> have 50 million dollars in assets, that they
> represented at least 50 American companies.

While all this was going on down south, a second group of
colonists up north were getting ready for their own voyage.
Harrsch had purchased a second vessel—the *Western Trader*,
a refrigerator ship of dubious virtue. At this point, one of
the passengers picks up the story.

In Oregon, Stan Bettis had read one of those newspaper accounts telling of the Island Development Company, and the impending departure of the *Western Trader*. Bettis, still a week short of his nineteenth birthday, scraped up enough to buy his share and join the other passengers on the vessel. Neither he, nor they, knew of the trouble brewing down in Ecuador. And so on March 25th, 1960—just 10 days after the *Alert* had arrived at its destination—another 66 men, women and children sailed off for Galápagos, with a brief stopover in Los Angeles to pick up their visas.

Above: The *Western Trader* waiting at dockside in Seattle.

There were no visas. Advance word of the colonization plan had created such a furor in Ecuador that the government in Quito had second thoughts about the project. The visas would have to wait until after the election, when the new regime could decide what to do about all this.

Meanwhile at Pier 227 in the Port of Los Angeles, American officialdom paid a visit and history repeated itself. The Coast Guard wanted a hull inspection, and that led to the *Trader* being sent off to dry-dock for extensive—and expensive— repair work. Bettis watched the welders' torches working along the flanks of the old rust bucket, torches fueled by the hard cash of the colonists.

More passengers arrived, and soon there were 90—one section of the hold for men, another for women and children. Three toilets and two showers for everyone. The *Western Trader* was a pest hole awaiting a pest. It arrived.

Infectious hepatitis sent three desperately ill passengers off to the hospital. The others dutifully dropped their drawers for the pleasure of a sadistic public health nurse wielding a dull needle.

But in the meantime, things were not going well down in Galápagos, and the prediction of the study group back at the University of Washington was coming to pass. Within two months of the first arrival, the papers reported that almost three dozen Americans had been left stranded in Ecuadorian seaports on the mainland, and "... the others at San Cristóbal in the Galápagos are destitute and short of food and supplies."

In late May, the *Seattle Times* phoned the American Consulate in Guayaquil for details. "The colonists on the Galápagos Islands apparently are doing just fine," said Consul General Frederick Somerford. "It's been many weeks, however, and they desperately need supplies, especially building materials." Apparently the paper did not press Somerford to explain how colonists with desperate needs could be doing "just fine."

At about the same time, Harrsch returned home after spending weeks in Guayaquil waiting for money to arrive to buy supplies. According to his wife Teresa, "When it became obvious that we were not going to get any money for supplies, Don decided to fly back to the United States to find out what was wrong. ... He worked day and night and raised more than $5,000." And then, "He was on his way back to Ecuador when he was advised that he no longer was president of the company."

Doing fine or otherwise, the colonists had taken advantage of a provision in their charter to vote Harrsch out of office by a 90 percent majority. He never returned to the island. His office was taken over by Alex Reuss, a former insurance salesman who quit his job to become Vice President of the group. Two months later he was in turn replaced by an ex-fireman from Seattle. Both failed to turn the colony around and make it a success. A handful asked Harrsch to come back, but he'd had enough and declined the invitation.

Disenchanted colonists began drifting back north. On his return to Seattle, contractor Emory Tomlinson was asked about all those passengers still sitting on the dock in California, waiting for their visas to show up. "They might as well go along for the ride—they've already paid their money. Getting back, however, might be a problem." Tomlinson had little encouragement for those who would stay there: "All they can do is live like the Ecuadorians and eat nothing but fish, rice and bananas. Bananas sell for 12 cents a stalk, but most of them don't have the 12 cents. Who wants to live like that?"

But the *Western Trader* colonists were still not ready to quit and the new leadership was enthusiastic, announcing in mid-June that "We are confident we will be at San Cristóbal within three weeks." Four weeks later they were still sitting at the dock. And then finally on July 15th the long-awaited visas arrived. The brief stopover of the *Western Trader* at Pier 227 had lasted a bit longer than anticipated; four months. But at last the vessel was ready for departure.

Stan Bettis waiting at Pier 227 for the *Western Trader* to resume its voyage to Galápagos.

Well, almost ready. Now the Coast Guard pulled out the book of regulations. A 130-foot freighter such as the *Western Trader* could carry 50 passengers. No more. The others were obliged to get off and wait for the next departure, which of course never took place. They kept company with several tons of vital equipment—tractors, a jeep, small boats, and so on. All this was left on the dock because the Ecuadorians now decided they needed a payoff—a 100% duty to let the hardware into the country. The Island Development Company no longer had sufficient funds to grease the right palms, and bankruptcy would soon take the company if the ship waited around until things could be worked out. And so, on August 2, 1960, the *Western Trader* finally pulled out of its Los Angeles berth, leaving equipment and people behind.

Some two weeks later, the ship passed Isla Genovesa and shortly after dawn on August 18th, the *Western Trader* dropped anchor in Wreck Bay, Isla San Cristóbal. Bettis described the day:

> It was a fine day—an expanse of clear, calm water resting between arms of black lava. At the head of the bay, a dock reached out from a broad beach of dazzling white sand. Behind the beach stood the homes and larger buildings of Baquerizo Moreno, the "small Ecuadorian village" we had heard of time and time again. It was more of a village than any of us had envisioned.

> Our dreams of a primitive tropical paradise faded completely later on, when we learned that almost 1,000 Ecuadorians lived in the village and that many of the homes possessed indoor plumbing, running water, and electric lights.

The next day, Bettis and a few others walked up into the highlands to discover what they were searching for.

> Trees weighted down with oranges, papayas, mangoes, avocados, and other tropical fruits bordered the road. Bright flowers peeped out through the vivid greens. Delightfully strange scents drifted in the warm moist air. Birds chattered. Here was the tropical paradise we had expected, even if it was far from undeveloped.

> Owners of crude shacks nestled in the forest welcomed us in the same open fashion that we had encountered in Baquerizo Moreno. They spoke little English, we spoke less Spanish, but we managed to communicate on the basic, simple level of friendship. We were offered a shot of Galápagos hooch—a vile-tasting, vile-smelling, heavy-bodied liquor known as *puro*. It was an all-purpose product—drink it, sterilize surgical instruments in it, or use it to slick down your hair.

A 1960 photo of the village of Progreso taken by Jacob Lundh at about the time the colonists arrived.

Bettis was convinced. He would stay in Galápagos, regardless. Regardless that within hours of coming to anchor, it was clear to him that the Island Development Company was finished. The morale of the earlier colonists suffered a blow when they learned that the *Western Trader* did not bring the long-expected equipment—equipment left sitting on a Los Angeles dock for want of money to pay the import duties. The *Trader's* refrigeration engineer took one look at the freezing plant, and that was enough for him. Short of an entirely new plant, there was no hope for it. The old gear was just too old, too dilapidated.

About 30 colonists decided they'd had enough and would return to the United States on the *Trader's* return voyage. Of those who remained, few had illusions. They didn't expect to see the *Western Trader* again, and they were right. But one prospective colonist was able to make the best of a rather bad situation: Alfred Moody had driven his wife and three children from Sacramento, California to Calina Cruz in Mexico, there to pick up the *Trader* and continue on to Galápagos. They were in for a surprise. As expected, the ship was in port. As not expected, it was deserted. Plagued by mechanical problems, the returning colonists had abandoned the vessel and made their way home overland.

But the Moody family was not about to quit. They camped aboard the deserted ship for a few months, then learned that Mexican authorities were making plans to seize it. Mr. Moody loaded his car onto the deck, sent his wife down to the engine room and he to the bridge. The engine miraculously started, and the Moody crew brought the ship out past the startled—or possibly, sleeping—port guards. No one in the family had ever before set foot on a ship, not even a rowboat. Despite that, they managed to bring the *Western Trader* back to San Diego, where they claimed salvage rights. Moody's attorney summed it all up for him:

> There's a law of the sea that provides when a ship is abandoned or deserted by her crew, the vessel is fair game for anyone who claims her.

> The *Western Trader* was up for grabs, and you
> grabbed her—just ahead of the Mexicans.

The good ship *Alert* did not fare as well for herself or her crew. Caught up in a legal battle back in Panama, it was tied to a dock by red tape and there it eventually sank.

Back on San Cristóbal, a few stragglers hung around for awhile, then left individually or in small groups, until none but a handful were left. One of them offered his assessment of island life:

> There is nothing ... absolutely nothing in the
> Galápagos in the way of making a living, in
> achieving a better life. A totally different life,
> yes. But a better life, never. There's just nothing
> there. No great quantities of lobster or fish. No
> transportation. No road. No way to clear the
> land. No way to farm. And most important,
> not enough water.

There was of course that "...lake large enough to insure an adequate water supply" but, as another colonist pointed out, "You couldn't drink it without getting dysentery."

Almost-always shrouded in mist, El Junco is the only fresh-water lake in Galápagos. Drink at your own risk.

The study group drew its conclusions:

> Many of the colonists had gone to Galápagos
> optimistically supposing they were without
> illusions. ... They not only uprooted themselves
> from their home communities and moved to a
> strange environment—strange geographically,
> culturally, climatically, and politically—but
> compounded the task of adjusting by trying to
> build a social system none of them had previously
> experienced. The illusion that they had no
> illusions probably aggravated their hardships.
> ... Every circumstance bore against success, and
> quick failure was perceptible in all stages of the
> short unhappy life of Filiate Science Antrorse.

And Stan Bettis drew his:

> The great dream ended, not with a bang but with
> a whimper. There were a few hard feelings, but
> the common emotion was sadness. There was
> an embarrassment about parting—the unspoken
> embarrassment of friends who have shared failure.

Bettis climbed down the side of the *Western Trader* for the
last time and up the side of an Ecuadorian lobster boat that
was working the island waters. He spent some time as crew,
but eventually lost his conviction to stay in Galápagos,
regardless. He moved back home, and that was the end
of the Island Development Company and *Filiate Science
Antrorse.*

CHAPTER TWENTY-TWO

A Brief History of History

Very few things happen at the right time,
and the rest do not happen at all:
The conscientious historian will correct
these defects.

Herodotus (?)

THERE IS A WELL-KNOWN RESEARCH THEOREM—or if there isn't, there should be—which defines the inverse relationship between a historical event and its description in The Literature. The Literature is here defined as that body of work written by people who were neither born, nor knew anyone born, at the time the alleged event took place. The theorem holds that the first time a significant event is chronicled in The Literature, the description may be accurate. When the same event appears a second time, the description may not be accurate. The third description is certainly not accurate, and so on, until by the time the event passes through the hands—or what seems more likely, the digestive system—of the modern conscientious historian, any similarity between the description and what actually happened is too remote to be seriously considered. To demonstrate the proof we need look no further than the subject of this little opus—the Galápagos Islands.

The early human history of the islands is sketchy at best and much of what little we know comes from the journals of buccaneers and explorers celebrated here on other pages. But these gentlemen usually had other things on their mind than history, so we can't always depend on them to give us the details we crave. There are, therefore, important facts missing throughout many original sources. Or rather, there were. It turns out that the early history of Galápagos continues to evolve, thanks to assorted twentieth-century authorities who, with few real facts on which to hang a tale, have conjured up their own. To follow the lead of those well-known historians Gilbert and Sullivan, these new facts deliver a certain "artistic verisimilitude to an otherwise bald and unconvincing narrative." Let's have a look at some of the more ludicrous examples of what we might call Creative History 101.

Many authorities agree on an important point first brought to public attention in 1803, when James Burney wrote that *"Los Galapagos"* appeared on a 1570 map created by the noted cartographer Abraham Ortelius. Selected 20th-century authorities now tell us that:

A.) [The islands] ... were named "Isolas de Galapagos" by Abraham Ortelius ... in 1574.

B.) The islands appear on Ortelius' *Theatrum Orbis Terrarum,* published at Antwerp in 1570, as *Insulae de los Galopegos.*

C.) Ortelius seems to have been the first to name them and he showed them as "Isolas de Galapagos" in his *Orbis Terrarum* published in 1574.

D.) The name Galápagos (tortoises) first appeared in the *Theatrum orbis terrarum* of Ortelius in 1570.

Isolas, Insulae, Galapagos, Galopegos, 1570, 1574, take your pick. No doubt one of the answers above is correct, but which shall it be? Those who are not quite sure about this may want to consult Ortelius himself, something that may not have occurred to the distinguished historians who study these things. His 1570 *Theatrum Orbis Terrarum* shows two island groups labeled "Ins. de los Galopegos" and "Ins. de los Galepegos." One is just above the  equator, the other slightly to the northeast. So, the fourth choice above appears to be the best answer, at least to those who have never studied geography.

To those who have though, the name Gerard Mercator may ring a bell. Seamen found a Mercator Projection map quite reliable in plotting a course across great expanses of open water. They also found the Galápagos Islands on it—in fact, they're also on it twice.

Above: A 1570 Ortelius map shows the Galápagos Islands—twice. But it's not the first even to do that.

So, it would appear that Mercator borrowed his Galápagos Islands from Ortelius, except for one little detail: it was the other way around—Mercator got there first. His map is dated 1569—one year pre-Ortelius. That's not much of a lead, but it is enough to show that Ortelius didn't name the islands. But then, neither did Mercator, for on page 10 we saw "Galapagos" on that vellum chart drawn perhaps a quarter-century earlier. Of course that chart is not very well known, and so quite easy to overlook. But how can one write of maps, and overlook the name of Mercator? One may wonder if some future authority will write a conscientious history of evolution and forget to mention Charles Darwin.

And now, we skip ahead a century or so, to rediscover the literary buccaneers whom we met earlier. Alas for history, the merry lads were not interviewed along their way, or if they were, the transcripts have not survived. So, about all we really know about them, and about their adventures, is what they themselves have told us. They may very well have been lying through their dagger-clamping teeth, but today we have no other accounts but their own for what went on way back then.

For example, whatever did happen along the coast of West Africa, on the way to Galápagos and beyond? About certain less-then-honorable exploits, William Dampier and Lionel Wafer say nothing and nothing, respectively. So, we're left with William Cowley's account of how he himself engineered the capture of a Danish ship. He's quite specific: they jumped aboard, overpowered the crew, set them onshore, and went on their merry way. As for their old ship, Cowley tells us the crew "set her on fire, by reason she should tell no tales." That's all we know. Lies? Perhaps. Omissions? No doubt, but who can say?

Who indeed? Why, the conscientious historian of course. Or better yet two of them, with apparently inside information about what *really* happened to that ship. According to a 1960 report by the British naval historians P. K. Kemp and Christopher Lloyd, "One account suggests that she was burned 'that she might tell no tales'." Well, so it did (*see* previous paragraph). But the modern authors tell us that

> ... another and possibly more likely statement
> is that she was exchanged farther down the
> coast for sixty young negro girls who served
> as a diversion for the buccaneers until they
> perished miserably one by one in the icy
> wastes of the Antarctic.

A more likely statement indeed, but one which seems to have originated in the fertile minds of Kemp and Lloyd, who apparently felt that a bit of artistic verisimilitude was needed to dress up Cowley's bald and unconvincing narrative. But alas, the authors may not have kept a record of their own inventions. A few years later Lloyd wrote a biography of William Dampier. In the intervening years, he may have forgotten a few trivial details, such as what happened to the ship, where the ladies came from, and where they went.

> How they disposed of the *Revenge* and of the
> sixty black girls they found on board their
> prize, we do not know.

Perhaps Lloyd hadn't read Kemp & Lloyd, but on that point, we do not know. But we do we know where Lloyd got the following tidbit about William Dampier at dinner with Samuel Pepys:

> One of the gentlemen of the Royal Society, of a
> higher station in life than he could ever aspire
> to, whom he met at the time that he dined
> with Evelyn and Pepys, called him "a blunt
> fellow, but of better understanding than would
> have been expected from one of his education."

The Diary of John Evelyn gives us the only known account of this dinner. He writes that "I dined with Pepys, where was Captain Dampier." If the table was indeed set for four, neither Evelyn nor Dampier thought enough of the gentleman of a higher station to mention his presence, and Pepys had given up writing his own diary years earlier. Well then, how did Christopher Lloyd come up with that "blunt fellow" description of our man Dampier? Perhaps he read a letter by Charles Hatton to his brother Christopher, written about one year before Dampier dined with Pepys. Hatton begins "I have discoursed with Dampier" and then offers the "blunt fellow" description. No doubt both the Hattons were gentlemen of high station—Christopher was in fact the first Viscount Hatton—but neither were gentlemen of the Royal Society. An earlier Christopher—the first Baron Hatton—had been in the Royal Society, but he died almost 30 years before Dampier's dinner with Evelyn and Pepys.

At about the time of that dinner, Sir Hans Sloane commissioned Thomas Murray to paint Dampier's portrait. The work must have been well-received, for in the introduction to an early 20th-century edition of Dampier's works, editor John Masefield tells us that, "An engraving of it, by Charles Sherwin, was published during Dampier's lifetime." William Bonner, one of Dampier's biographers, apparently consulted Masefield, for he writes of the portrait that "An engraving was made from it and published during Dampier's lifetime."

The Sherwin engraving was in fact published on March 2, 1787, which is about 40 years after Dampier's death. And there's little reason to suspect it had been created while its subject was still alive. For when Sherwin was born, Dampier had already been in the ground for some 15 years.

Another Dampier-watcher furnishes background on his personal life. In the late 19th century, biographer W. Clark Russell wrote that "I think we may take it that he never married whilst he pursued his sea-life." Perhaps Russell did not wish to tire himself by actually reading Dampier's first book, in which he mentions his marriage. And then about a century later, in a book about the cartographer

Herman Moll, we learn that Dampier set out on one of his voyages "after buying some land in Dorset and setting his now-pregnant wife upon it." And, to complete the fable,

> Dampier made enough money, coupled with the
> royalties from his books, to live well until his death
> in 1715 and leave his family comfortably situated.

Other than these late twentieth-century statements, there is no record of Judith being left in a family way, or of Dampier receiving royalties of any amount from his books—although one may certainly hope he saw at least a little something for all that work. If he lived well and left his family comfortably situated, that information has also escaped notice.

In addition to the interesting Dampierian details perpetrated on history by Kemp & Lloyd, we may suspect that other "authorities" went no further than these writers when concocting their own accounts of Dampier, Cowley and friends. One tells us what happened after the Danish ship was captured.

> They rechristened her the *Batchelor's Delight*, and
> seem to have made her live up to her name by
> taking on a company of black girls, to perish in the
> cold of Cape Horn.

Another inverts the sequence:

> Nor do they say what fate befell the sixty black
> girls they found on the Danish ship, although
> there is a jocular clue in the fact that they
> promptly renamed their ship the *Batchelor's Delight*.

Or, if you prefer ethnic cleansing, …

> Captain Cowley and his crew once allowed five
> dozen captive women to perish from the cold as
> they sailed southward along the coast toward Cape
> Horn.

But whether it's sixty black girls, or five dozen captive women, the unfortunate females have one thing in common: they are never mentioned by William Dampier, William Ambrosia Cowley, or Lionel Wafer. Cowley did however mention a capture that may have set the stage for this fanciful fable. In a September 30th entry in his journal, he describes the capture of a ship "… having sixty men on board, and we having but twenty in the canoe." But this was in 1685, some two *years* later, and in a different sea. At the time, Cowley and company were in the Pacific, the captured ship was on its way to Japan, and its crew were not female. In fact, the only similarity between the reports of Cowley and Kemp & Lloyd is the number of captives. Is this all it took to inspire their invention, or just a coincidence? As the authors themselves might have put it, "we do not know." Perhaps they were simply following Mark Twain's suggestion: "Truth is the most valuable thing we have. Let us economize it."

As for the ship which carried Cowley and friends to Galápagos, Lionel Wafer is the one—the *only* one—who ever mentions it by name. He tells us of a time when Mr. Dampier went off to the Westward on another ship but, as for himself, "I staid with Captain Davis, in the *Batchelors Delight*." Period. The time was late August, 1685, or about two years after the capture of the Danish vessel. No doubt their prize's former name was something suitably Danish, but why and when did the merry lads decide to call it *Batchelors Delight?* We have no idea, and neither do the modern historians, who are therefore free to invent their own time line.

And speaking of William Ambrosia, the 1924 edition of Philip Gosse's *The Pirates' Who's Who* describes him as Captain William C. Cowley, and introduces new intelligence: he is now the possessor of a Master of Arts degree from Cambridge University, "a man of high intelligence and an able navigator." And then just a few years later, William Dampier's biographer Clennel Wilkinson puts his own subject aside for a moment to tell us something about Cowley: "Although an M. A. of Cambridge University, he is neither a very lively nor a very reliable historian."

Now if William Ambrosia was not a very reliable historian, neither was critic Wilkinson, who clearly didn't like him very much. He notes that Cowley irresponsibly named a tiny island in Galápagos for himself, for which the biographer pronounces him "A conceited ass!" The exclamation mark is by Wilkinson, who might have left it out if he'd studied another mariner's words on the subject of name-calling.

> "These islands having no particular names in
> the drafts, some or other of us made use of the
> Seamens priviledge, to give them what names
> we please."

Although the quotation does not refer to the Galápagos Islands, it comes from the works of William Dampier, with which (one hopes) Mr. Wilkinson was familiar.

Here's another excerpt from Cowley that did not escape Wilkinson's critical attention:

> "We steer'd away S. W. finding the Sea as red
> as Blood about the lat. of 40 deg. South, which
> was occasioned by great Shoals of Shrimps,
> which lay upon the water in great patches for
> many Leagues together."

Apparently this was too much for Dampier's biographer, who dismissed the commentary with "The value of some of Cowley's observations may be judged from his assertion that the sea was 'red as blood,' owing to the number of 'shrimps' swimming about in it." Again, Wilkinson overlooked a little something written by Dampier himself:

> "We saw great shoals of small Lobsters, which
> coloured the Sea in red spots, for a Mile in
> compass, and we drew some of them out of
> the Sea in our Water-buckets."

The same phenomenon was also reported by another observer of some note, and we may wonder what value Wilkinson would have placed on this observation by Charles Darwin:

> "In the sea around Tierra del Fuego, and at
> no great distance from the land, I have seen
> narrow lines of water of a bright red colour,
> from the number of crustacea, which somewhat
> resemble in form large prawns."

But let's get back to our man Cowley, to his education and, of all things, to a piratical pen name. In that 1960 account mentioned earlier, Kemp & Lloyd describe him as

> ... a man who had taken a Master of Arts
> degree at Cambridge and had some skill
> as a navigator. Although, for a reason not
> hard to discover, he concealed for a time his
> name under the pseudonym of "an ingenious
> Englishman", he was in fact William Ambrose
> Cowley.

Unlike these ingenious Englishmen, the modern reader may have a bit of trouble with the concept of a man signing himself onto a buccaneering vessel as Master's Mate, taking that vessel around the Horn, yet not telling the Master — or anyone else — his name. The modern reader may also wonder what source inspired this little bit of historic nonsense. Perhaps the fable can be traced to one of several surviving copies of Cowley's manuscript journal, where an unknown copyist penned the following introduction:

An exact Journal of A voyage sail'd from the Gorgona to Batavia & from thence north about Scotland to Holland by an Ingenious English man &c/

Four other copies of the same journal clearly identify its author by name. No doubt Cowley was ingenious, and surely an Englishman too, but it does take a bit of creative imagination to deduce from this introduction that an entire ship's company would put themselves in the hands of a man with no name. But as evidence that this might indeed have been so, Kemp and Lloyd note that Dampier made no mention of Cowley. Perhaps they should have followed his example.

And what of Cowley? Did he ever mention his more-famous shipmate? According to one author, yes and no. Or rather, no and yes: In his Introduction to a 1927 edition of Dampier's *New Voyage,* Sir Albert Gray notes that Dampier "... is not even mentioned by ... Cowley." And then, later in the same introduction, "He is once respectfully mentioned as 'Mr. William Dampier' by Cowley." Well, was he or wasn't he? The conscientious historian will find the answer in Cowley's own book, where he describes a reunion with a Moskito Indian left behind on Juan Fernandez Island some years before. When Cowley and the others called at the island, he tells us there were "... several of our Ships Company who were at the leaving of this *Indian* there by Capt. *Sharpe,* and among others Capt. *Edmund Cook* and Mr. William Dampier."

But to return to Master Cowley's credentials. The fable evolves: some thirty years after Kemp and Lloyd concocted that "ingenious Englishman" nonsense, Kemp—now Editor of the *Oxford Companion to Ships and the Sea*—informs us that our man was an "English mathematician and navigator" and offers even more details about his penchant for secrecy.

> Cowley, as a man of some education,
> attempted to preserve his anonymity
> throughout, and hid his name as author
> of his journal under the pseudonym "an
> ingenious Englishman." The whole [journal]
> was published in William Hack's *Collection of
> Voyages* in 1699, still under Cowley's original
> pseudonym.

In fact, Cowley's whole journal was *never* published, though there is a much-abridged version in *A Collection of Original Voyages*, published in 1699 by Capt William Hacke (with an "e"). According to the title page, the first entry in the collection is "Capt. *Cowley's* Voyage round the GLOBE" (italics in original). His "original pseudonym" appears nowhere in the book.

Readers who would seek more information about Cowley's academic credentials are advised not to consult the pages of the venerable *Alumni Cantabrigiensis*. Cambridge University has no record of a 17th-century graduate named William Cowley. Nor is there anything for Ingenious Englishman.

In addition to rewarding Cowley with his advanced degree, *The Pirate's Who's Who* by Philip Gosse claims he "was addicted to giving new names to islands," including an unspecified place that he dubbed "Pepys Island." Dampier's biographer Clennell Wilkinson decrees that this island "simply did not exist." Well then, if it did not exist, then what? In Cowley's printed account of the voyage, one reads that "We came into the latitude of 47 degrees where we saw land; the same being an island not before known. It was not inhabited [how on earth could he know that?] and I gave it the name of Pepys Island." This angers Wilkinson, who inserts the bracketed question in the narrative and speculates that Cowley's publisher may have been deceived by this erroneous latitude for the Sibble de Wards Islands— better known today as the Falkland Islands. So he took it to be both a new discovery and an opportunity to compliment Samuel Pepys. After all, Cowley had named many of the Galápagos Islands, so it would follow that he might have done the same with other islands, if only he had thought of it. But he hadn't, so the publisher thought of it for him.

But how could this be? Wilkinson offers a suggestion: "In his manuscript journal, Cowley merely states that they espied an island in latitude 47° 40'." He doesn't trouble us with a little something else that Cowley wrote: "These islands that we saw I supposed to be the Sibble de Wards." In short, Cowley knew exactly where he was, and Wilkinson knew that Cowley knew it too.

It was the publisher who "moved" the islands slightly north to 47 degrees (instead of the 47° 40' as in the journal), then deleted Cowley's correct identification and inserted the Pepysian tribute. Did he do all this with or without the author's consent? Of course we don't know, and no doubt never will. But motivation need not be a mystery if we remember William Dampier's dinner date with Sam Pepys. If this literary buccaneer's exploits brought him to the favorable notice of Pepys and his circle, perhaps naming a "new" island after the great man would do the same for Cowley, for his publisher, or for both of them.

Cowley is treated with a bit more sympathy in George Wycherly's *Buccaneers of the Pacific*, where the author describes him as "a very intelligent, amiable man and a skilful navigator." Wycherly then has a go at describing Captain Edward Davis who, he tells us, "landed at the Island of Jamaica, with a booty said, by one account, to amount to fifty thousand pieces-of-eight, besides much silver and many jewels." That "one account" may have been Gosse's *Who's Who*, which reports the same inventory. By the late twentieth century the Davis loot had appreciated significantly, due no doubt to inflation. Perhaps that's why it was moved to Coco Island, where as one writer informs us:

> In 1685, according to journals, Davis left "733
> bars of pure gold, each four by three inches
> in measure and two inches thick ... and
> bejeweled swords, precious stones and three
> kettles of gold coins." Later, Davis surrendered
> to an offer of amnesty from King James II, king
> of England, Scotland and Ireland. It is not clear
> if he ever recovered his treasure.

Needless to say, the writer does not identify the "journals" which he consulted. The only known potential journalist along at the time was Lionel Wafer, who makes the following confession in his own book: "I was but Young when I was abroad, and I kept no Journal."

When Davis and Wafer left the Pacific, both Gosse and Wycherly inform us that Davis accepted an offer of pardon from King James while at Jamaica (he didn't), settled down in comfort at the well-named Point Comfort in Virginia (didn't do that either), then lapsed back into his old habits some fourteen years later (ditto).

In fact, Captain Davis and Lionel Wafer did not voluntarily surrender to anyone. They were subsequently captured in Chesapeake Bay, and after some stout denials that they were pirates, eventually appealed for His Majesty's gracious pardon. It took them some years to get it, and transcripts from James Towne Court show that Davis was illiterate. Although Lionel Wafer signed the depositions, Davis scratched out an awkward "E" and had to let it go at that. Sometimes even that was too much, and the "E" would tumble on its side, like a crude "M." But in any case, the court clerk would write "his mark" and "Edward Davis" above and below these rustic signatures.

In his 1949 *Ecuador and the Galápagos Islands,* anthropologist Victor Wolfgang von Hagen identifies the Captain as Edward "Iron Ass" Davis. Some twenty years later, an unsigned Galápagos feature appeared in a magazine for doctors. With many "facts" lifted from von Hagen, apparently the editors felt the new identity too indelicate for medical sensitivities—accordingly, the Captain became Edward "Iron Pants" Davis. Neither von Hagen nor his anonymous plagiarist explain how (or why) Davis acquired his ferrous fanny.

Edward Davis signed himself "E" and John Hinson was "2" on James Towne court records. The court clerk wrote "his mark" and the name of the person around each such mark. Apparently only Lionel Wafer—who styled himself "Delawafer"—was up to the task of signing his name.

When Lionel Wafer's book was eventually published some years after his detention in Virginia, it contained a brief account of *Davis's Expedition to the Gold Mines, in 1702.* Wycherly and other historians have concluded that the *Expedition's* author was none other than our friend Captain Davis, late of the *Batchelors Delight.* The evidence against this possibility is in plain sight yet apparently invisible to scholars. Cowley and Dampier have both told us their Captain's first name was Edward, as do the court transcripts.

Although Wafer refers to him simply as Captain Davis, he takes the trouble to identify the author of *Expedition* as a *Mister Nathaniel* Davis. So, in order for the Captain to be the author, he would have had to learn how to read and write almost overnight, and learned so well that he could become an author. He would also need to have changed his name from Edward to Nathaniel, get back to Central America from England and then back to England in time to be included in Wafers' book. And Wafer, who spent years as shipmate, and no little time later as cell mate to Davis, would have had to find his friend's hasty transformation from an illiterate *Captain Edward* to a literary *Mr. Nathaniel* not worthy of an explanation to the reader.

Although we may never know the real identity of our Mr. Nathaniel, we do know that he possessed a certain gift for geographical detail, especially when it came to measuring hills. As his little group went off in search of the mines, he tells us that

> We mounted one of their mountains ... it was above a Mile and a half high, and not twenty yards of plain Ground on it, so that some of the Men fainted and were ordered back again to the House we came from.

Two pages later ...

> We rested at Night on the top of a very high Mountain, which according to the best of my Computation could not be less that four or five Miles in heighth.

Same page, a few days later ...

We were incommoded with getting up to a prodigious Mountain, which, I believe, could not be less than six Miles high.

We were incommoded with getting up to a prodigious Mountain, which, I believe, could not be less than six Miles high.

And then, the very next day ...

This Day we marched over the highest of all the Mountains; and such a one as I thought Man could not be able to get up: I do really believe it could not be less than seven or eight miles high. Some of our Men imagin'd it to be within a stone's cast of Heaven.

This Mr. Davis—whoever he is—has the distinction of being the first in the long series of historical liars celebrated in this chapter. But, having nothing further to add to our story, we leave him at his summit and wonder how he might have coped with the highest spot in all the Americas—Argentina's Mount Aconcagua, a comparative mole hill not quite 4½ real miles high.

To return to Messrs. Cowley and Dampier, Victor Wolfgang von Hagen describes their return from Galápagos:

After months of terrifying weather in which Ambrose Cowley, Lionel Wafer, and William Dampier almost went down in the Fuegian gales, they put into Montevideo. There the curtain falls on the *Bachelor's Delight*.

Long before the *Batchelors Delight* began its return voyage, the two Williams had transferred to other ships and eventually made their well-documented *westward* returns to England, across the Pacific and around the Cape of Good Hope. Nor was there much chance of a final curtain in Montevideo anyway, for a stage with that name would not exist for another quarter of a century. Or as Lionel Wafer put it, "The Country hereabouts is well watered, but without any inhabitants." And as for the *Batchelors Delight,* Wafer has already told us that he (and it) made it all the way back to the Caribbean without much incident.

No doubt William Ambrosia Cowley will be getting his doctorate in short order, but while waiting for news of that event, we might take a closer look at early Yankee Imperialism. After dropping Dampier and the others off at Montevideo, von Hagen goes on to re-write the role of Captain David Porter, U. S. Navy, in Galápagos history:

> Captain Porter claimed the Galápagos for the
> United States. Not being able to garrison any
> of the islands, he raised the Stars and Stripes
> over Chatham Island, and nailed under it title
> to the islands in the name of the United States
> of America.

Well, yes—Porter did raise the Stars and Stripes on an island claimed for his country, and he named it Madison in honor of the President. The island was (still is) Nuka Hiva, now part of the French Marquesas archipelago and about 3,000 miles west of Ecuador's Chatham. All the thanks Porter received for his initiative, von Hagen tells us, was a reprimand followed by a court-martial for the twin offenses of disobedience and exceeding orders. The verdict and consequences of the court martial were not pleasant:

> Found guilty of "taking" the Galápagos, he was
> suspended for six months without pay. That
> was too much for America's greatest seaman.

> He resigned his commission and sailed for
> Mexico, where he organized its navy.

Right again, almost. Porter was indeed suspended for six months. For an action taken in Puerto Rico, which is in a different sea. It all took place more than ten *years* after he claimed an island in the Marquesas—not Galápagos—group for the United States. Porter requested a leave of absence, which was granted, and received full pay during the period of his suspension. He resigned his commission about one year after the trial.

Of course buccaneers and U. S. Navy captains are not the only ones to fall victim to the conscientious historian. Even poor old Lorenz and Nuggerud eventually became the subject for other historians with a flair for creative writing. After their bodies were discovered on Isla Marchena, a February 18, 1935 account in the Ecuadorian newspaper *El Universo* by reporter Carlos Luna R. spun a fanciful tale that Lorenz was not in fact trying to leave the islands after the disappearance of the Baroness. Instead, he had talked Nuggerud into taking him to Isla Santiago, where he could hide out for awhile. The pair landed on Isla Marchena, but by the time they realized their mistake, Nuggerud's boat— with his boatman José Pazmiño—had drifted away, never to be seen again. The pair had nothing to do but await their fate.

The same newspaper report published a photo showing the burial of their mummified remains on the island's sandy beach.

El Entierro de Los Cadáveres

Guayaquil, Ecuador: *El Universo*, February 18, 1935.

"The cadavers of Lorenz and Nuggerud were interred in a pit dug with difficulty in the sand. In solemn silence, the mummified bodies of the victims of the Marchena tragedy were covered with sand."

In 1952, William Albert Robinson paid a return visit to the Galápagos Islands, and he later wrote about it in his book *To the Great Southern Sea*. He had met Trygve Nuggerud many years earlier, and of course knew the story of his death on Isla Marchena. And now, almost 20 years later, Robinson found himself near the very beach where Lorenz and Nuggerud lay buried in their sandy tomb. Apparently the author had a pair of most remarkable field glasses on board:

> The remains were still visible with the binoculars, just around the point from the cove where we anchored. ... We had thought of staying there at anchor for the night, but the place was ominous. ... We left, almost in a hurry.

In the middle of the twentieth century, Joseph Slevin's *Galápagos Islands: A History of their Exploration* was published by the California Academy of Sciences. The author had made extensive use of old manuscript journals, and at some unknown point their identities were mixed up. Unfortunately Slevin died before the history was published, and it was left to his editors to see the work through the press, which may account for a few errors. The manuscript of William Dampier is attributed to Ambrose Cowley, and credit for Cowley's own manuscript is given to the illiterate Edward Davis, who is called Davies here. A footnote explains that this is the spelling found in the Cowley manuscript, which means it's really in the Dampier manuscript.

These unique juxtapositions make it possible to determine which post-Slevin historians have consulted original sources, and which have been content to plagiarize Slevin. Not a few have chosen the latter option, and it's not difficult to find out who they are. Some have even copied the misspelling of Captain Edward D's last name.

In 1970, the Sierra Club published an elegant two-volume *Galápagos: The Flow of Wildness*, in which Loren Eiseley offers a superb one-line definition which speaks volumes. Natural selection, he writes, "is, in essence, a selective death rate which promotes the survival of those creatures whose genetic qualities most successfully meet the needs of a given environment." While clearing up that little mystery of mysteries, the book introduces a new one. The first chapter of the first volume presents an excerpt from the journal of Edward Davis (that is, of Ambrosia Cowley), followed by a few pages written by Salvator R. Tarnmoor. The work is not identified, nor is information offered about its author. The next chapter offers an extensive excerpt from Herman Melville's *The Encantadas,* and the perceptive reader may note a stylistic similarity between these writers. Indeed, it would be surprising if there were no similarity, for Tarnmoor *is* Melville. The unidentified excerpt is also taken from *The Encantadas,* which was first published in three issues of *Putnam's Monthly Magazine* under the pseudonym, Salvator R. Tarnmoor. Why is part of the story credited to Tarnmoor and another part to Melville? That is just one more mystery of mysteries.

It appears that creative history is still alive and well in the 21st century: In his 2002 book *Galápagos,* author John Kricher tells us that,

> ... in the case of the tortoises, Darwin believed
> that they were not native to the archipelago
> but instead represented a species that had been
> brought by sailors from elsewhere, probably
> to serve as a food source. ... Darwin never
> regarded them as native and thus paid little
> attention to them other than for amusement.

But could it be that the famed Galápagos visitor would ignore the famed Galápagos residents? Or did modern scholarship ignore Darwin? Well, we already know that he didn't pay sufficient attention to the differences between one tortoise and another, but he did reach the following conclusion in *Voyage of the Beagle:*

There can be little doubt that this tortoise is an aboriginal inhabitant of the Galápagos; for it is found on all, or nearly all, the islands, even on some of the smaller ones where there is no water; had it been an imported species, this would hardly have been the case in a group which has been so little frequented.

And as for the origin of the tortoise species, it was FitzRoy (not Darwin) who wrote that

... in simple truth, there is no other animal in the whole creation so easily caught, so portable, requiring so little food for a long period, and at the same time so likely to have been carried, for food, by the aborigines who probably visited the Galapagos Islands.

FitzRoy doesn't explain why these aborigines went to the bother of dropping off different species on different islands though. Perhaps to torment conscientious naturalists years later.

Herodotus is often credited with a perceptive observation about historians, all because of a 19th-century author who once wrote:

Herodotus says, "Very few things happen at the right time, and the rest do not happen at all: The conscientious historian will correct these defects."

Well, if "the Father of History" said it is so, then it must be so. Right? Not quite. That 19th-century writer was Mark Twain, spinner of the tall tale and inventor of the catchy quote which introduces this chapter, and before that appeared in the Acknowledgements for his *A Horse's Tale*. It's just the sort of thing that Twain certainly would—and Herodotus certainly would not—write on the subject. Yet despite the improbable attribution, and the reputation of the attributor, today's conscientious historians often look no further than the 19th century for their facts. And in the case of Galápagos historians, some don't even look that far back.

And that's a fact.

CHAPTER TWENTY-THREE

WHAT'S IN A NAME?

*The Main Islands of the Galápagos
are twice-named.*

Tom Stoppard, 1981

TWICE-NAMED, AND THEN SOME. Many islands of the Galápagos are more than twice-named, and two have been named about a dozen times. Even "Galápagos" itself has not escaped—the "Man and the Galápagos" chapter in William Beebe's 1924 *Galápagos: World's End*, pointed out that "Ecuador, in a recent (1892) commemorative frenzy, renamed it the Archipelago of Colon." Ruth Rose, who wrote that chapter, put the matter in perspective:

> As the White Knight would say, "Galápagos
> isn't its *name*; it's only what it's *called*."

At that time the nation celebrated the 400ᵗʰ anniversary of Columbus' discovery of—not Ecuador, not even Galápagos, but of what he thought was a suburb of Japan. And even if the Ecuadorians were not really that frenzied, they nevertheless did go to a lot of bother to honor the great admiral who died neither seeing nor suspecting the Pacific Ocean, nor any of its islands—enchanted or otherwise.

But then, why shouldn't Ecuador go to a lot of bother?—When it comes to names, just about everyone else has. Of course today's visitor needn't go to any bother at all to sort out the names that have been given to this or that island by this or that visitor. It's just not that important, especially since the Ecuadorians themselves have given us the last, the final, and the official word on the subject. But it is a lot of fun, provided one doesn't go to the bother of trying to make much sense out of it all. For names have come and names have gone, and names have moved from one island to another. Some islands have had many names, but at least one doesn't have any (that too is official). Let's have a look.

Popular folklore has it that in the old days the islands had the annoying habit of drifting about and were rarely found where one expected to find them. And so the Spaniards marked them on their charts as Las Encantadas—The Enchanteds—because surely an enchanted spell was the best way to explain the unexplainable. It's a charming—one might say, enchanting—legend, but it doesn't hold up well under scrutiny. To this day, no one has found an old Spanish chart with anything but Galápagos on it, and in fact Encantadas never appears on any map.

Laurie & Whittle's 1794 chart is one of only two known to refer to the islands as enchanted (or here, Inchanted).

Well, almost never. In 1775, Galapagos or Inchanted Is. appeared on an English map drawn by Robert Sayer, and again on a 1794 map by Laurie & Whittle. And then the label disappeared until Herman Melville wrote his *Las Encantadas* in the middle of the following century. Everyone else, Spaniards included, preferred Galápagos.

Eventually the enchanted Galápagos attracted the favorable notice of British buccaneers, notably our friends the two Williams—Dampier and Cowley. These pugnacious Protestants found the islands a convenient resting place after the fatigue of harassing the ships and shores of his Catholic Spanish majesty. But a good buccaneer—that is, a good *British* buccaneer—would surely consider it an impropriety to visit an island that did not have a proper name of its own, an important point yet one apparently overlooked—with one known exception—by both Spanish sailors and European cartographers.

To compensate for the oversight, the first round of name-calling began in 1684, under the personal supervision of William Ambrosia Cowley, whose adventures were described here in another chapter. Back in pre-Cowley days, the Spaniards spoke of a place called Santa María de l'Aquada. Although we now know this to be one of the Galápagos Islands, it doesn't show up on Cowley's own chart, and other charts of his era placed it out of reach, much farther south and west than it actually is. Given his penchant for name-dropping, it's safe to assume that Cowley didn't know anything about it. Cowley's shipmate and fellow author William Dampier speculates that Captain Davis eventually went there, some time after both he and Cowley had left the *Batchelors Delight*.

A few years later some French visitors stopped by. Add Mascarin, Tabac and Sante to the mix. And then about twenty years later, Captain Woodes Rogers followed the crowd out to Galápagos, after the obligatory sack of Guayaquil. The event had become somewhat of a buccaneering tradition, if not quite the highlight of the mainland social season. Rogers also conjectures that Davis may indeed have led his merry lads to Santa María de l'Aquada. But then again, maybe he didn't. He gripes that although Davis claims to have eventually found an island with water on it (as Santa María had, and still has),

> ... all the light he has left to find it again is,
> that it lies to the Westward of those Islands he
> was at with the other Buccaneers.

But in any case Rogers doesn't think the account of a buccaneer can stand too much scrutiny, no doubt with the possible exception of his own:

> These sort of men, and others I have convers'd
> with, or whose Books I have read, have given
> very blind or false Relations of their Navigation,
> for supposing the Places too remote to have
> their Stories disprov'd, they imposed on the
> Credulous, amongst whom I was one, till now I
> too plainly see, that we cannot find any of their
> Relations to be relied on.

Rogers eventually found his way home again and his opinion of his predecessors found its way to the bottom of Herman Moll's Galápagos chart when it was redrawn (*see* page 61) by Emanuel Bowen, who may have wanted to cash in on Rogers' fame. His own Relations to be relied on, *A Cruising Voyage Round the World*, was published some years earlier and became an instant best-seller. Fortunately he resisted the renaming bug, which instead bit his colleague Edward Cooke, who wrote the very forgettable *Voyage to the South Sea and Round the World in the Years 1708 to 1711* in which he leaves us with the names Duke, Dutchess and Marquesas, after the three ships which were sailing in consort. Neither the Cooke book nor his three island names made much of an impression on anyone.

Meanwhile even the Spaniards had begun to take more notice: in 1793 the frigate *Santa Gertrudis*, Alonso Torres in command, bequeathed their respective names to two of the islands, and left one more chart for the possible benefit and certain confusion of succeeding travelers. Here we discover the islands of Guerra, Tierra de Gil, and Carlos IV (of course not to be confused with Charles II). Perhaps capitan Torres had a rough go of it in the enchanted waters, for his chart of the area bears little resemblance to reality. We have at least one clue to his apparent frustration: he's labeled one of the islands Quita Sueña (Sleepless).

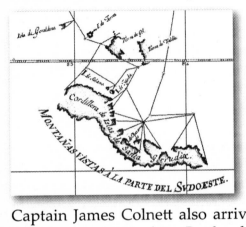

A section of Alonso Torres' 1793 chart shows *Cordilleras de Islas de Santa Gertrudix* (note plural), which may be the modern Isla Isabela. Or it may be something else.

Captain James Colnett also arrived in 1793, on board the British merchant ship *Rattler*, bringing with him fresh names to plant. His opportunity came when he discovered a pair of islands that seemed fair game: "As I could not trace these islands by any accounts or maps in my possession, I named one Chatham Isle, and the other Hood's Island," and for those who have difficulty following things, he helpfully adds "after the Lords Chatham and Hood." On the chart accompanying Colnett's book, these became Lord Chathams Isle and simply, Hoods Isle. Perhaps Hood was not as title-conscious as my Lord Chatham.

One of Colnett's discoveries was in fact a re-discovery, for Chatham Isle was actually Cowley's Charles. But Colnett thought that Charles was yet another island, none other than the wandering Santa María, finally anchored in its proper place. And so it appears on his chart, but labeled Charles. The error has been faithfully copied by map makers ever since, and is now part of the Galápagos tradition of enchantment by confusion.

Next it was our turn: in 1813 the American frigate *Essex*, Captain David Porter, sailed these waters. As we learned in Chapter 6, the Reverend David Adams, ship's chaplain, went ashore on Cowley's Duke of Norfolk's Island, didn't recognize it (or did, but pretended he didn't), and re-christened it as Porter's. There is no record of the Captain objecting. On Porter's own chart we find a Phillip's Island, which no one else has been able to find since, at least not by that name. And who was Phillip anyway? Porter doesn't say, but perhaps he doesn't have to: the 1823 London edition of his *A Voyage in The South Seas* was published by Sir Richard Phillips & Co. The same island is shown unnamed in the American edition published the previous year.

While sailing near the island temporarily bearing his own name, Captain Porter was told of a sail sighted off to the northwest. On taking a closer look it turned out to be a few rocks jutting from the water, which the captain decided to call Bainbridge's Rocks. The name stuck, but poorly. Soon enough the names sailed off to quite a different set of rocks near the coast of San Salvador. Porter's original Bainbridge's are now called Gordon Rocks.

The rocks that Captain Porter called Bainbridge's Rocks (left) are Gordon Rocks today, while a cluster of eight small islets (six shown on the right) are now named Bainbridge's Rocks.

A few years post-Porter, settlers began arriving from mainland Ecuador, which had recently declared its independence from Simon Bolívar's republic of Gran Colombia. Along with everything else, the Ecuadorians brought ... what else? *more* names. President José María Flores was rewarded with his very own island of Floreana, and his wife Mercedes was also immortalized, however briefly. Some of the settlers arrived on the bark *Mercedes* and the name found its way to one of the islands as well. But before long Mercedes all but disappeared from the island now called San Cristóbal. Just to keep things perfectly clear, San Cristóbal is the former Chatham of Colnett, which means it is really the Charles of Cowley.

Eventually a few other presidents, Plaza and Caamaño, made it all the way to the official approved list, while Floreana has to make do as the popular local name for the island the officials now call Santa María, after Columbus's flagship. Of course, no one could possibly confuse this with the same island of the same name formerly called Santa María de l'Aguada—which may have been so named to commemorate a drink of water enjoyed by a thirsty Spaniard.

To keep things properly enchanted, the British still think of Floreana as Charles, remembering it was their own Ambrosia Cowley who wrote of the island "the which I called King Charles's Island," and forgetting that he was talking about someplace else.

Since the days of Cowley, Colnett, Porter and the others, visitors have come, visitors have gone, and names have piled on top of names. For the moment, the record holder seems to be San Salvador, a/k/a Carenero, James, Olmedo, San Marco, Santiago, Tabac, Tierra de Gil, York's, and a few others. Running a close second is Santa Cruz, which has not yet sunk under the combined weight of Bolivia, Chavez, Indefatigable (very British), Norfolk, Porter's, San Clemente and Valdez.

Eventually, the government of Ecuador made its move. Perhaps emboldened by pulling off the annexation of the islands in 1832 (much to the relief of everyone else, who wanted nothing to do with them), they decided to go all the way. In 1892, the Ecuadorians cast off many of those hand-me-down names and started fresh. Not content with giving the Great Admiral's Spanish name of Colón to the whole works, islands within the chain now celebrate various chapters of the Columbian saga. His birthplace gives its name to Isla Genovesa, while San Salvador is after the island of the same name in the Caribbean which Columbus mistook for the Orient. And then we have Pinta and Santa María (after the ship, not the drink of water) but alas no Niña, even though that little vessel was the admiral's favorite. However, Niña's captain, the faithful Vicente Yañez Pinzón is remembered, although he shares the honor with his slightly-less-faithful captain brother Martin Alonzo who had a nasty habit of wandering off with the Pinta when things got sticky.

Las Islas Rábida and Santa Fe immortalize the convent and the city in which Queen Isabela I finally got off her throne long enough to send Columbus on his way. A friendly friar by the name of Marchena is also commemorated, and of course Isabela and her Fernando aren't forgotten either — although His Majesty undergoes a gender crisis (an old Spanish custom) to become Fernandina.

With their traditional reverence for all official utterances, contemporary Ecuadorians faithfully use the officially designated names at all times, except when it doesn't suit them. In this case the official name is pushed aside by some other name that has become popular through long years of usage. In fact, even the officials themselves seem to ignore *el Archipiélago de Colón* in favor of Galápagos. And perhaps as a concession to reality, when the archipelago was designated as a province in 1973, its name was entered in the record as *Provincia de Galápagos*. Be that as it may though, scientific journals (and often enough, British visitors) still refer to the islands by the names given them by Cowley and Colnett. And so with all that, we find that each island may now enjoy an official name, a Spanish name, an English name, a popular name and perhaps one or more other names. In fact, there are very few exceptions to this rule of names, very few islands with a single officially-popular Spanish-English name. One of the few is Isla Cowley.

Among the 150 odd names (some odder than others), there's one to prove that even the most avid island christener may run out of steam every now and again. For we have amongst the profusion, Nameless Island. And that's official, even if most people—including the English—call it by its unofficial name of Sin Nombre.

A little island with no name: labeled "Nameless" on many maps, its "Sin Nombre" to most island watchers.

When there aren't enough names to go around, why not share? That's just what happened on Gardner Isle, off the coast of Santa María/Floreana, of course not to be confused with Gardner Isle off the coast of Española/Hood. Some modern charts label both of them Jardinero, which is Spanish for gardener. Naturally, Gardner was not a gardener. He—that is, one of them—was Admiral Sir Alan Gardner, immortalized in the Galápagos by Colnett, but only at the isle near Floreana. Which is of course Santa María. Unless you call it Charles.

In 1892, the United States Bureau of the American Republics marked the Columban quarto-centenary with its publication *Ecuador*. Demonstrating a grasp on Latin American affairs which has since become a tradition, in the bulletin Floreana becomes Carlos, while the French Mascarin is St. Charles. Keeping an eye on the Italian vote, Bindlos's gets translated to Bindolese, and a San Bernardo appears out of nowhere to make a cameo appearance. The manual also chastises Cowley for changing some of the French names—names that were bestowed a few years after he wrote his journal. In still another account there's the explanation that Floreana comes from "floriferous," which probably has poor old president/general Flores spinning beneath the flowers surrounding his grave.

This chapter's preoccupation with names follows a long tradition. For ever since people have taken on the task of assigning names, other people have busied themselves chronicling the assignments. Each new account usually manages to introduce a few inversions, perhaps a new spelling variation, and every now and then, an explanation that is both delightfully original, decidedly creative, and definitely wrong.

Of course not everything in Galápagos is so confusing as this matter of names. For example, how many islands are out there, and, where are they? The first question has been answered many times by many authorities. For example:

> Some fourscore leagues (about 250 miles) to the westward.
>
> Richard Hawkins, 1593

> ... about 140 Spanish leagues West from the Island Plata, but I believe it's at least 30 Leagues more (that is, about 500 miles off the coast of Ecuador).
>
> Woodes Rogers, 1712

> ... nine hundred miles from the nearest land ...
>
> An early 20th-century account

... several hundred miles west of Peru (!!).

A 1981 book

That last quote comes from a book that offers yet another little surprise—especially for Ecuador: "The Government of Peru is now considering building an airport on the largest of these islands."

And now for the final word(s) on pinpointing the islands, we turn again to William Beebe, who apparently bought all that enchanted business. In the preface to his *Galápagos: World's End* he writes that the islands are

... directly on the equator, in the Pacific, five hundred miles off the coast of Ecuador, to which country they belong.

With the preface out of the way Beebe turns his attention to Chapter 1, where he now reports sailing

... straight to the Galápagos Islands, six hundred miles off Ecuador.

No wonder the Spaniards had such a hard time finding them.

But now let's answer another question: how many? We need go no further than Cowley, Charles Darwin, or perhaps the latter's Captain:

These are about 14 in number, most of them large considerable Ilands.

William Cowley

This archipelago consists of ten principal islands, of which five exceed the others in size.

Charles Darwin

There are six principal ones, nine smaller, and many islets ... .

Robert FitzRoy

Apparently Darwin and FitzRoy did not compare notes as they voyaged together through the enchanted waters. And from assorted other authorities …

> The Galápagos archipelago … consists of five large and numerous small oceanic islands …

> The archipelago, consisting of some fifteen islands and numerous islets and rocks, …

> … in all, no less than 50.

> … a tiny group of about sixty islands and islets.

And so it may be said here that there is little doubt there are more than two of them, and even less that some are bigger than others.

As the White Knight would say, "Galápagos isn't its *name*; it's only what it's *called*."

NOTES

In some cases, background information about an image did not fit well on the page where that image was displayed. And elsewhere, inserting an important detail about something in the text would have required an awkward break in that text. Therefore, these omissions are presented here. Refer to the bibliography which follows for more details about any source mentioned below.

Frontispiece. The Galápagos Satellite photo may be downloaded from NASA's Visible Earth website (http://visibleearth.nasa.gov/view_rec.php?id=2538).

1 – THE INCA VISITS GALÁPAGOS

facing p. 1. The village of Tumbez (now, Tumbes, Peru) is seen here on a mid-eighteenth century map Carta de la Provincia de Quito y de sus Adjacentes by Pedro Maldonado. Drawn some two centuries after the voyage of Inca Tupac, it's "modern" enough to display an accurate position for the village, just a few miles from the border with Ecuador.

p. 1. The opening quotation is an excerpt from Chapter XLVI of Sarmiento's History of the Incas, in which Tupac Inca Yupanqui learns of islands to the west. As noted, the islands were surely not in the Galápagos chain, and yet the legend persists—which is good enough excuse to include it here.

p. 4. The balsa (balza here) engraving is taken from Juan and Ulloa's Voyage to South America.

2 – THE BISHOP PAYS A CALL

pp. 5 & 18. The illustration which opens and closes the chapter is from the chart "Septentrionalium Regionum Descrip." in the 1570 Atlas *Theatrum Orbis Terrarum* (Theater of the World) by Abraham Ortelius. Unfortunately, Fray Tomás offered no description of the ship in which he sailed, so this will have to do as a stand-in.

3 – WILLIAM DAMPIER: PIRATE & HYDROGRAPHER

Much of this chapter is based on Dampier's own *A New Voyage Round the World.*

p. 19. The chapter title comes from a 1914 identification tablet placed next to Thomas Murray's portrait of Dampier, which prompted this remark from his biographer Clennell Wilkinson:

> It is as though we were to describe a man as "John Smith, burglar and mathematician," or "Tom Jones, bush-ranger and astronomer."

In later years the portrait went out on loan to Lyme Park and eventually found its way back to the Portrait Gallery's storage area. The tablet itself has gone missing—perhaps it too is in storage, or perhaps it was discarded when its subject was banished to the basement.

NATIONAL   PORTRAIT   GALLERY.

INSCRIPTION FOR TABLET.

William Dampier.

1652 – 1712.

Pirate and hydrographer. Author of 'A Voyage round the World'. Afterwards Captain, R. N.

Painted by Thomas Murray.

Directions for text to be inscribed on tablet when Dampier's portrait was exhibited in 1914.

pp. 31-33. All illustrations on these pages are from Edward Cooke's *Voyage to the South Sea. ...*

p. 35. The map section is from Herman Moll's 1726 *New and Exact Map of the Coast, Countries and Islands within ye Limits of ye South Sea Company.* ...

pp. 36 & 41. The mariner's calipers in the National Library of Australia's collection are, according to the Library, "traditionally thought to have belonged to William Dampier." Dampier visited the west coast of Australia long before it was Australia, and there had a brief encounter with a group of naked spear-waving aborigines. After a skirmish in which one of his men was injured, he gave up further attempts at communication. It would be more than 100 years until eastern Australia was settled, mostly by convicts transported from England. So the prospect that Dampier's calipers survived the years and an overland journey of several thousand miles may be more wishful thinking than reality.

p. 38. If we are to take him at his word, Lemuel Gulliver was not only related to William Dampier, but was also on friendly terms with his cartographer. On reaching the south-east point of New Holland (Dampier reached the north-west point), the famous voyager noted that

> ... the maps and charts place this country at least
> three degrees more to the east than it really is;
> which thought I communicated many years ago to
> my worthy friend, Mr. Herman Moll, and gave him
> my reasons for it, although he has rather chosen to
> follow other authors.

Jonathan Swift's friend Lemuel was not the only one acquainted with Dampier: Swift himself wrote his own *A New Voyage Round the World.* The fictional voyage owes much to Dampier, although Swift's ship sailed in the opposite direction, hence his addition of *by a Course never sailed before* to the title.

p. 41. In telling of a visit to Bahia, Brazil in his *Voyage to New Holland,* Dampier observed the "clocking-hens" — so called by the English, he says, because of the cluck noise they make. He recalls similar birds in the Bay of Campeachy and remarks that "There are both here and there four sorts of these long-legg'd

Fowls, near a-kin to each other, as so many Sub-Species of the same kind."

Dampier's many other achievements are well-told elsewhere, notably in Diana and Michael Preston's biography, *A Pirate of Exquisite Mind*. But one indicator of his influence which has escaped general notice is recounted here, even though it has nothing to do with Galápagos.

Among the many accomplishments of the poet John Dryden was his translation from the Latin of Virgil's *Aeneid*, completed in his old age and just a few years before the ailing poet's death. In his lengthy Dedication to the Earl of Mulgrave, Dryden writes that were it not for his ambition, he "could never had done anything at this age, when the fire of poetry is commonly extinguish'd in other men." But he drew some inspiration from an incident recounted in Book V of Virgil's poem — a boxing match between the elderly Entellus and a younger man. Entellus triumphs, "... proud of his prize, but prouder of his fame." Dryden observes that "...the elder contended not for the gift, but for the honor." And then he adds a puzzling comment:

> For Dampier has inform'd us, in his *Voyages,* that the air of a country which produces gold is never wholesome.

Dryden refers here to a remark made by Dampier in his *New Voyage*. After mentioning that the mountains surrounding Quito abound with gold, he cautions his readers:

> I know no place where Gold is found but what is very unhealthy.

But what does an observation about gold have to do with a translation from the Latin? It would seem that Dryden chose to draw on the authority of the buccaneer to put across his notion that, like the gold of Quito, other things of great worth may be discovered in unlikely places. He says no more though, leaving it his readers to understand his allusion to the value of verse from an unhealthy poet. It is not known if those readers appreciated the subtlety. Perhaps they simply wondered what the old man was talking about, and moved on to the next page.

Were it not for the dedicatory remark, one would hardly seek a connection between Dampier's *Voyage* and Dryden's Virgil. And yet there is another: both were published in the same year. Notices in the January and February, 1697 issues of the *London Gazette* announced Dampier's work, and Dryden's is thought to have appeared a few months later. That would mean that he was writing his Dedication to the Earl of Mulgrave at about the time Dampier's book was coming off the press. And that would mean that he put aside his work to spend a bit of time reading the *Voyage*. Was it just coincidence that he found Dampier's remark in time to insert it in his own text? Or did he know of it in advance from reading a pre-publication manuscript? Were he and Dampier acquainted? Both men had dined with Samuel Pepys, and perhaps therefore, with each other. But beyond the appearance of Dampier's name in Dryden's dedication, we know nothing of their relationship. About all we can conclude is that the poet thought the name of the buccaneer would not be out of place in the dedication of a tale of an earlier voyager.

One hopes that William Dampier was pleased to discover that his observations were of some value to his distinguished contemporary.

4 – WILLIAM AMBROSIA COWLEY, MARRINER

p. 43. The last word in the title did not slide unnoticed past the spell checker. It's just the way the word is spelled in two of the extant manuscript journals of the voyage.

p. 44. Cowley's disingenuous complaint about being "forced" to be away for several years was in his letter to the unknown "Your Grace." The complaint becomes a matter-of-fact remark at the end of his manuscript journals.

> The 12th of October 1686, I arrived at London, thus
> have I sailed round the whole globe of the World,
> keeping still a continuous course to the West-ward,
> till I arrived at the same place, cutting the same
> line, which I had formerly crossed in 3 yeares and
> 4 months.

From this we know that he left London in June of the year 1683. Both he and Dampier tell us they departed Virginia in August of the same year, so that would mean he signed on to Captain Cook's *Revenge* almost immediately after his arrival in Virginia. Now, was this arrival and departure just a remarkable coincidence of timing, or something that had been arranged in advance? The evidence, such as it is, further suggests that Cowley was no unwilling participant in the voyage, but had come to Virginia with all due haste to participate in the adventure.

p. 52. The aerial photo of Isla Cowley was taken by Galápagos National Park photographer Heidi Snell (© 2002, Heidi Snell.)

pp. 55, 62. The segments of William Hacke's Galápagos chart are from his *Description of the Islands of the Gallapagos, delineated exactly according to the prescription of Mr. William Ambrose Cowley.* The original is at the British Library [Add. 5414. 27].

5 – THE LEGEND OF IRISH PAT

pp. 63-64. Captain Porter may be the first author to mention the Galápagos post-office, where the letter from Captain Macy was found. However the famous landmark had not yet become the barrel that it is today. Porter wrote that Lieutenant Downes "returned ... with several papers, taken from a *box* (my emphasis) which he found nailed to a post, over which was a black sign, on which was painted *Hathaway's Postoffice."*

James Colnett, Captain of H. M. S. *Rattler* is often credited with setting up the first Galápagos post office barrel, probably because the phrase "Post Office" appeared on a chart by Aaron Arrowsmith. The first edition of this chart was inserted into the 1798 edition of Colnett's *Voyage.* However, the phrase does not appear on the chart until an 1820 reprint. Arrowsmith apparently used John Fyffe's 1815 chart, which cited a "Post Office" as his source when he updated this chart. Fyffe did not state if it was a box or a barrel.

The original edition of the chart shows that Colnett did not stop at Charles Island (the modern Isla Floreana), nor does Colnett mention the post office in his text. Therefore the post office was established by someone else—perhaps someone named Hathaway—who visited the island a year or so before Porter's arrival.

p. 63. Captain Porter was not the only one to comment on Captain Macy's writing style. In *Harper's Magazine,* vol XIX, July 1859:

> Captain Macy, of the *Sukey,* was more successful, it
> is hoped, in handling the harpoon than the pen, in
> the use of which he had boldly committed to the
> world this specimen of his skill:

There follows the letter that Porter included in his *Journal,* by way of introduction to his description of Patrick Watkins. Some years later, Macy's son Roland joined his father's profession for a time, then decided that he'd rather go into the dry goods business. So he opened up a small shop which eventually did rather well. Today it's known as R. H. Macy & Co.

p. 64. Both Macy and Porter state that Pat's Landing is on the east side of the island. They may have meant the *north*-east side, or what is more likely, the *west* side, in the area of the present Black Beach.

p. 65. Patrick "by some means became possessed of an old musket," perhaps similar to the one shown here—a Whitney 1798 flintlock musket manufactured during the first decade of the 19th century. *Flayderman's Guide to Antique American Firearms* is an excellent source for information about this and other weapons.

6 – JOURNAL OF A CRUISE

p. 84. Farragut's famous "Damn the torpedoes! Full speed ahead!" has been quoted innumerable times, although that's not exactly what he said. According to *1,001 Things Everyone Should Know About American History,* by John A. Garraty (1989):

> What Admiral David Farragut actually said when he
> ordered his ship to enter Mobile Bay in 1864 was
> more precise. To Percival Drayton, the commander
> of his flagship, USS Hartford, he said, "Damn the
> torpedoes! Four bells (i.e., full speed)! Captain
> Drayton, go ahead!" To James E. Jouett, commander
> of the gunboat Metacomet, which was lashed to
> the Hartford, he said, "Jouett, full speed!"

But the abbreviated quote does make for a better "sound bite."

p. 89. The stone enclosure was discovered and photographed by Thalia Grant Estes in 2004 (© 2004, Thalia Grant Estes).

p. 97. An unsigned "Cruise of the Essex" account in *Harper's* devotes four pages to Galápagos, including the "Gallapagos Turtle" engraving seen here. Nothing, however, is said of the Gamble/Cowan duel described in the next chapter.

p. 100. The aerial photo of MacGowen Reef was taken by Galápagos National Park photographer Heidi Snell (© 2002, Heidi Snell.)

pp. 105, 106. The life mask of David Porter created by Browere, and the Captain's opinion of it, may be found in Charles Henry Hart's *Browere's Life Masks of Great Americans*. Bronze castings of this and other Browere masks are on display at the Fenimore Art Museum in Cooperstown, New York.

7 – THE SEARCH FOR LIEUTENANT COWAN

p. 110. As in Chapter 5, *Flayderman's Guide to Antique American Firearms* provides information about the type of pistol that might have been used in the duel.

pp. 114-115. As noted, it's puzzling that neither Slevin nor Schmitt were aware that Darwin knew of Captain Porter, when in fact Darwin makes direct reference to Porter's remarks in the paragraph directly following the Lawson anecdote. It's true that Porter's comments did not appear in Darwin's work when it was first published in 1839, but were added to the very popular second edition of 1845. Furthermore, Schmitt referred to the work by a title—*Voyage of the Beagle*—that first appeared in 1905. Is it possible that he read nothing but the rare first edition, referred to it by a title that did not come into existence for another 50 years, and Slevin didn't notice this? That seems unlikely at best, which leaves us with no other conclusion than that both men were not as attentive readers as we might have expected them to be.

p. 119. Slevin sketched the area where he thought Cowan's grave might be found on a copy of a James Bay inset on British Admiralty chart 1375 of the Galápagos Islands.

pp. 119-120. Notwithstanding the duel, Lieutenant John Gamble rose steadily within the service, eventually to the rank of brevet Lieutenant-Colonel. He retired from the Marines in 1834 and died two years later at the age of 46.

In his 1938 letter to Schmitt, Slevin states the portrait is of a *Colonel* Gamble, and in a 1941 letter to Captain Picking, he refers to the subject as *Lieutenant* Gamble. Since it is known that Gamble was promoted to Captain in 1814, he probably held that rank when the portrait was painted about two years later. He was promoted to Major before 1822, as indicated by the phrase "Lieut. (now Major) Gamble" in the lengthy title to the second edition of Porter's *Voyage,* which was published in that year. He may have been promoted to the honorary brevet Lieutenant-Colonel rank on or shortly before his retirement.

Gamble married Hannah, daughter of prominent New York publisher John Lang, who may have commissioned Samuel Lovett Waldo to paint the portrait seen here. Another portrait was painted ca. 1830 by Anthony Lewis DeRose.

p. 125. The photo of Sherwood Picking is taken from the 1911 edition of *The Lucky Bag,* vol. XVIII, the yearbook of the U. S. Naval Academy.

p. 128. The photo of the rectangular rock formation was taken by Galápagos National Park photographer Heidi Snell (© 2005, Heidi Snell.) The location agrees with the descriptions written by David Porter and John Shillibeer, and the marginal notes of James Wilkie described here on p. 125.

8 – CHARLES DARWIN SLEPT HERE

p. 131. The opening "Finches from Galápagos Archipelago" illustration appeared for the first time in the 1845 edition of Darwin's *Journal of Researches.*

p. 132. In *Charles Darwin: A Man of Enlarged Curiosity,* author Peter Brent noted that "… the clerical profession was often chosen as the last resort of the family dullard. …" Brent's sub-title comes from Darwin's uncle Josiah Wedgewood, who remarked about the benefit to his nephew of the proposed voyage: "… looking on him as a man of enlarged curiosity, it affords him such an opportunity of seeing men and things as happens to few."

p. 137. Darwin made the remark about his "bump of reverence" in his autobiography.

p. 147. Lord Byron is often credited as the author of *Voyage of H. M. S. Blonde ...*, but the book is in fact a compilation of journals kept by various crew members and edited for publication by Maria Graham (later, Maria Lady Calcott). The identity of the person who coined the "imps of darkness" expression is unknown. The imp himself (or perhaps, herself) is from the 1890 illustrated edition of Darwin's *Journal of Researches*.

pp. 153-155. There are many versions of what really happened at the Oxford Debate, and the late Stephen Jay Gould's "Knight Takes Bishop?" presents an excellent overview of what was, and what was not, said by Huxley. The anecdote about FitzRoy and his Bible is told in Poulton's *Charles Darwin and the Origin of Species*.

p. 158. Lindley Sambourne's "Man is but a Worm" caricature appeared in *Punch's Almanac for 1882*, an unpaginated supplement bound into volume LXXX.

9 – THE GEOGRAPHY OF HERMAN MELVILLE

p. 165-166. Melville himself does not reveal the identity of his "Dog King" and writes simply that the man "proposed to a group of soldiers that they come live on one of his islands." In his Epilogue to the 1940 Wreden edition of *The Encantadas*, editor Victor Wolfgang von Hagen makes the connection between His Majesty and José Villamil. And in his own *Ecuador and the Galápagos Islands*, he writes of Villamil that "... for his own protection, he had need of a pack of dogs which ran at his heels." In *The Enchanted Islands*, author John Hickman offers the explanation of why the invited were in no position to decline, and also notes that Villamil "... had acquired a pack of dogs ... and the island became known as the Dog Kingdom." The author's source for these assertions is unknown, but was perhaps von Hagen, who also does not identify his sources—other than Melville himself of course.

pp. 166-167. The illustrations are from Abel du Petit-Thouars' *Voyage Autour Du Monde Sur La Frégate Vénus Pendant Les Annees,*

1836-1839 (Voyage Around the World on the Frigate La Vénus, during the Years 1836-1839). Melville was in Galápagos on the whaleship *Acushnet* in 1841 and 1842.

p. 170. The "cursed man" is an illustration by Walter Crane for an 1894 edition of Spenser's *The Fairie Queene*. Although Melville borrowed Spenser's verse to introduce his "Sketch Ninth," it's unlikely (to say the least) that Irish Pat would recognize himself in either the verse of in Crane's illustration.

p. 171. Thomas Russell's "Melville's Use of some Sources in *The Encantadas*" is an excellent resource for details on that subject. The author has, however, taken Melville's sly reference to his "reliable sources" as being serious.

p. 173. The "Giant Tortoises of the Galapagos Islands" is from Lydekker's *The Royal Natural History*. Published some 40 years after *The Encantadas*, it nevertheless goes well with Melville's description of tortoises and wicked officers.

10 – THE SMALL WORLD OF MANUEL J. COBOS

In the days of Manuel J. Cobos, his island was popularly known as Chatham Island, but it is called Isla San Cristóbal here in recognition of modern usage.

Much of the information in this chapter is drawn from Bognoly and Espinosa's *Las Islas Encantadas, ó el Archipielago de Colon*. In addition, Jacob Lundh's unpublished manuscript, *Galápagos: A Brief History*, presents more-detailed accounts from the same source.

p. 175. The opening illustration is taken from a photograph of the Cobos family mausoleum in the cemetery at Guayaquil. Don Manuel Augusto Cobos's habit of carrying a pistol at all times was also noted in Sidney Howard's *Isles of Escape*. The book offers additional details about the assassination of Manuel Julian Cobos, presumably as related by his son Manuel Augusto.

p. 176. *"C'est ne pas gay ici"* ("It is not gay here"). Don Manuel used the word some years before it took on a rather different meaning.

pp. 175-176. The anecdote about Manuel Augusto Cobos and the Norwegian journalists is from Stein Hoff's *Drømmen om Galápagos* (*The Galápagos Dream*).

p. 176. The photo of Cobos and Aguilera was taken on January 31st, 1933 by John Garth during the Third Allan Hancock *Velero III* Expedition.

pp. 177, 179, 180. The reproduction of the 50 centavos note and photos of Elias Puertas and Camilo Casanova are from Bognoly and Espinosa's *Las Islas Encantadas, ó el Archipielago de Colon.*

p. 183. The painting of the gunship *Cotapaxi*—now *Calderón*—is at the Museo Naval in Guayaquil. The ship itself is on display outside the Ecuadorian First Naval Zone headquarters in Guayaquil.

11 – HOW ACADEMY BAY GOT ITS NAME

Much of the material in this chapter comes from two sources; Joseph Slevin's *Log of the Schooner "Academy"* and Thomas H. and Patricia R. Fritts' *Race with Extinction: Herpetological Field Notes of J. R. Slevin's Journey to the Galápagos, 1905-1906.* Slevin consistently referred to the islands by their English names, and his usage is followed here.

pp. 187, 205. The aerial photo of Academy Bay was taken by Galápagos National Park photographer Heidi Snell (© 2002, Heidi Snell.)

pp. 188-189. The 1905 photos of the schooner *Academy* and its crew © California Academy of Sciences, Special Collections. Used by permission.

p. 192. The H. M. S. *Lancaster* visited Post Office Bay on November 28, 1917. The photo is from a postcard printed in Canada. Date and publication details are unknown.

p. 194. See p. 343 for more details about the Galápagos home brew known as "puro."

p. 196. The chart of Academy Bay is an inset on the 1948 edition of British Admiralty chart 1375, based on data from an unidentified United States chart of 1936.

p. 198. The aerial photo of Isla Daphne Major was taken during a 1943 mapping mission by the U. S. Army Air Forces (now, U. S. Air Force).

p. 206. The track of the schooner *Academy* is based on the cover illustration to Fritts & Fritts' *Race with Extinction*.

12 – THE LIGHTHOUSE KEEPER OF WRECK BAY

One of the first mentions—perhaps *the* first mention—of a treasure-hunting old man was in Rothschild and Hartert's "A Review of the Ornithology of the Galápagos Islands, with Notes on the Webster-Harris Expedition." This includes the diaries of Charles Miller Harris and F. P. Drowne. Harris mentions "… an Englishman, T. Levick" and refers to him on another page as "Captain Levick." Both diaries state that Levick, who was living on Charles Island at the time, accompanied them from time to time, but there's no mention of his interest in buried treasure.

In the introduction to Robert Cushman Murphy's 1936 *Oceanic Birds of South America,* the author includes a biographical sketch written by Rollo Beck, and it is here that we first hear of an old sailor (now on Chatham Island) and the treasure on Tower Island.

pp. 207, 217. The lighthouse illustration is from the 1917 edition of Bognoly & Espinosa's *Las Islas Encantadas.*

p. 211. The photo of the lighthouse keeper's shack is from Ralph Stock's *Cruise of the Dream Ship.*

p. 223-24. The conversation between Rolf Blomberg and Doña Karin Guldberg is based on Jacob Lundh's unpublished English translation of Blomberg's *Underliga Människor och Underliga Djur* (Strange People and Strange Animals).

p. 230. Both photos were taken in 1919 by Ralph Stock.

13 – THE GALÁPAGOS DREAM

This chapter is based on Stein Hoff's *Drømmen om Galapagos,* published in Norwegian only. Hoff's fascinating history has been translated into English by Friedel Horneman and edited by Robert J. Bowman, but is not yet available in print. There is an online version of the translation on this author's website at *http://www.galapagos.to/texts/hoff-0.htm.*

All photos are from *Drømmen om Galapagos,* © 1985, Stein Hoff. Used by permission.

14 – THE VOYAGES OF THE VELERO III

pp. 243, 245, 250. The drawings and photo of the *Velero III* are from DeWitt Meredith's *Voyages of the Velero III.*

p. 244. The photo of Captain Hancock is from Sam T. Clover's biography of the Captain, *A Pioneer Heritage.*

p. 247. The photo of the iguanas being released on Isla Seymour Norte was taken on January 17th, 1932 by John Garth during the First Allan Hancock *Velero III* Expedition.

p. 249. The aerial photo of Banco Hancock was taken by Galápagos National Park photographer Heidi Snell (© 2002, Heidi Snell.)

15 – MARGRET AND THE BARONESS

In addition to the credits given below, much of the background information for this chapter comes from Margret Wittmer's *Floreana Adventure* and Dore Strauch's *Satan Came to Eden.*

p. 251. The opening illustration is one of several postmark stamps used by Margret Wittmer.

p. 253. Rolf Sønderskov's discovery of the lava tube is mentioned in Stein Hoff's *Drømmen om Galápagos.*

p. 254. The photo of the young Freidrich Ritter is taken from Ritter's *Als Robinson auf Galapagos,* published posthumously, presumably by Dore Strauch on her return to Germany after Ritter's death.

p. 255. It was Dore herself who wrote down Friedrich's remark about "a love-sick woman full of romantic notions" in her *Satan Came to Eden*.

p. 256. The photo of Paul Bruun is from Stein Hoff's *Drømmen om Galápagos*. Dore Strauch's claim that he had done some spying is unfounded. In *Drømmen*, Hoff presents ample evidence that Bruun was innocent of such charges.

p. 257. Details on the death of Captain Bruun will be found in Temple Utley's *A Modern Sea Beggar*. Dr. Utley was a witness to the accident and assisted in the burial of Bruun.

p. 259. The two-hour stroll may no longer be necessary to reach the highland caves; in recent years the road has been improved and there are now a few vehicles on the island to transport visitors there and back.

pp. 259, 263-264, 267. Photos of the Wittmers, the Ritters, the Baroness, Lorenz and Phillipson were taken by members of several of the Allan Hancock *Velero III* Expeditions.

pp. 261, 262, 269. The caricatures of the Baroness and the Ritters are from Hakon Mielche's *Let's See if the World is Round*.

p. 267. Although Ritter's letter to Captain Hancock is mentioned in Margret Wittmer's *Floreana Adventure*, in John Treherne's *The Galápagos Affair* and John Hickman's *The Enchanted Islands*, none of these authors reveal the source of their information. The direct "We hope you will come ..." quotation is from Stein Hoff's *Drømmen om Galapagos*.

p. 268. The illustration is from *Aboard the Seth Parker*, a booklet published by Frigidaire Sales Corp. to publicize the use of their equipment aboard the ship.

16 – A MONUMENTAL TALE

p. 273. The illustration of Charles Darwin is from a recent photo of the Darwin Monument on Isla San Cristóbal.

p. 280. For reasons best known to themselves (one hopes), the Christ's College Council declined a request for a photograph of their Darwin monument.

p. 280. The letters between Henry Fairfield Osborne and William Couper are in the archives of the American Museum of Natural History Library in New York City.

p. 282. G. T. Corley-Smith's reference to the "Galápagos Memorial Expedition" should of course be to the *"Darwin* Memorial Expedition."

p. 284. Of the people whose names are on the Darwin Monument plaque, only Dr. and Mrs. von Hagen were actually present at the dedication. Members of Mrs. von Hagen's family were included in recognition of the family's financial support. Dard Hunter had hoped to participate, but did not.

p. 285. The photo of the Darwin bust at Down House © 2005 Richard Milner. Used by permission.

17 — THE GALÁPAGOS FILES

Information about U. S. Navy ship visits to Galápagos is based largely on information found in the U. S. Navy *Field Monograph of Galápagos Islands,* with additional details from Victor Wolfgang von Hagen's books and unpublished manuscript.

The aircraft photos are from the collections of various American veterans of the WWII occupation of the islands.

p. 288. The photo of the U. S. S. West Virginia is from a postcard printed in the United States. Date and publication details are unknown.

p. 289. The cartoon of Uncle Sam making an offer for the Galápagos Islands probably appeared in an Ecuadorian newspaper, but details are unknown. The "galápago" looks more like a sea turtle, but that could just be artistic license.

p. 293. Reporter Galvarino Gallardo's comments about President Roosevelt's 1938 visit were reported in the New York Times on July 31st, 1938. The report does not identify the source of its information.

p. 296. Count Felix von Luckner was universally admired for his humanitarian actions during the First World War, during which he always treated his prisoners with the greatest kindness and respect. At home he was a hero, and before the Second World War enjoyed cordial relations with the emerging Nazi Party. In fact, Propaganda Minister Goebbels made the following comment to an inquiry from the German Foreign Office:

> I inform you that Count Felix von Luckner's world trip was at the time to a large extent supported conceptually and financially by me.

With Nazi money supporting von Luckner's 1937-39 world cruise on his yacht *Seeteufel* (Sea Devil), he may indeed have distributed photographs and other propaganda material along the way, as part of Goebbels' plan "to elicit understanding for National Socialism."

Later on the Count fell out with the Nazis, and Hitler banned his books and forbade him to make public appearances. When ordered to renounce various honors received from foreign governments, he refused. Near war's end, he successfully negotiated with advancing American forces to save the city of Halle from destruction.

See Blain Pardoe's *Cruise of the Sea Eagle* for additional details about Count von Luckner.

p. 297. The photo of the Conways with lunch was taken on January 24th, 1938 by John Garth during the Seventh Allan Hancock *Velero III* Expedition.

18 – WHO KILLED THE IGUANAS?

As in the previous chapter, the wartime photos and Goat's Whisker illustration are from the collections of various American veterans of the WWII occupation of the islands. Correspondence from State Department and other wartime sources is taken from numerous microfilm records of the military occupation of the islands.

pp. 299, 313. The illustration is the emblem of the Sixth Air Force.

p. 302. The photo of the nose section of the crashed fighter plane was taken in 2001, during the filming of The Rock, an Ecuadorian documentary on the WWII occupation of the islands.

p. 307-308. Dr. Schmitt's 1942 diary excerpts are in the Smithsonian Institution Archives.

p. 308. The cartoon of Dr. Schmitt is by Robert E. Hogue, seen on the dust jacket cover of Richard E. Blackwelder's biography of Schmitt, *The Zest for Life*.

19 – A SOCIAL VISIT EXTRAORDINARY

p. 315. The photo is of the observation plane flown to Isla Floreana by Vernon Lange and Ernest Reimer, with Lt. Reimer standing next to it.

20 - ISLANDS FOR SALE OR LEASE

p. 325. The cartoon of Ecuador contemplating the value of the Galápagos Islands is from Stein Hoff's *Drømmen om Galapagos*. The original source, presumably a newspaper in Ecuador, is unknown.

p. 328. The Coat of Arms of Ecuador was established at the National Congress of 1900.

21 – THE SHORT UNHAPPY LIFE OF FILIATE SCIENCE ANTRORSE

The information in this chapter comes from four primary sources, the first of which is Don Harrsch's *Filiate Science Antrorse*, a 10-page brochure sent to those who expressed interest in the venture. A paper by Faris, Catton and Larsen supplied information from the University of Washington group that studied the project. Another valuable resource was the series of reports in the *Seattle Times* published between 1959 and 1961. Finally, the personal account by Stan Bettis, published in *Old Oregon* Magazine gave much background detail about the *Western Trader* and the second wave of colonists.

Additional details came from phone conversations with Don Harrsch, who states that the details of his discharge as reported in the Faris et al paper were wrong. The distinction is important to him, because "a bad-conduct discharge is less severe than a dishonorable discharge and is designed as a punishment for bad conduct rather than as a punishment for serious offenses of either a civilian or military nature" (U. S. Court of Appeals for the Armed Forces).

p. 335. The track of the tuna clipper *Alert* is superimposed on a Satellite photo downloaded from NASA's Visible Earth website.

p. 339, 341. The 1960 *Western Trader* photos are from the Bettis essay in *Old Oregon* Magazine © 1971 University of Oregon. Used by permission.

p. 343. See page 194 for an earlier appearance of the "puro" offered to Bettis and his group.

p. 345. The *El Junco* photo was taken by Galápagos National Park photographer Heidi Snell (© 2002, Heidi Snell.)

22 – A BRIEF HISTORY OF HISTORY

p. 347. Sculptor James Christensen describes some of his work as being "just a little to the left of reality." Therefore, his "The Scholar" makes an appropriate introduction to a chapter where many of the sources dwell in the same land.

pp. 350-364. Perhaps there's a bit too much commentary on Dampier and Cowley here, but it can't be helped. Their stories have been so often mangled that the temptation to comment on the commentators proved irresistible.

p. 348. The observation about "artistic verisimilitude" was first uttered by His Grace, the Archbishop of Titipu (*and* Lord High Everything Else) Poo-Bah, in Gilbert and Sullivan's *The Mikado*.

p. 354. Mark Twain's observation about truth is from his *Following the Equator*.

p. 360-361. Much information on the capture of Edward Davis & Lionel Wafer is in the British National Archives (formerly, Public Record Office), and also Edward Berkeley's "Three Philanthropic Pirates."

23 – WHAT'S IN A NAME?

p. 371, 382. The illustration of Alice and the White Knight is from a wood engraving by the Dalziel Brothers for Lewis Carroll's *Alice in Wonderland*.

p. 371. The Tom Stoppard quotation is from a working manuscript. The "main island" phrase—deleted when the article was published in *The Observer*—is reinserted here for clarity.

p. 373. Le Sieur de Villefort added *Mascarin* and other names to some of the islands.

p. 375. The Torres chart drawn by Thomas de Cruz Goblado is in the Museo Naval archives in Madrid, Spain.

p. 376, 379. The photos of Gordon and Bainbridge's Rocks and Nameless Island were taken by Galápagos National Park photographer Heidi Snell (© 2002, Heidi Snell.)

BIBLIOGRAPHY

A bracketed number indicates the chapter(s) for which each listed author's work was consulted.

Adams, F. Colburn [Notes]
1876   *High Old Salts. Stories Intended for the Marines, but told before an Enlightened Committee of Congress.* Washington, DC: (publisher not identified)

Admiralty, British [7, Notes]
1841   Map: Galapagos Islands Surveyed by Capt. Robt. Fitz Roy R. N. and the Officers of H. M. S. *Beagle*, 1836.

Alumni Cantabrigiensis (*see* J. A. Venn)

Anonymous
ca. 1530 Untitled vellum chart of Pacific coast from Guatemala to Northern Perú. Chart 9 in *Nautical Charts on Vellum in the Library of Congress*, compiled by Walter W. Ristow and R. A. Skelton. Washington: Library of Congress, 1977. [2]

1909   "The Darwin Celebration." In *The American Museum Journal*, Vol. IX, No. 3 (March). New York: American Museum of Natural History. [16]

1919   *The U. S. S. South Dakota Cruises in the South Seas: Compiled from Extracts of the "Ess Dee" the Weekly Journal of the Crew.* Manila: E. C. McCullough & Co. [17]

Arrowsmith, Aaron [6]
1798   Map: "Chart of the Galápagos, Surveyed in the
        Merchant-Ship Rattler, and Drawn by Capt: James
        Colnett. ..." In Colnett's *A Voyage to the South Atlantic.*

1820   Map: *Chart of the Galápagos, ... Additions & Corrections
        to 1817.* Revised edition, published separately. London:
        Aaron Arrowsmith.

Banning, George Hugh [14]
1933   "Hancock Expedition to the Galápagos Islands, 1933:
        General Report." In *Bulletin of the Zoological Society of
        San Diego,* No. 10 (May). San Diego: Zoological Society
        of San Diego.

Beebe, William [8, 12, 15, 18, 23]
1924   *Galápagos: World's End.* New York: G. P. Putnam's Sons.

Berkeley, Jr., Edward [24]
1966   "Three Philanthropic Pirates." In *The Virginia Magazine,*
        Vol 74, No. 4, pp. 433-444 (October). Richmond,
        Virginia: Virginia Historical Society.

Berlanga, Tomás de [2]
1535   "Letter to His Majesty ... describing his Voyage from
        Panamá to Puerto Viejo." In *Colleccion de Documentos
        Ineditos relativos al Descubrimiento, Conquista y
        Organizacion de las Antiguas Posesiones Españolas de
        América y Oceania.* Tomo XLI, Cuaderno II. Madrid.
        Imprenta de Manuel G. Hernandez (1884, pp. 538-544).

Bettis, Stan [21]
1971   "A Voyage to World's End." In *Old Oregon Magazine,*
        January/February. Eugene, Oregon: University of
        Oregon Alumni Association.

Blackwelder, Richard E. [Notes]
1979   *The Zest for Life, or Waldo Had a Pretty Good Run: The
        Life of Waldo Lasalle Schmitt.* Lawrence, Kansas: The
        Allen Press, Inc.

Blomberg, Rolf [12, Notes]
1936   *Underliga Människor och Underliga Djur* (Strange
        People and Strange Animals). Stockholm: (Publisher
        unknown).

Bognoly, José A., & José Moises Espinosa [10, Notes]
1917   *Las Islas Encantadas ó Archipielago de Colón.* Guayaquil,
        Ecuador: Libreria e Imp. "Gutenberg" de Elicio A.
        Uzcátegui.

Boswell, James [8]
1876   *Boswell's Life of Johnson: including their Tour of the
        Hebrides.* London: John Murray.

Bowen, Emanuel [4, 23]
1744   Map: "The Gallapagos Islands Discovered and
        Described by Capt. Cowley in 1684." In John Harris'
        *Navigantium atque Itinerantium Bibliotheca, or A Complete
        Collection of Voyages and Travels* ... . 2nd ed. London: T.
        Woodward et al.

Brent, Peter [8, Notes]
1981   *Charles Darwin: A Man of Enlarged Curiosity.* New York:
        Harper & Row.

Brower, Kenneth (Editor) [9]
1970   *Galápagos: The Flow of Wildness.* 2 volumes. San
        Francisco: The Sierra Club.

Browere, John Henry Isaac (*see* Hart, Charles) [6]

Browne, Janet [8]
1995   *Charles Darwin: Voyaging.* New York: Alfred A. Knopf.

2002   *Charles Darwin: The Power of Place.* New York: Alfred A.
        Knopf.

Browne, Sir Thomas [8]
1927   *The Works of Sir Thomas Browne.* 3 volume reprint.
        Edinburgh: John Grant.

[Burnett, James, Lord Monboddo] [8]
1917   Biographical entry. In *Dictionary of National Biography.*
        London: Oxford University Press.

Burney, James [22]
1816   *A Chronological History of the Discoveries in the South Sea or Pacific Ocean.* Vol. 4. London: G. & W. Nicol.

Byron, John [8]
1768   *The Narrative of the Honourable John Byron, Containing an Account of the Great Distresses. ...* London: S. Baker, G. Leigh, T. Davies.

[Byron, Lord George Anson] [8, Notes]
1826   *Voyage of H. M. S. Blonde to the Sandwich Islands in the Years 1824-1825.* London: John Murray.

Cabello Valboa, Miguel [1]
1586   *Miscelánea Antártica.* 1951 reprint. Lima, Peru: Universidád Nacional Mayor de San Marco.

Cayot, Linda J., & Rafael Menoscal [18]
1992   "Land Iguanas Return to Baltra." In *Noticias de Galápagos*, No. 51, 1992. Quito, Ecuador: Charles Darwin Foundation.

Clover, Sam T. [Notes]
1932   *A Pioneer Heritage.* Los Angeles: Saturday Night Publishing Co.

Colnett, James [6, 9, 23, Notes]
1798   *A Voyage to the South Atlantic and Round Cape Horn into the Pacific Ocean. ...* London: W. Bennett.

Conway, Ainslee & Frances [17, Notes]
1948   *The Enchanted Islands.* London: Geoffrey Bles.

Cooke, Edward [3, 23]
1712   *A Voyage to the South Sea, and Round the World, Perform'd in the Years 1708, 1709, 1710, and 1711, by the Ships Duke and Dutchess of Bristol.* 2 vols. London: B. Lintot & R. Gosling.

Corley-Smith, G. T. [16]
1979   "Looking Back on 20 Years of the Charles Darwin Foundation." In *Noticias de Galápagos*, No. 30. n. p. Charles Darwin Foundation.

Coulter, John [5]
1845   *Adventures in the Pacific.* ... Dublin: William Curry, Jun.
        & Co.

Couper, William [16]
1909   September 2 letter to Henry Fairfield Osborn. Folder
        764. New York: American Museum of Natural History
        Archives.

Cowley, William Ambrosia [3, 4, 6, 9, 11, 22, 23, Notes]
1686   "A Short Account of my Voyage Round this Terestiall
        Globe. ... In *Miscellanea Curiosa*. Richmond, Virginia:
        Virginia Historical Society Mss1. T8525a3, Vol IV.

1687   "The Voyage of Capt. Cowley. Papist." In *Codex
        Chartaceus*. Lambeth Ms. 642, pp. 441-485. London:
        Lambeth Palace Library.

16__   *Cowley's Voyage Round the World.* Sloane Ms. 1050.
        London: British Library.

1699   "Cowley's Voyage Round the Globe." In *A Collection of
        Original Voyages.* ... London: James Knapton.

Cox, William E. [7, 18]
1983   *Guide to the Papers of Waldo Lasalle Schmitt.* Washington,
        DC: Archives and Special Collections, Smithsonian
        Institution.
        Joseph R. Slevin Correspondence. Box 31, Folder 26.
        Diary, June 8-July 2, 1942. Box 100, Folder 8.

Cruz Goblado, Thomas de [24]
1794   Map: *Carta Espherica que comprehended una parte del
        Archipielego de los Galapagos.* Madrid: Museo Naval.

Dampier, William [3, 4, 6, 9, 22, 23, Notes]
16__   *The Adventures of William Dampier, with others who
        Left Capt. Sharpe in the South Seas.* ... Sloane Ms. 3236.
        London: British Library.

1697   *A New Voyage Round the World.* London: James
        Knapton.

Dampier, William (continued)

1703   *A Voyage to New Holland, &c. in the Year 1699.* London: James Knapton.

1906   *The Voyages of Captain William Dampier.* 2 volume reprint edited by John Masefield. London: E. Grant Richards.

1927   *A New Voyage Round the World.* Reprint edited by Sir Albert Gray. London: Argonaut Press.

Darwin, Charles [3, 8]

1839   *Journal and Remarks.* Volume III of *Narrative of the Surveying voyages of His Majesty's Ships Adventure and Beagle.* London: Henry Colburn.

1839   *Journal of Researches into the Geology and Natural History of the various countries visited by H. M. S. Beagle.* London: Henry Colburn.

1890   *Journal of Researches into the Natural History and Geology of the Countries Visited During the Voyage Round the World of H. M. S. "Beagle."* London: John Murray.

1899   *The Descent of Man.* New York: D. Appleton & Co.

1899   *On the Origin of Species.* New York: D. Appleton & Co.

1899   *The Life and Letters of Charles Darwin.* 2 volumes. New York: D. Appleton & Co.

1903   *More Letters of Charles Darwin.* 2 volumes. London: John Murray.

1934   *Charles Darwin's Diary of the Voyage of H. M. S. "Beagle."* Edited from the ms. by Nora Barlow. Cambridge, England: Cambridge University Press.

1958   *The Autobiography of Charles Darwin.* Edited by Nora Barlow. London: Collins.

Darwin, Erasmus [8]

1796   *Zoonomia; or, the Laws of Organic Life.* 2 volumes. London: J. Johnson.

David, Edwin [6]
1815   Engraving of David Porter. In *Analectic Magazine*, accompanying "Biographical Memoir of Captain David Porter. (*see* Irving, Washington)

De Maillet, Benoît [8]
1797   *Telliamed; or, the World Explained: containing Discourses on ... the Origin of Man & Animals. ...* Baltimore: D. Porter.

D'Orso, Michael [18]
2002   *Plundering Paradise: The Hand of Man on the Galápagos Islands.* New York: HarperCollins.

Drowne, F. P. [12, Notes]
1899   Diary excerpts, in Rothschild & Hartett's "Review of the Ornithology of the Galápagos Islands" (q. v.).

Dryden, John [Notes]
1987   *The Works of John Dryden. Poems: The works of Virgil in English, 1697.* Vol. 5, p. 328 of 20-volume reprint. Berkeley: University of California Press.

Eibl-Eibesfeldt, Irenäus [18]
1960   *Galápagos.* London: Macgibbon & Kee.

Eiseley, Loren (*see* Kenneth Brower)

Enock, C. Reginald [17]
1914   *Ecuador.* New York: Charles Scribner's Sons.

Evelyn, John [3, 22]
1698   Diary entry, 6 August. In *The Diary of John Evelyn.* 1901 reprint. New York & London: M. Walter Dunne.

Faris, E. L. & William B. Catton, Jr., Otto N. Larsen [21]
1964   "The Galápagos Expedition: Failure in the Pursuit of a Contemporary Secular Utopia." pp. 48-54. In *Pacific Sociological Review*, Vol. 7. No. 1 (Spring) . Portland, Oregon: Pacific Sociological Society.

FitzRoy, Robert [3, 8]
1839   *Proceedings of the Second Expedition, 1831-1836.* Volume
        II of *Narrative of the Surveying voyages of His Majesty's
        Ships Adventure and Beagle.* London: Henry Colburn.

Flayderman, Norm [Notes]
2001   *Flayderman's Guide to Antique American Firearms.* 8th
        edition. Iola, Wisconsin: Krause Publications.

Fraser, C. McLean [14]
1943   *General Account of the Scientific Work of the Velero III in
        the Eastern Pacific, 1931-41.* Los Angeles: University of
        Southern California Press.

Fritts, Thomas H. & Patricia R. Fritts (Eds.) [11]
1982   *Race with Extinction: Herpetological Field Notes of J. R.
        Slevin's Journey to the Galápagos, 1905-1906.* Lawrence,
        Kansas: Herpetologist's League.

Fyffe, John [6]
1815   *A Chart of the Gallapagos Islands.* Chart #103, Shelf Pa.
        Taunton, England: United Kingdom Hydrographic
        Office.

Gallardo, Galvarino [17, Notes]
1938   "Sees Defense Move in Roosevelt Trip: Chilean Writer
        Hints Visit to Galápagos was More Than a Fishing
        Expedition." In *New York Times,* July 31, p. 5:1. New
        York.

Garraty, John A. [Notes]
1989   *1,001 Things Everyone Should Know about American
        History.* New York: Doubleday & Co.

Gerbault, Alain [13]
1929   *In Quest of the Sun: The Journal of the "Firecrest."*
        London: Hodder and Stoughton.

Gifford, William [6]
1815   "Journal of A Cruise made to the Pacific Ocean. ..."
        Review in *The Quarterly Review.* Vol. XXVI (July), pp.
        352-383. London.

Gilbert, W. S., & Arthur Sullivan [22]
1885   *The Mikado*. Operetta in 2 Acts. London.

Gosse, Philip [22]
1924   *The Pirates' Who's Who*. Boston: Charles E. Lauriat.

Gould, Stephen Jay [Notes]
1991   "Knight Takes Bishop?" In *Bully for Brontosaurus*. New
         York: W. W. Norton & Co.

Hacke, William [4]
1687   Map: *A Description of the Islands of Gallapagos, delineated
         exactly according to the prescription of Mr. William
         Ambrose Cowley*. Ms. Add. 5414.27. London: British
         Library.

1687   Map: *A general draught of the Islands of Gallapagos*. ...
         16 charts in Sloane Ms. 45. part ii. London: British
         Library.

Harris, Charles Miller [12, Notes]
1899   Diary excerpts, in Rothschild & Hartett's "Review of
         the Ornithology of the Galápagos Islands" (q. v.).

Harrsch, Don [21]
1959   *Filiate Science Antrorse*. Seattle, Washington. Privately
         circulated brochure.

Hart, Charles Henry [6, Notes]
1899   *Browere's Life Masks of Great Americans*. Plate XIII of
         David Porter. np: Doubleday and McClure Company.

Hatton, Charles [22]
1878   May 1697 letter to his brother Christopher. In *Hatton
         Correspondence*, Vol. XXII. London: Camden Society
         Publications.

Hawkins, Richard [4, 23]
[1622]   *The Observations of Sir Richard Hawkins Knight, in his
         Voyage into the South Sea. Anno Domini 1593*. 1933
         Argonaut Press reprint. London: John Jaggard.

Herschel, John [8]
1836   February 20 Letter to Charles Lyell. Complete text in
         Walter F. Cannon's "The Impact of Uniformitarianism."
         In *Proceedings of the American Philosophical Society,*
         Vol. 105, No. 3, June 1961. Philadelphia: American
         Philosophical Society.

Hoff, Stein [13]
1985   *Drømmen om Galápagos: En Ukjent Norsk
         Utvandrerhistorie.* (The Galápagos Dream: An Unknown
         History of Norwegian Emigration.) Oslo: Grødahl &
         Søn Forlag A. s.

Hogue, Robert E. [Notes]
1979   Cartoon of Waldo Schmitt. Cover art for Richard E.
         Blackwelder's *The Zest for Life* (q. v.).

Hooker, William [6]
1822   Map: "Gallapagos Islands." In David Porter's *Journal of
         a Cruise,* 1822 edition.

Howard, Sidney [Notes]
1934   *Isles of Escape: being the adventures of Roydon Bristow.*
         London: G. Bell & Sons.

Humboldt, Alexander von [8]
1814   *Personal Narrative of Travels to the Equinoctial Regions of
         America.* London: Longman, Hurst, Rees, Orme, Brown.

Hunter, Joseph [11]
1905-06 *Typed Field Notes of Joseph Slayton Hunter, 1905-1906
         Galápagos Expedition, California Academy of Sciences.*
         Special Collections, San Francisco: California Academy
         of Sciences.

Huyot, Jules & E. de Berard [9]
ca. 1850 Engraving of Albemarle Island. Publication details
         unknown.

Irving, Washington (Editor) [6]
1814   "Biographical Memoir of Captain David Porter." In
         Analectic Magazine, Vol. IV, September, pp. 225-243.
         Philadelphia: Moses Thomas.

James Towne Court Records (*see* United Kingdom National Archives)

Juan, Jorge, & Antonio de Ulloa [1, Notes]
1806   *A Voyage to South America, ... Translated from the Original Spanish.* London: John Stockdale et al.

Kelly, James [4]
1700   "A Full and Due Discovery of all the Robberies, Pyracies, and other Notorious Actions of that Famous English Pyrate, Capt. James Kelly, who was Executed on Fryday the 12th of July 1700 ... Written with his own Hand." In a July 11 newspaper account. London: (Details unknown).

Kemp, Peter [22]
1976   *The Oxford Companion to Ships & The Sea.* London & New York: Oxford University Press.

Kemp, P[eter]. K., & Christopher Lloyd [22]
1960   *Brethren of the Coast: Buccaneers of the South Seas.* New York: St. Martin's Press.

Keynes, Richard Darwin (Editor) [8]
1988   *Charles Darwin's Beagle Diary.* Cambridge, England: Cambridge University Press.

Kricher, John [22]
2002   *Galápagos.* Washington, DC: Smithsonian Institution Press.

Laing, Jr., F. W. [7]
1957   Letter to Joseph R. Slevin. San Francisco: California Academy of Sciences.

Lange, Vernon [19]
1984   "The Wittmers of Floreana." In *Echoes of My Life.* Unpublished manuscript.

Laurie [Robert] & [James] Whittle [22]
1794   Map: *South America, as Divided amongst the Spaniards and the Portuguese, the French and the Dutch. By Samuel Dunn, Mathematician.*

Leong, S/Sgt. Sing [18]
1944   "The Awful Truth: The 'Rock.' " Cartoon in *The Caribbean Breeze*, Vol. 4, No. 10 (November). New Orleans: Sixth Air Force.

Library of Congress (*see* Anonymous) [2]

Lloyd, Christopher [22]
1966   *William Dampier*. London: Faber & Faber, Ltd.

Long, David [6]
1970   *Nothing Too Daring*. Annapolis: United States Naval Institute.

Luna R., Carlos [22]
1935   "Los Misteriosos Crimenes del Archipielago." In *El Universo*, February 18. Guayaquil, Ecuador.

Lundh, Jacob [12]
2004   *Galápagos: A Brief History*. Oslo, Norway: Unpublished manuscript.

Lydekker, Richard (Ed.) [9, Notes]
1893-94 Engraving: "Giant Tortoises of the Galapagos Islands." In The *Royal Natural History*, Vol. V, *Reptiles and Fishes*. London: Frederick Warne & Co.

Macy, William H. [5]
1869   "King Pat, the Crusoe of the Galápagos." In *Ballou's Monthly Magazine*, Vol. XXIX, No. 6 (June), pp. 528-534. Boston.

Maldonado, Pedro [1]
1750   Map: *Carta de la Provincia de Quito y de sus Adjacentes*. Paris?

Markham, C. R. [1]
1892   "Discovery of the Galapagos Islands" in *Proceedings of the Royal Geographical Society*, Vol. XIV, pp. 314-316. London: Royal Geographical Society.

Melville, Herman [5, 7, 9, 15, 22]
1854   "The Encantadas or, Enchanted Isles." In *Putnam's Monthly Magazine,* Vol. III (March, April, May issues). New York: G. P. Putnam's & Co.

1856   "The Encantadas or, Enchanted Isles." In *The Piazza Tales.* New York: Dix & Edwards.

        See also Victor Wolfgang von Hagen (Ed.).

Mercator, Gerard [22, 23]
1569   Map: *Nova et aucta terrae descriptio ed usum navigantium emendate accomodata.*

Meredith, DeWitt [14]
1939   *Voyages of the Velero III.* Los Angeles: Brookhaven Press.

1964   *G. Allan Hancock: A Pictorial Account of One Man's Score in Fourscore Years.* San Jose, California: Privately printed.

Mielche, Hakon [15]
ca. 1935 *Let's See if the World is Round.* London: Travel Book Club.

Milner, Richard [8]
1993   *Encyclopedia of Evolution: Humanity's Search for its Origins.* New York: Henry Holt & Co.

Moll, Herman [3, 4]
1697   Map: "A Map of the World, Shewing the Course of Mr. Dampier's Voyage Round it." In Dampier's *A New Voyage.* ...

1699   Map: "The Gallapagos Islands, Discovered by Capt. John Eaton." In *Cowley's Voyage Round the Globe.*]

1711   *A View of the Coasts, Countries and Islands within the Limits of the South-Sea-Company.* London: J. Morphew.

1726   Map: *A New & Exact Map of the Coast, Countries and Islands within ye Limits of ye South Sea Company.* ...

Murphy, Robert Cushman [16, Notes]
1936   *Oceanic Birds of South America.* New York: Macmillan Company.

Newby, G. Bruce [14]
1931   "A New Type Business and Research Cruiser." In Vol. 28, No. 9 (September) *Pacific Marine Review.*

New York Times [17]
1936   "31 Canal Zone Planes will Drill in the Pacific: First Tests Will be Made of Use of Galápagos Islands as Base for Defense Forces." In *New York Times*, February 3, p. 11:2. New York.

Niles, Hezikiah (Editor) [7]
1815   "Midshipman Cowan." Obituary notice in *Niles Weekly Record—Supplement to Volume Seven.* Baltimore: Hezikiah Niles.

Ortelius, Abraham [2, 22]
1570   Map: "Americae Sive Novi Orbis, Nova Description." In his Atlas *Theatrum Orbis Terrarum.*

Osborn, Henry Fairfield [16]
1909   August 30 letter to William Cooper. Folder 764. New York: American Museum of Natural History Archives.

Palmer, Edwin O. [14]
1934   *Third Galapagos Trip of the Velero III in the Winter of 1933-1934: From the Log Book of the "Medicine Man" of the Trip.* Privately printed.

Pardoe, Blaine [17, Notes]
2005   *The Cruise of the Sea Eagle: The Amazing True Story of Imperial Germany's Gentleman Pirate.* Lyons Press.

Pazmiño, R. [10]
1904   *Disembarkation of the Galápagos Insurrectionists.* Postcard issued in Guayaquil.

Peale, Charles Willson [6]
1818-19 Portrait of David Porter. Philadelphia: Independence National Historical Park.

Peeler, Sgt. Ernest (Editor) [18]
1945   "Goats May be Banned from PX." In *Goat's Whisker*,
        Vol. 2, No. 25 (June 19) (Base Newspaper). Isla Baltra,
        Galápagos: Sixth Air Force.

Pepys, Samuel [3, 4, 22]
1660-69 *The Diary of Samuel Pepys.* 1970-83, 11-volume reprint.
        Berkeley: University of California Press.

Petit-Thouars, Abel du [5, 8]
1841   *Voyage Autour Du Monde.* ... (Voyage Around the World
        on the Frigate La Vénus, during the years 1836-1839.)
        Vol. 2. Paris: Gide et Cie.

Picking, Sherwood [7]
1941   April 24 letter to Captain Dudley W. Knox, Office of
        Naval Intelligence. Navy Department Library "ZB"
        (Personnel) files. Washington: Naval Historical Center.

Porter, David [5-9, 22, 23]
1815   *Journal of a Cruise made to the Pacific Ocean.* ...
        Philadelphia: Bradford & Inskeep.

1822   *Journal of a Cruise made to the Pacific Ocean.* ... New
        York: Wiley & Halstead.

1823   *A Voyage to the South Seas.* ... London: Sir Richard
        Phillips & Co.

Porter, David Dixon [6, 8]
1875   *Memoir of Commodore David Porter of the United States
        Navy.* Albany: J. Munsell.

Poulton, Edward Bagnall [Notes]
1909   *Charles Darwin and the Origin of Species.* London:
        Longmans, Green & Co.

Preston, Diana & Michael [Notes]
2004   *A Pirate of Exquisite Mind: Explorer, Naturalist, and
        Buccaneer: The Life of William Dampier.* New York:
        Walker & Co.

Reimer, Ernest [19]
1984   *A Social Visit Extraordinary.* Unpublished manuscript.

Ritter, Friedrich [Notes]
1935   *Friedrich Ritter † Als Robinson auf Galapagos.* ("The
        Robinson [Crusoe] of Galápagos."). Leipzig: Grethlein
        & Co Nachf.

Robinson, William Albert [22]
1957   *To the Great Southern Sea.* London: Peter Davies.

Rogers, Woodes [8, 22]
1712   *A Cruising Voyage Round the World.* 1928 reprint. New
        York: Longmans, Green & Co.

[Roosevelt, Franklin Delano] [7, 18]
1938   *The Inspection Cruise and Fishing Expedition of President
        Franklin D. Roosevelt on board USS Houston, 16 July 1938
        – 9 August 1938.* Hyde Park, NY: Franklin D. Roosevelt
        Presidential Library.

Rose, Ruth [8, 22]
1924   "Man and the Galápagos." In William Beebe's
        Galápagos: World's End. New York: G. P. Putnam's Sons.

Rothschild, Walter, & Ernst Hartert [Notes]
1899   "A Review of the Ornithology of the Galápagos
        Islands." In *Novitates Zoologicae,* Vol. VI, No. 2
        (August). (Contains diary excerpts of Charles Miller
        Harris and F. P. Drowne.) Tring, United Kingdom:
        Walter Rothschild Zoological Museum.

Russell, W. Clark [22]
1889   *William Dampier.* London: Macmillan & Co.

Sambourne, Linley [8]
1881   Cartoon: "Man is but a worm." In *Punch,* Vol. LXXX.
        London.

Sarmiento de Gamboa, Pedro [1]
[1572] *History of the Incas.* 1999 republication of a 1907
        Hakluyt Society reprint, translated by Sir Clements
        Markham. Mineola, NY: Dover Publications, Inc.

Sato, General Kiyokatsu [17]
1940   "How to Conquer the United States." In *New Current
        Digest.* August. Tokyo: (publisher unknown).

Sayer, Robert [22]
1775   Map: *A Map of South America Containing Tierra-Firma,*
          Guayana, New Granada, Amazonia, Brasil, Peru, Paraguay,
          Chaco, Tucuman, Chili and Patagonia.

Schmitt, Waldo Lasalle (*see* Cox, William E.)

Seattle Times [21]
1959-61 News reports about Island Development Company
          colonization project. Seattle, Washington.

Shelley, Mary Wollstonecraft [8]
1818   *Frankenstein, or the Modern Prometheus.* 1992 reprint.
          New York: Penguin Books.

Shillibeer, John [7]
1817   *A Narrative of the Briton's Voyage to Pitcairn's Island. ...*
          London: Law and Whittaker.

Slevin, Joseph Richard [7, 11, 22]
1931   *Log of the Schooner "Academy" on a Voyage of Scientific*
          Research to the Galápagos Islands, 1905-1906. Occasional
          Papers XVII. San Francisco: California Academy of
          Sciences.

1935-57 Correspondence with Waldo Lasalle Schmitt. San
          Francisco: California Academy of Sciences.

1959   *Galápagos Islands: A History of their Exploration.* San
          Francisco: California Academy of Sciences.

Solberg, Carl [18]
1946   "Beachhead on the Moon." In *Time Magazine,* Vol.
          XLVIII, No. 3 (July 15). New York: Time, Inc.

Spenser, Edmund [9, Notes]
1596   *The Faerie Queene.* 1981 reprint. New Haven: Yale
          University Press.

Staples, M. M. [10]
1881   Letter to General Hurlbut, American Minister in Lima,
          Peru. Private collection.

Stock, Ralph [12]
1921   *The Cruise of the Dream Ship.* London: William
          Heinemann, Ltd.

Stoppard, Tom [23]
1981   "Wildlife Observed - The Galápagos." in *The Observer*, November 29. London: Guardian Newspapers, Ltd.

Strauch, Dore [15]
1935   *Satan Came to Eden*. London: Jarrolds Ltd.

Swift, Jonathan [3, Notes]
1725   *A New Voyage Round the World, by a Course never sailed before*. London: A. Bettesworth & W. Mears.

1726   *Travels into Several Remote Nations of the World*. 1906 reprint. London: George Routledge and Sons.

Thomas, Russell [Notes]
1932   "Melville's Use of some Sources in *The Encantadas*." In *American Literature*, Vol 3, No. 4 (January). Durham, North Carolina: Duke University Press.

Time Magazine [20]
1944   "Brotherly Greed." In *Time Magazine*, Vol. XLIV, No. 9 (August 28). New York: Time, Inc.

Treherne, John [15]
1983   *The Galapagos Affair*. New York: Random House.

Trueb, Linda [11]
1982   Map: "The Galápagos Islands: Course of the Schooner 'Academy'." Cover illustration for Fritts' *Race with Extinction*.

Twain, Mark [22]
1907   *A Horse's Tale*. New York. Harper & Brothers.

United Kingdom National Archives [Notes]
1687-90 *State Papers: Colonial Series, America and West Indies*. Kew: National Archives.

U. S. Bureau of the American Republics [23]
1894   *Ecuador*. Bulletin No. 64, 1892 revised to April 1, 1894. Washington, DC: U. S. Government Printing Office.

U. S. Congress [20]
1944   *Congressional Record: Proceedings and Debates of the 78th Congress, Second Session.* Vol. 90, Part 5: June 13,1944 to August 24, 1944 (pp. 5825-7302). Washington, DC: U. S. Government Printing Office.

U. S. Naval Academy [7, Notes]
1911   Photo of Sherwood Picking. In *The Lucky Bag,* vol XVIII (Naval Academy Yearbook).

U. S. Navy [16, 17, 20]
1942   *Field Monograph of Galápagos Islands.* College Park, MD: National Archives and Records Administration, Document. ONI-78, Item 23c, Record Group 38.

Utley, Temple [Notes]
1938   *A Modern Sea Beggar.* London: Peter Davies.

Venn, J. A. [22]
1922-54 *Alumni Cantabrigiensis.* Cambridge: Cambridge University Press.

Villefort, Le Sieur de [23]
ca. 1700 Journal abstract in *Navigation aux Terres Australes,* cited in Burney's *Chronological History of Voyages.*

von Hagen, Victor Wolfgang (Ed.) [Notes]
1940   *The Encantadas, or, Enchanted Isles, by Herman Melville. With an Introduction, Critical Epilogue & Bibliographical Notes by Victor Wolfgang von Hagen.* Burlingame, California: William P. Wreden.

von Hagen, Victor Wolfgang [16, 17, 22]
1940   *Ecuador the Unknown.* New York: Oxford University Press.

1949   *Ecuador and the Galápagos Islands.* Norman, Oklahoma: University of Oklahoma Press.

1982   *The Galápagos Revisited: Return to the Enchanted Isles.* Unpublished manuscript.

Wafer, Lionel [22]
1704   *A New Voyage and Description of the Isthmus of America. Giving an Account of the Author's Abode there, ...* London: James Knapton.

Waldo, Samuel Everett [7]
ca. 1816 Painting: Lieutenant John Marshall Gamble. Privately
          owned.

Weiner, Jonathan [8]
1994   *The Beak of the Finch: A Story of Evolution in Our Time.*
        New York: Alfred A. Knopf.

West, Paul [5]
1809   *Log of the whaleship Cyrus,* May 14th entry. Nantucket,
        Massachusetts: Nantucket Historical Association
        Research Library.

Wilkinson, Clennell [22, Notes]
1929   *Dampier: Explorer and Buccaneer.* New York: Harper &
        Brothers.

Wittmer, Margret [15, 17, 19, Notes]
1936   *What Happened On Galápagos?* Unpublished manuscript
        translated from the German *Was Ging Auf Galapagos
        Vor?* by Sidney Skamser.

1961   *Floreana Adventure.* New York: E. P. Dutton & Co.

Wolf, Theodor [12]
1879   *Ein Besuch der Galápagos-Inseln.* (A Visit to the
        Galápagos Islands.) Heidelberg: Wilhelm Frommel.

Woram, John [18]
1991   "Who Killed the Iguanas?" In *Noticias de Galápagos,* No.
        50, 1991. Quito: Charles Darwin Foundation.

1992   "The First Iguana Transfer." In *Noticias de Galápagos,*
        No. 51, 1992. Quito: Charles Darwin Foundation.

Wycherly, George [22]
1928   *Buccaneers of the Pacific.* Indianapolis: Bobbs-Merrill.

INDEX

Boldface font indicates entire chapter.

D

V

W

Illustrations

Breinigsville, PA USA
21 November 2010
249770BV00001B/4/A

9 780976 933601